Citizenship Education and the Curriculum

Recent Titles in
International Perspectives on Curriculum Studies
David Scott, Series Editor

Volume 1: Curriculum and Assessment
David Scott, editor

Citizenship Education and the Curriculum ———

Edited by
David Scott
and Helen Lawson

International Perspectives on Curriculum Studies

ABLEX PUBLISHING
Westport, Connecticut • London

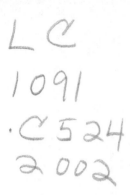

Library of Congress Cataloging-in-Publication Data

Citizenship education and the curriculum / edited by David Scott and Helen Lawson.
    p. cm.—(International perspectives on curriculum studies, ISSN 1530–5465 ; v. 2)
    Includes bibliographical references and index.
    ISBN 1–56750–651–8 (alk. paper)
    1. Citizenship—Study and teaching—Cross-cultural studies. 2. Curriculum
planning—Cross-cultural studies. I. Scott, David, 1951– II. Lawson, Helen, 1966– III.
Series.
    LC1091.C524 2002
    370.11'5—dc21   2002016340

British Library Cataloguing in Publication Data is available.

Library of Congress Catalog Card Number: 2002016340
ISBN: 1–56750–651–8
ISSN: 1530–5465

First published in 2002

Ablex Publishing, 88 Post Road West, Westport, CT 06881
An imprint of Greenwood Publishing Group, Inc.
www.ablexbooks.com

Printed in the United States of America

The paper used in this book complies with the
Permanent Paper Standard issued by the National
Information Standards Organization (Z39.48–1984).

10 9 8 7 6 5 4 3 2 1

Contents

Series Foreword

The purpose of the series *International Perspectives on Curriculum Studies* is to provide scholarly and authoritative debate about current curriculum issues. The series includes overviews of research in this area, examination of theoretical models and principles, discussion of the work of key curriculum theorists, and the reporting of new empirical research. Contributors to the various volumes in the series are not asked to provide definitive answers to questions that theorists and practitioners working in this field are asking. What they have been asked to do is to critically assess ways of thinking, influential models and current policy initiatives that relate to the curriculum.

The curriculum is defined in its widest sense and refers to programs of teaching and learning that take place in formal settings. Examples of formal settings are schools, colleges, and universities. A curriculum may refer to a system, as in a national curriculum; an institution, as in a school curriculum; or even to an individual school, as in a school geography curriculum. The four dimensions of a curriculum are (1) aims and objectives, (2) content or subject matter, (3) methods or procedures, and (4) evaluation or assessment. The first refers to the reasons for including specific items in the curriculum and excluding others. The second refers to the knowledge, skills, or dispositions that are implicit in the choice of items, and the way that they are arranged. Objectives may be understood as broad, general justifications for including particular items and particular pedagogical processes in the curriculum, or as clearly defined and closely delineated outcomes or behaviors, or as a set of appropriate procedures or experiences. The third dimension is methods or procedures. This refers to pedagogy and is determined by choices made about the first two dimensions. The fourth dimension is assessment or evaluation, which refers to the means for determining whether the curriculum has been successfully implemented. A range of issues have been brought to the surface and debated in relation to these four dimensions.

The series focuses on these issues and debates. The first volume examined the relationship between curriculum, pedagogy, and assessment. This second volume focuses on citizenship education. Each volume will take a cross-sector and comparative approach. This series is timely, as administrators and policy makers in different parts of the world have taken an increased interest in education, and as moves to centralize curriculum provision have gathered pace. This has in some cases driven a wedge between curriculum theory and curriculum practice, as policy makers have developed and implemented proposals without referring to academic debates about these issues. It therefore seems to be an important task to reassert the need to discuss and debate the curriculum in a critical manner before implementation occurs. This series will attempt this difficult, but much needed, task.

David Scott, Series Editor
The Open University, UK

1
Introduction

Helen Lawson and David Scott

The concept of citizenship is composed of a number of key elements. These are the notion of participation in public life, the idea that a citizen is one who both governs and is governed, a sense of identity, an acceptance of societal values, and rights and responsibilities. While there is general agreement over the core components of citizenship, there is no universal agreement about the precise meaning of each of these components, and this gives rise to very different understandings of what citizenship entails. Indeed, competing citizenship models (Scott and Lawson 2001) have been developed in relation to the following: knowledge (cf. Usher 1996); action (cf. Habermas 1994); community (cf. Etzioni 1995); rights and responsibilities (cf. Giddens 1994); public and private morality (cf. Beck 1998); inclusivity (cf. Arnot 1997; Lister 1997); and locality (cf. Gellner 1983; Wringe 1999; Cogan and Derricott 2000).

The current revival of interest in citizenship has been brought about by significant social and economic change, specifically in relation to the means of communication, population growth and movement, and the environment (Cogan and Derricott 2000). In the past citizenship tended to be equated with membership in, and relationship with, the nation-state. The nation-state was the principal community with which a person identified. From it, an absolute set of core values and rules was derived by which everyone lived. However, globalization, the generic term used to describe the above changes, has affected the notion of citizenship in such a way that there now exist a multiplicity of communities of which an individual can be a member and with which he or she can identify. As Giddens (1999: 12) argues, "Globalisation isn't only about what is 'out there,' remote and far away from the individual. It is an 'in here' phenomenon too, influencing intimate and personal aspects of our lives." It has been argued that the multiplicity of communities that exist leads individuals to uncertainty and insecurity about their identity and where their loyalties lie (Marr 2000). Loyalty at one level may mean being considered disloyal at another. How individuals understand their place in the various communities of which they are a part will influence not only how they participate in society at the different levels but also the other communities with which they align themselves.

More importantly, the globalization process has been recognized as a contributing factor to the way individuals behave politically as citizens. Giddens (1999) refers to the paradox of democracy which is that democracy is spreading throughout the world, yet at the same time people in mature democracies are becoming increasingly disillusioned with democratic processes. This in turn has meant that fewer people are turning out to vote, and trust in politicians is low. Giddens suggests that the lack of interest in democracy is due, in part, to the impact of globalization. Democracy at the level of the nation-state has a limited impact on global changes such as increased ecological risks, globalization of the economy, and technological change. Individuals therefore feel that little difference can be made by participating in national politics. In contrast, public distrust in traditional democratic processes has led to an increase in groups involved in "single-issue" politics. Moreover, the globalization process is affecting nation-states in such a way that they are increasingly unable to make unilateral decisions, which in turn enhances the view that individuals have little control over decisions made by national governments. A further point of contention in the citizenship debate is that the relationship of the individual with each of the communities to which they might belong varies depending on the person's political orientation. For example, liberal individualism is based on a rights approach to citizenship, and the protection of the civil and political rights of the individual has been seen as the main function of the political system. Communitarian approaches, on the other hand, understand the individual to be part of a community and to have rights as an individual but also obligations as a member of that community.

The aims and objectives of citizenship education will be influenced by understandings of citizenship itself which, as we have suggested, is a contested concept. It is a concept that has evolved over the years, and citizenship education has consequently had a number of purposes. In the past citizenship was chiefly concerned with an individual's relationship to the nation state. Consequently the principal aims of citizenship education were to build a common identity and a shared history, and to encourage patriotism and loyalty to the nation. However, globalization and the fragmentation of a national consensus about values have challenged the idea of a monolithic nation state.

These competing definitions of citizenship and citizenship education form the backdrop for this book. The contributors come with a wide range of perspectives and from different backgrounds. The rationale for this book is not to reach an agreement about citizenship education, but to air the various debates referred to above and develop new frameworks for understanding these important issues.

Mark Olssen in chapter 2 examines the two central principles characteristic of the development of education in New Zealand: universality and equality of opportunity in relation to notions of citizenship and citizenship education. Alfred Marshall's concept of citizenship was based on a belief in universal citizenship entitlement. A precondition for achieving this was compulsory schooling, which was to have common elements for all children irrespective of locality, socio-economic background, or religion. Significantly to Marshall, formal education is the only obligatory right and duty of the citizen. Under the period of the welfare state, citizenship was formulated in terms of a "social contract." That is, the state promised rights to work, education, and health in return for respect for law and order and property. Such reciprocal obligations were an essential component of the social democratic arrangements at the beginning of the twentieth century. Toward the latter part of the century there was a shift in emphasis, and citizenship was redefined in a more individualist sense. This led to a revival in New Zealand of a traditional welfare state notion of citizenship. However a major criticism of social-democratic citizenship is that treating all individuals as equal does not counterbalance the disadvantages that some groups will experience. With regard to education processes not everyone will be starting from the same point, and furthermore education is not neutral but reproduces the normative and cognitive codes of the dominant groups in society. By treating all individuals as the same when they clearly are not reinforces the inequalities that exist. This criticism led Young to suggest a notion of differentiated citizenship which "preserves and facilitates minority group differences" (Young 1997). Olssen argues for a form of education that recognizes difference and examines New Zealand's attempts to achieve this. He then goes on to suggest that there needs to be some form of common ground in order for difference to flourish, which raises the question of which practices can be tolerated/respected in relation to difference, and which must be part of the common agenda.

James Arthur and Jon Davison in chapter 3 examine the relationship between social literacy, citizenship education, and involvement in the community. They argue that experiential learning is an essential part of the development of active citizenship. The authors examine the types of values that might support a curriculum for citizenship education, and ways in which values are acquired. They offer four different accounts of citizenship: libertine, paleoconservative, libertarian, and communitarian, each underpinned by a set of different values and from which markedly different curricula would be constructed. They go on to suggest that the Labour government in the United Kingdom aspires to a communitarian vision of citizenship and seeks to promote this vision through schools, specifically through the community learning element of citizenship education. However, there exists a tension between the government's goals of citizenship education and the design of a school curriculum that continues to focus on academic subjects, competition within and between schools, and a reliance on classroom-based pedagogies. The authors acknowledge that experiential learning does not automatically lead to positive outcomes/benefits for the pupil. It needs to be accompanied by preparation, action, reflection, and celebration in order that values such as appreciation of cultural diversity may be acquired.

Alistair Ross in chapter 4 explores the important issues of identity and citizenship, the reasons for the current interest in citizenship education, and the relationship between citizenship and citizenship education. He suggests that concerns around identity and the democratic deficit are the major forces behind the recent revival of interest in citizenship education. He examines three distinct approaches to curriculum construction: content-driven, objectives-driven, and process-driven. Each determines a particular pedagogic style, and citizenship education will belong to a different tradition depending on who is advocating such education and why. Ross uses examples from a number of European countries to identify their intentions regarding citizenship education, and examines how these intentions correspond to different types of curricula. Though new programs of citizenship education in England do not easily fit any of them, Ross argues that the motivation for citizenship education in England is inspired by social considerations and is thus instrumental—it is education for planned social change. However, the current curriculum is based on a behavioral objectives model with clearly defined learning outcomes. It leads to a view of citizenship education that is at odds with the stated purposes of curriculum makers.

Identity is also the principal theme of Audrey Osler (chapter 5), specifically in the context of diversity. The author provides an analysis of a number of policy documents developed by the United Kingdom government that are aimed at promoting racial equality. One such document is the Race Relations Amendment Act 2000, which mandates that it is no longer sufficient for public bodies to avoid discrimination. Instead, they must actively promote racial equality. In spite of this, however, government initiatives to actively promote a vision of a multicultural society have not been manifest. Osler argues that while policy is important it is not sufficient to ensure the full participation of all citizens in society. She suggests that what is needed is a new multicultural vision that is inclusive of all—including white communities. Moreover, schools are implicated as part of the problem of institutional racism, but are also seen as being able to contribute to its solution and as such should address and prevent racism. The United Kingdom government has indicated that citizenship education should meet the challenges for preventing racism and valuing cultural diversity, yet no indication is given of just how this will happen. Osler therefore argues that government statements of commitment to race equality need to be translated into practical action at both the level of education policy and curriculum advice for schools.

Orit Ichilov in chapter 6 characterizes citizenship as a universal condition that transcends difference, and challenges the notion that citizenship education is taught equally to all students. Through a detailed analysis of educational documents produced for Israeli citizenship courses, Ichilov examines the type of citizenship roles that academic and vocational schools promote and argues that differential educational experiences produce dissimilar citizenship roles. Furthermore, she suggests that an individual's placement in schools is linked to the development of those activities associated with active citizenship such as voting and involvement in public affairs. Thus a link and a pattern are established between formal educational experiences and adult behaviors. Based on the premise that differentiated curricula guide students to dissimilar citizenship roles, Ichilov argues that all pupils should be taught the same curriculum regardless of ability. An important question she raises is, How should educators and curriculum developers react to differences in ability among students?

Marie Clarke in chapter 7 examines the relationship between assessment and citizenship education with particular reference to the Irish educational system. She suggests that certain forms of citizenship education are inappropriately assessed by formal testing and that to attempt this distorts the nature of the educational experiences offered to children in schools. Her chapter deals with the issue of citizenship education and assessment, focussing on the complexity of issues that face those involved in promoting an active participatory citizenship education model. She documents the development of political education, analyzes the manner in which values that underpin education systems have evolved, and offers a range of citizenship education curriculum models. This serves as a context for exploring the role of assessment in the area of citizenship education, and the challenges that this presents.

Sigrún Adalbjarnardóttir in chapter 8 examines the role of the teacher in citizenship education programs and how teachers' understandings of citizenship influence the outcomes of citizenship education programs. Furthermore, she suggests that the quality of these teacher interventions directly influences the levels of interpersonal understanding achieved by students.

Cameron White and Roger Openshaw in chapter 9 focus on one of the most contentious debates in this field: the place and role of the nation-state in the development of civic virtue. They examine the role of the nation-state in the construction of citizenship identity and contrast this with multinational and global citizenships. They also examine issues of globalization and fragmentation through two contrasting case studies in New Zealand and the United States. They conclude by suggesting that programs of citizenship education, if they are conceived as democratic and empowering, can facilitate critical democracy and vibrant forms of citizenship.

Ann McCollum, in the concluding chapter of this book, suggests that rather than producing overly prescriptive models for citizenship education, curriculum makers and theorists need to identify core principles and concepts that are tested collaboratively in the development of new practices. The book does not offer definitive answers to many of the questions it raises. What it does do is bring a number of the key issues in relation to citizenship education to the surface and problematize them. This is an essential part of the process of reaching consensus on what it means to be a citizen at the beginning of the twenty-first century.

REFERENCES

Arnot, M. 1997. " 'Gendered Citizenry': New Feminist Perspectives on Education and Citizenship." *British Educational Research Journal* 23 (3): 275–293.

Beck, J. 1998. *Morality and Citizenship in Education*. London: Cassell.

Cogan, J. and Derricott, R. 2000. *Citizenship for the 21st Century. An International Perspective on Education*. London: Kogan Page.

Etzioni, A. 1995. *The Spirit of Community: Rights and Responsibilities and the Communitarian Agenda*. London: Fontana.

Gellner, E. 1983. *Nations and Nationalism*. London: Blackwell.

Giddens, A. 1994. *Beyond Left and Right: The Future of Radical Politics*. Cambridge: Polity Press.

Giddens, A. 1999. *Runaway World. How Globalisation Is Reshaping Our Lives*. London: Profile Books.

Habermas, J. 1994. "Citizenship and National Identity." In *The Condition of Citizenship*. ed. B. van Steenbergen. London: Sage Publications.

Lister, R. 1997. *Citizenship: Feminist Perspectives*. London: Macmillan.

Marr, A. 2000. *The Day Britain Died*. London: Profile Books.

Scott, D. and Lawson, H. 2001. "Citizenship Education: Models and Discourses." In *Learning for a Democratic Europe*. ed. A. Ross. London: Children's Identity and Citizenship in Europe (CiCe).

Usher, R. 1996. "A Critique of the Neglected Assumptions of Educational Research." In *Understanding Educational Research*. eds. D. Scott and R. Usher. London: Routledge.

Wringe, C. 1999. "Social Exclusion, Citizenship and Global Education." *Development Education Journal* 6 (1).

Young, I.M. 1997. "Policy and Group Difference: A Politics of Ideas or a Politics of Presence?" *Contemporary Political Philosophy*. eds. Robert E. Goodin and Philip Pettit. Oxford: Blackwell.

2

Citizenship Education and Difference

Mark Olssen

INTRODUCTION

The welfare state was characterized by two central principles: *universality* and *equality of opportunity*. It can be argued that the development of education in New Zealand was shaped and maintained by both these ideals. The public benefits of education were not, however, simply the sum of individual private benefits, for norms such as political or civic tolerance, literacy, or the values required for democratic functioning adhere to the quality of a community and are not reducible to, or contained in, the psychological characteristics of individuals. The early New Zealand educators claimed that in order that public benefits might be derived from schooling, and as an essential precondition of citizenship, all children should receive an education with common features whether they lived in town or in rural districts, whether they were rich or poor, black or white, and irrespective of their religion or their cultural practices. As Fraser expressed it in 1939, "The government's objective, broadly expressed, is that every person, whatever the level of his academic ability, whether he be rich or poor, whether he live in town or country, has a right *as a citizen* [emphasis added] to a free education of a kind for which he is best fitted and to the fullest extent of his powers" (AJHR 1939: 2–3). This statement not only became the benchmark for all subsequent education policy, at least up until the 1980s, but expressed the political commitment to citizenship, to which most New Zealanders aspired.

It was a conception of citizenship that can be seen philosophically and socially located in writers such as Alfred Marshall (1842–1924). In his paper to the

Cambridge Reform Club in 1873 Marshall (1925: 3–4) poses the question "whether there be valid ground for the opinion that the amelioration of the working classes has limits beyond which it cannot pass." "The question," he said, "is not whether all men will ultimately be equal, but whether progress may not go on steadily, if slowly, till by occupation at least, every man is a gentleman. I hold that it may and that it will." His faith was based on the belief in a universal citizenship entitlement that included labor, as well as leisure, a general social condition that he foresaw as the ultimate achievement of all. While Marshall realized that his system resembled those of the socialists in some respects, he held that his own system differed fundamentally from the socialists' in that it would preserve the essentials of a free market. There would be a role for state compulsion in some respects, however, for all children must be compelled to go to school: "It is bound to compel them and to help them to take the first step upwards; and it is bound to help them, if they will, to make many steps upwards" (1925: 15). Importantly, only the first step is compulsory; free choice sets in once the conditions for freedom have been established. Herein is embodied Marshall's conception of citizenship wherein the state, as the collective embodiment of the aspirations of the people, must seek the realization of a standard of civilized life that was the standard regarded by his generation as appropriate to a gentleman. It was a general claim insofar as it was a claim for all to enjoy these conditions: a claim to be admitted to a share in the social heritage, a claim to be admitted as full members of society, that is, a claim to be *citizens*.

Citizenship is represented by Marshall as both a right and a duty. In his 1950 essay "Citizenship and Social Class," presented in commemoration of Alfred Marshall, T.H. Marshall (1997: 300) defines citizenship as an institution that developed in the latter part of the seventeenth century, its growth coinciding with the rise of capitalism. He writes,

Citizenship is a status bestowed on those who are full members of a community. All who possess the status are equal with respect to the rights and duties with which the status is endowed. There is no universal principle that determines what those rights and duties shall be, but societies in which citizenship is a developing institution create an image of an ideal citizen against which achievement can be measured and towards which aspiration can be directed. (1997: 300)

In the nineteenth century, it was to become one of the new "Rights of Man." Building on the philosophical preconceptions of John Stuart Mill, the "new liberals" such as T.H. Green, L.T. Hobhouse, and Alfred Marshall himself, they advanced citizenship as a positive freedom, to supplement the negative rights of "Life, Liberty, and Property" advocated since the seventeenth century by the classical liberals. As a right and duty for all, citizenship becomes a basic principle of equality. It implies a way of life that constitutes reciprocal obligations between a person and the community. Rather than something presented from without, it is a way of life that grows within a man and to which a person seeks entry. Because it affords rights, it is simply an equal right to membership as well as a right to participation. Alfred Marshall clearly saw such rights as limited, acknowledging only education as entailing a specific right that could legitimate the compulsory powers of the state. During the period of the welfare state, however, the entitlement to membership and participation also came to embody rights to work, to health, and to security. As such, citizenship expressed the new positive role of the state as the embodiment of social democracy. Formulated in the language of the "social contract," it promised a new series of entitlements to work, education, and healthcare in return for an acceptance of law and order and a respect for property. While in this sense citizenship was quite compatible with a certain level of class inequality, it presumed a commitment to formal rights to equality, and, more importantly, to access to equality of opportunity and the institutional structures of opportunity in the society.

Citizenship, in this sense, was only possible in a postfeudal society, for it embodied an equality of status that can be seen as entailing a principle of equality inherent in the formation of a social contract. As T.H. Marshall (1997: 302) expresses it, "modern contract is essentially an agreement between men who are free and equal in status, though not necessarily in power. Status was not eliminated from the social system. Differential status associated with class, function and family, was replaced by the single uniform status of citizenship, which provided the foundation of equality on which the structure of inequality would be built." Citizenship in this sense was an increase in the rights that could be enjoyed by all. In his essay T.H. Marshall identifies three aspects of citizenship—civil, political and social. The civil element is composed of "rights necessary for individual freedom—liberty of the person, freedom of speech, the right to own property and conclude valid contracts, and the right to justice" (p. 294). The political element pertains to the "right to participate in the exercise of political power, as a member of a body invested with political authority or as an elector of the members of such a body" and by the social element he means the "right to a modicum of economic welfare and security to the right to share in the full social heritage and to live the life of a civilised being according to the standards prevailing in the society" (p. 294). While in times past these three elements could be found "wound into a single thread," in more recent centuries

the three elements of citizenship parted company. . . . So complete was the divorce between them that it is possible, without doing too much violence to historical accuracy, to assign the formative period in the life of each to a different century—civil rights to the eighteenth, political to the nineteenth and social to the twentieth. (p. 294)

The story of civil rights in their formative period was embodied in the principle of individual economic freedom. By the beginning of the nineteenth century this was accepted as axiomatic. Civil Rights were established in something like their modern form by the time of the first Reform Act of 1832 (p. 299).

The story of political rights was different in terms of both time and character. It consisted in giving old rights to new sections of the population. Their extension was one of the main features of the nineteenth century, although universal political citizenship was only finally realized in 1918. The original source of social rights was participation in local communities and associations, which were gradually replaced by a national system of wage regulation. While social rights were almost nonexistent in the eighteenth and nineteenth centuries, their revival started with the onset of public education. Only in the twentieth century, however, did they attain equal importance with the other two elements of citizenship.

The emergence of citizenship also embodied a conflict, says Marshall, between "the planned (or patterned) society and the competitive economy" (p. 298). Marshall identifies the emergence of the Speenhamland system of poor relief which came into existence at the end of the eighteenth century, as an important factor in the history of citizenship in that it offered, in effect, guarantees of a minimum wage and family security, together with the right to work. With the Speenhamland system the Poor Law became for the first time "an aggressive champion of the social rights of citizenship [for] it was fully realised by the originators of the scheme that the Poor Law was being invoked to do what wage regulation was no longer able to accomplish. For the Poor Law was the last remains of a system which tried to adjust real income to the social needs and status of the citizen and not simply to the market value of his labour" (p. 298).

In the succeeding period the Poor Law effected a divorce between economic security and the status of citizenship in that it treated the poor, not as citizens in themselves, but as an excluded category—that is, as people who were not citizens in any true sense of the word. By the end of the nineteenth century, however, the conception of a social democratic concept of citizenship was firmly entrenched.

The history of education also shows the nineteenth century to have been a period in which the foundations of social rights were laid. Yet education was a service of a unique kind, as children cannot be citizens. Yet, for Alfred Marshall, the education of children has a direct bearing on citizenship, for when the state compels all children to be educated it has the requirements of citizenship clearly in mind. It is trying to "stimulate the growth of citizens in the making. The right to education is a genuine social right of citizenship, because the aim of education during childhood is to shape the future adult. Fundamentally it should be regarded, not as the right of the child to go to school, but as the right of the adult citizen to have been educated. . . . Education is a necessary prerequisite to civil freedom" (1997: 299). The state's obligation to educate its people, just as the individual's obligation to improve him or herself, is therefore a social duty and not merely a personal one, because the social health of a community depends on the education of its members. In short, political democracy needs an educated electorate, just as economic production needs educated workers and technicians. And it was in this sense that the development of public elementary education during the nineteenth century became a major support to the reestablishment of the social rights of citizenship in the twentieth.

It is pertinent at this juncture to reexamine Alfred Marshall's conceptions afresh, for under neoliberal regimes that have become ascendant in the Organization for Economic Cooperation and Development (OECD) countries since the 1980s, the level and extent of inequality pose serious threats to mutual obligations embodied in claims of citizenship, giving rise to the rather worrying suggestion that if the social democratic state reneges on its obligations to employment, health, education, and security, then the reciprocal obligations embodied as fundamental components of the social contract—of a respect for law and order, and property, by the citizenry—may also lapse. Such reciprocal obligations, embodying both rights and duties, were an essential component of the revised social democratic settlement of the late nineteenth and early twentieth centuries. Under neoliberal regimes, also, there has been a shift from *duties* to *rights*, meaning that the double emphasis embodied in the nineteenth-century conception involving the reciprocal obligation between an individual and the community has become fundamentally redefined in a more individualist sense. It was the worrying possibility of such an inherent threat to peace and stability in our country in present times that provided support for a return to center-left politics, which occurred in New Zealand with the election of a Labour government in November 1999. While this may temporally revive a traditional welfare state conception of citizenship involving equality of opportunity and equal treatment before the law, we must ask whether such a conception is not now revealing deficiencies that have been inherent in it all along—deficiencies that were the specific focus of criticisms of the welfare state from the Left in the 1980s and that also became embodied in neoliberal arguments for devolution and choice.

This criticism of social-democratic citizenship essentially takes the following form: structures of theoretical equality based on formal equal status do not offset the disadvantages that groups experience because they lack the resources that are necessary to participate in the various forms of social opportunity in the first place. To invoke an old adage from Aristotle, the problem with the social-democratic conception of citizenship is that injustice arises as much from treating unequals equally as it does from assuring equal access to the opportunities available in society. In relation to education, for instance, one of the central criticisms of education under a unified national system of provision was that it simply reproduced existing class inequalities. That is, treating as equals participants from social class, race, and ethnic groups who are in fact very different— who have different language systems, different orientations toward the future, different motivational patterns, different levels or amounts of cultural capital— would only ensure a true and fair equality of opportunity if the curriculum and assessment structures of the educational system were indeed neutral. Which, of course, they are not. There is no need to remind readers here of the fact that several decades of research and debate in the sociology of education contradict such a claim. Far from being neutral, school structures were found to embody the normative and cognitive codes of dominant and already privileged sections of the community. Curriculum and assessment practices were coded in the dominant language and rewarded individualized, competitive attainment, which depended upon socially learned abstract reasoning processes and involved bodies of knowledge that expressed, as often as not, the partisan interests of the already well-off. By treating everyone the same, in other words, the structures of our single public education system unfairly treated children who were differentially equipped to cope with it. Although such a criticism came initially from neo-Marxists in the 1980s and from the educational sociology of Pierre Bourdieu, it is interesting that the Treasury brief to the incoming Labour government in 1987, *Government Management*, embodied a version of the same criticism. Drawing on Le Grand's work in England, it charged the central system of public education with "middle class capture" in that it was the children of the middle class who benefited most because their culture was most like that of the schools. To point out to a young Polynesian girl living in Otara that she too can be a brain surgeon because of her formal rights of citizenship may certainly be true in theory, but is also trite. From the young girl's perspective, in fact, it is a form of quibbling.

DIFFERENTIATED CITIZENSHIP

It is this criticism of the social democratic ideal of universal citizenship for failing to recognize and take account of group differences that constitutes the basis of Iris Marion Young's notion of "differentiated citizenship as the best way of realising the inclusion and participation of everyone in full citizenship" (Young 1997: 257).

According to Young, the ideal of universal citizenship embodied in the social democratic conception incorporates a sense of universality as (a) generality, and (b) equal treatment. In the first sense the ideal of citizenship that serves to "express or create a general will that transcends the particular differences of group affiliation, situation, and interest has in practice excluded groups judged not capable of adopting that general point of view" (p. 257). In the second sense, universality functions "in the sense of laws or rules that stay the same for all and apply to all in the same way" (p. 257). Her argument is that such a representation results in exclusions and/or homogeneity, and thus the inclusion or participation of everyone on a fair basis is only possible if (a) there exist specific mechanisms for group representation, (b) the rule of equal treatment is departed from in specific cases so as to ensure fair and just treatment, and (c) where special rights that attend to group differences are articulated so as to combat oppression and disadvantage.

The emergence of universal citizenship simply suppressed differences between peoples and acted on the basis of subgroup exclusions and oppressions. Feminists in particular have analyzed how the discourse of citizenship was founded by men, and how it paraded values and norms derived from masculine experience as universal. No one can express this point better than Young:

The bourgeois world instituted a moral division of labour between reason and sentiment, identifying masculinity with reason and femininity with sentiment, desire, and the needs of the body. Extolling a public realm of manly virtue and citizenship as independence, generality, and dispassionate reason entailed creating the private sphere of the family as the place to which emotion, sentiment, and bodily needs must be confined. The generality of the public thus depends on excluding women, who are responsible for attending to that private realm, and who lack the dispassionate rationality and independence required of good citizens. (1997: 258)

It was not only women but people of color as well as the poor and the working class who were excluded because of the requirement that all citizens be the same, or be willing or able to adopt the general perspective. The early American republicans as well as their European counterparts were explicit "about the need for the homogeneity of citizens fearing that group differences would tend to undermine commitment to the general interest" (p. 259).

This assumption of unity or generality that infected the ideal of citizenship also infected the social democratic ideal of the late nineteenth and twentieth centuries. Young represents it as a metaphysical postulate that inhabits the enlightenment urge to reduce differences to unity, reinforced by the idea of a single truth in accord with universal reason, a single morality, and a concern with normality. It embodies the ideal of a community that submits to the logic of identity, an ideal of a community that expresses a longing for harmony among persons. It is what Foucault calls the Rousseauist dream of a shared subjectivity or common consciousness, where community is represented as a "copresence of subjects" (Young 1990: 231), as a system of mutuality or reciprocity. Whether among the new bourgeoisie of the seventeenth or eighteenth centuries or the new liberals of the nineteenth, the striving for commonness threatened to suppress differences among citizens.

Such a conception of universal citizenship will put some groups at a disadvantage even though they have formal equal rights to citizenship status. That which is different becomes relegated and bracketed off as private, while what is common and universal is public. Because citizenship is a public status, it is assumed that all citizens will adopt a point of view that is impartial and general, and from which particular interests and differences are transcended.

Instead of universal citizenship, Young advocates a differentiated citizenship of a heterogeneous public where differences, which are irreducible, are publicly recognized and accepted, coexisting with supposedly common procedural commitments in a process of communication stretching across the differences involved. In Young's view this reconfiguration of political life does not require the creation of a unified public realm in which group differences are suppressed in preference of a common citizenship ideal, but preserves and facilitates minority group differences, based on the institutionalization of mechanisms of minority group representation.

It is through mechanisms of group representation that difference can operate. Such a recommendation is distinct from a mere quantitative increase in the indices of participatory democracy, which unless systematically untied from a universalistic conception of citizenship only lead to increased segregation and reproduce existing group oppression. Young cites Gutmann (1988: 33) in her analysis of the politics of race in the United States. Gutmann argues that an increase in participatory democratic structures tended to silence disadvantaged groups and increase segregation in cities because the more articulate, better-off whites were better able to promote their interests against African Americans' demands for equal treatment in an integrated system.

To install mechanisms for specific group representation is to increase political equality and "institutionalize means for the explicit recognition and representation of oppressed groups" (1997: 261). In this analysis the concept of a social group becomes all-important, for what Young proposes is that minority groups be given the right to do things differently. Rejecting an individualist contract model of society, she maintains that rather than see group identity substantively in terms of an essence or nature, it should be understood in relational terms, as generated through social processes. In this sense, group existence and identity is fluid and changeable over time. Moreover, every group has differences cutting across it.

It is a failure to acknowledge the processes of group differentiation and oppression that becomes the key to understanding the weaknesses of the liberal model of citizenship. What such a model ignores is that there are differences of power between groups—that some are privileged and others are oppressed. Oppression leads to imbalances of power to which the liberal model of citizenship is largely blind. It can take the form of systematic exploitation, marginalization, powerlessness, cultural imperialism, or violence. Such differences in power undermine the axiom, inherent in the ideal of universal citizenship, of a level playing field where the structures of the system are somehow neutral or agnostic, allowing all to participate on a fair and equal basis. It is because of such differences in power that different race or ethnic groups cannot hope to participate in education on the basis of a single set of rules and procedures.

It is on this basis, then, that Young advocates specific mechanisms of representation to adequately represent and recognize the different voices and perspectives of different groups. Included among such mechanisms are public resources to support (1) self-organization of group members so that they can gain a sense of collective empowerment, (2) voicing a group's analysis of how social policy proposals affect them, and generating policy proposals themselves, in institutional contexts where decision-makers are obliged to show that they have taken these perspectives into consideration, and (3) having veto power regarding specific policies that affect a group directly (Young 1997: 264–266).

"Group representation," says Young, "best institutionalises fairness under circumstances of social oppression" (1997: 264). Hence, a society should always "be committed to representation of oppressed or disadvantaged groups" (1997: 263). As individuals' lives are structured partly through group-based experience and identity, "no one can claim to speak in the general interest—[t]he existence of social groups implies different, though not necessarily exclusive, histories, experiences, and perspectives on social life that people have" (1997: 263). Her model implies the ideal of a "rainbow coalition" as expressing the diverse interests of a heterogeneous public in which each group maintains autonomy, and decision-making bodies and procedures provide for group representation (1997: 264–265).

Such a model is different from interest-group or pluralist conceptions of the social order, for these models assume a level playing field and neutral rule systems. In addition, says Young, her model involves the granting of special rights only to groups that are disadvantaged or oppressed by the structures of the system. Such rights should be granted to "only those groups that describe the major identities and major status relationships constituting the society or particular institutions and which are oppressed or disadvantaged" (1997: 265–266). In addition, special rights are given to groups, not on the basis of some interest or goal, but according to their social location and relative lack of power. Finally, whereas pluralist models of power operate on the basis of forestalling public discussion and decision-making, her conception of a heterogeneous public seeks to institute a larger program for democratized decision-making processes.

JUSTICE AND THE MĀORI

In her article "Together in Difference: Transforming the Logic of Group Political Conflict," Young (1995) introduces an analysis of Andrew Sharp's (1997) book *Justice and the Māori* as a case study exemplar of how her conception of political difference can be seen to work. The debate over Māori claims under the Treaty of Waitangi, she argues, "succeeded at some level in creating a heterogeneous public" (1995: 171). While initially the arguments were assimilationist, what succeeded them were claims and arguments based on distinctness. To establish this point she cites Sharp (1990: 43):

Although the tension between unity and difference was always likely to be resolved in a way which denied justice to the Māori people (by insisting on seeing them as so many separate individuals who were part of the New Zealand nation), yet they persisted in, and won, a propaganda battle with politicians over their separateness. Perhaps this is the best that can be said of the history of the conflicts of the 1970s and 1980s, with respect to justice.

Further, she points to the fact that Māori identity as an *ethne* or common group was constituted relationally out of many tribal groups only in confrontation with and differentiation from the European settlers. This became the basis for the

Treaty of Waitangi in 1840. Her thesis is that a theory of cultural and political difference as indicated by biculturalism is preferable to a political theory of assimilation, which dominated New Zealand race relations up until the 1970s. Sharp (1990: 43–45) notes, for instance, the prevalent assimilationist view as expressed by Keith Holyoake, who was prime minister from 1960–1972, and Robert Muldoon, who occupied the position from 1975 to mid-1984, which asserted a "one people" view of "fading race differences" in what was only a cultural reassertion of Hobson's words on the day the treaty was signed: "he iwi kotahi tatou" (now we are one people). This was but an assertion of what Sharp (p. 48) calls the "unity-in-melding" or "one people" view that lay behind Holyoake's hope for a "pale brown New Zealand."

It was not until 1981 that the basic cultural logic of biculturalism was given official sanction when Sir David Beattie, the then governor general, suggested that "we are not one people, despite Hobson's oft quoted words, nor should we try to be." Rather we are "two people, one nation" (Sharp 1997: 45). The prospect for an officially endorsed multiculturalism was by-passed, says Sharp (pp. 46–47), when Sir Paul Reeves stressed the existence of two, not many peoples. Thus biculturalism, the doctrine that distributions of things in Aotearoa/New Zealand should be made primarily between the two main cultures, Māori and Pākehā, and that "since Māori and Pākehā were *ethnie* worthy of equal respect, the distributions should be equal between them. It was not numbers of persons within each *ethnie* that weighted the balance; it was the equal value of each culture" (1990: 227). This did not mean that other minority groups were not accorded special rights, or that their different requirements and needs were not to be recognized. What it meant was that Māori had a different order of right based on historical arguments, which gave them an effective equality with Pākehā over many different claims.

One interesting example concerning the nature of claims made relates, says Sharp, to the Manukau Report of 1983 by the Tainui people of the Manukau Harbor and Lower Waikato River areas in their arguments that they were entitled to what they claimed. At the basis of these claims were:

- That land confiscations that they had suffered since the 1860s were legally void because they proceeded without due process of law, that is, it was claimed that Tainui had undertaken simply defensive wars since 1863 onwards against Pākehā aggression and that this had been overlooked.

- It was also argued that the Treaty of Waitangi promised them that their possessions would not be alienated without their consent, yet land and water had been taken by "colour of statute; regulation and by-law without their consent."

- It was also argued that they were morally entitled to what they claimed because the Treaty of Waitangi was morally binding.

- It was also argued that they were *tangata whenua* whose claims to land and fisheries, *mana* and *rangatiratanga*, were historically and morally prior to the alien law imposed by Pākehā.

- These rights claims "demonstrate that arguments for just rights really depend on specific and varying conceptions of good human lives."

- Hence Tainui argued, says Sharp, that they were better conservators of nature than Pākehā had shown themselves to be, and hence Māori deserved the office of *kaitaki* (guardians) of the harbor.

- It was argued further that Māori needed control of the environment if they were to live the lives that had meaning and value for them, and they argued that the harbour needed their protection.

- Finally, they argued that Tainui had a "cosmically irreducible duty" as *tangata whenua* to act as *kaitaki*, and that therefore they had a right to do so. (Sharp 1990: 31)

These special rights, accorded on the basis of difference, constitute a mix of legal and moral rights, which serves to reinforce, says Sharp, that "justice appears in practical life as a complex set of conceptions" (pp. 31–32).

In relation to New Zealand education, the *National Education Guidelines* (Ministry of Education 1997) now endorse the principles of biculturalism in terms of which all school boards of trustees must contain a mandate within their charters, as specified in section 62 of the Education Act of 1989, to "seek and consider the concerns of Māori in their community." In addition, under section 63, every charter is deemed to contain "(a) The aim of developing concerned policies and practices for the school that reflect New Zealand's cultural diversity, the unique position of the Māori culture, and (b) The aim of taking all reasonable steps to ensure that instruction in *tikanga Māori* (Māori culture) and *te reo Māori* (the Māori language) are provided for full-time students whose parents ask for it" (Ministry of Education 1997: 11).

Although it is on the basis of Sharp's analysis that Young maintains that Māori claims under the Treaty of Waitangi constitute an exemplar of the politics of difference, I will shortly qualify her reading of Sharp's book, as well as her interpretation of biculturalism as premised on difference, by reinstating a concept of community. Before doing so, however, let me turn briefly to the issue of difference and education.

JUSTICE AND EDUCATION: REFUGEE GROUPS IN NEW ZEALAND

In relation to education, it can be argued that effective citizenship rights are increased by the acknowledgement of group differences in capacities, needs, cognitive styles, and other forms of cultural capital that cannot be accounted for through a single system of institutional processes governing assessment, pedagogy, and learning. A unified system of rules and procedures ends by representing certain differences as deviance or deficiency, just as it presumes that some capacities, needs, attitudes and cognitive styles are normal. It is indeed through such a "structuration," to use Anthony Giddens' term, that dominant groups are able to assert their experience of and perspectives on life as impartial, objective, and the only valid norms to which all children should be required to conform. Such a structuration of education, which processes all children through a single system and subjects them all to equal treatment according to strict meritocratic procedures (screwed even tighter by institutions such as scaling), simply reproduces disadvantage and perpetuates unequal outcomes. It does this because it was built on the assumptions of neutralist liberalism. But in education, at least, there are no neutral norms of behavior or performance, for when groups come from very different backgrounds the formulation of law, policy, and the rules of the game tend to be biased in favor of the privileged groups. It is their experiences and their perspectives on life that implicitly establish those norms that will be deemed appropriate.

One possible correction of this problem is the idea of a differentiated education that enables different systems of schooling to exist, as evidenced in New Zealand by Kohanga Reo and Kura Kaupapa schooling and in various kinds of private schooling. Moreover, the difference principle could be extended to enable different forms of organization, pedagogy, and assessment both between and within schools. Many other groups have had their citizenship diminished within the context of education. And with changes in immigration policy that have permitted the entry of a greater diversity of immigrant groups, the systemic bias of the dominant system has become more insidious since many groups of refugees are poorly equipped by background, language or perspective to succeed within the country's education system. In this sense, in fact, the eurocentric bias of schooling serves to marginalize some groups of students through cognitive and organizational rituals as well as norms of behavior.

In a recent paper, Louise Humpage and Augie Fleras (2000) trace the systematic bias and the marginalization of Somali refugee adolescents within New Zealand education, providing an interesting and insightful ethnography of the rules, roles and rituals that contributed to this group's effective marginalization within New Zealand society. Of particular note is their conclusion that this group of refugees is, because of its cultural experiences, poorly disposed to fit into the country's education system. Using interview data on Somali refugee adolescents at a secondary school in Christchurch, they argue that "immigrant students are marginalised by consequence, if not necessarily by intent, through practices that diminish their full and equal participation within the school system" (2000: 1). They argue that schooling manifests a eurocentric bias that is "systematically discriminatory at the level of rituals, rules, and roles" (2000: 1). Systematic bias operates, they claim, through the application of "ostensibly neutral rules and universal standards to unequal situations that have the effect of discriminating against some because of their differences" (2000: 3). In their account of the rituals of exclusion they refer to

- A lack of familiarity with the rituals of learning and teaching
- Unfamiliarity with book based learning

- Unfamiliarity with group-based work patterns
- Conceptualization problems linked to unfamiliarity with dominant language
- Lack of linguistically and culturally appropriate educational resources (e.g., books)
- Forms of assessment (exams, tests, assignments) dependent on dominant language familiarity
- Unfamiliarity with organizational rituals and practices concerned with learning, classroom management, the presentation of schoolwork, homework routines, etc.
- Unfamiliarity with appropriate education style
- Lack of differentiated culturally specific educational support
- Different cultural orientations to time, scheduling of activities, and the prioritizing of school work relative to other cultural activities, such as festivities, religious observances, holidays, etc.
- Conflicting understandings over roles relating to age, gender, classroom, or playground behavior
- Different expectations of rules concerning such practices as "entrance procedures," "school uniforms," or "appropriate individual behavior" (Humpage and Fleras 2000: passim)

Although some of the schools studied had run segregated classes or offered subject specific support "in class" for the Somali refugee students, such interventions had only been occasional and had only lasted a short time. Although teachers at the schools studied did not convey obvious personal prejudice, they inadvertently put Somalis at a disadvantage by adhering to "universal" educational standards of teaching and assessment.

Such practices are clearly cases where school practices depart from the written rule of Tomorrow's Schools' reforms. In addition to implementing a market liberal model that encouraged competition between schools and among parents as the consumers of education, the Tomorrow's Schools' reforms also saw the introduction of a concept of equity that was compatible in important ways with the politics of cultural difference. There was, in a sense, an endorsement of a differentiated concept of equity, which—it could be argued even by those who abhorred the competitive consequences of the privatization agenda—if abstracted from a market context could be seen as a positive feature of the Tomorrow's Schools' reforms. Thus, instead of upholding universal standards and treating all children the same, the new conception of equity specified different rules and treatments for different groups.

Under the *National Education Guidelines*, first established in 1990 as part of the reform of school management that followed the passing of the Education Act of 1989, boards of trustees were charged with implementing the National Education Goals (NEGs), the National Curriculum statements (NCS) and the National Administration Guidelines (NAGs). The NEGs constitute the government's goals for the New Zealand state education system. Among the goals listed was that boards of trustees were obligated to "encourage respect for the ethnic diversity of New Zealand" as well as to "contain specific references to Māori students and to Māori initiatives" (Ministry of Education 1997: 7). For each of the ten goals stated, "boards of trustees are required to consider the implications for their schools as to how they can best contribute to the goal given their local circumstances" (ibid.: 7). Their responses will vary depending upon such factors as the size of the school, the needs of the students, and the aspirations of the school community" (ibid.: 7).

The National Curriculum Statements (NCS) identify the essential learning areas and essential skills for all students and make specific reference to the Māori language curriculum, as well as to specific subjects in Māori (mathematics, science, social studies). In addition, they make reference to curriculum concerned with the "language and languages learning area" for Chinese, Somoan, Spanish, Japanese, and Korean students. Notwithstanding these references, the overall requirements placed on schools in the NCS, as they concern the treatment of minority cultures, lacks specificity in relation to treatment or application, especially as regards the educational use of alternative languages to English.

Turning to the NAG, one finds more specific support for the educational practices that respect cultural difference. Not only is there general support for the "health and safety" of all pupils, as listed in the six areas of school operations, but in their charters, boards of trustees are responsible for taking into account the "local character" of the school, with an emphasis on the "special features of the school's community including its cultural and religious character." In addition, boards of trustees are specifically required to "analyze," "identify," and "where possible remove . . . barriers to learning and achievement." Such goals are to include "both female and male students, students of all ethnic groups; students with different abilities and disabilities; and students of different social and religious backgrounds. Inequalities will be recognised and addressed. All programmes will be gender inclusive, non-racist, and non-discriminatory, to help insure that learning opportunities are not restricted" (Ministry of Education 1993: 7).

In identifying and analyzing barriers to learning, schools must be able to collect information, utilize specialist diagnostic and special services, and determine possible effective changes that might be implemented. Such barriers to learning may arise from students' characteristics, their home circumstances, a school's systems and practices (such as "learning styles" or "restrictive timetables"). Or they may arise from "cultural differences," which might involve such things as "attitudes towards discipline or the role of women" (Ministry of Education 1997: 16). The Education Review Office has also published material on this issue. In their booklet *Barriers to Learning* (Education Review Office 1995: 1) the point is made that "there are a number of ways in which school administration structures and teacher behaviour are themselves disincentives to student learning." In addition to "external" factors such as student characteristics or home circumstances, schools must also consider their own "internal" processes with regard to issues such as timetabling, course fees, course prerequisites, ineffective policies on truancy and lateness, over-reliance on suspensions or expulsions, inappropriate resourcing of different needs, or practices linked to teaching or knowledge of the curriculum. Boards of trustees were specifically charged to design and implement strategies that address identifying learning needs to overcome barriers to student learning. Such strategies could involve practices in relation to the classroom, the school, or the outside community.

The NAGs are required for all schools in New Zealand in accordance with Section 60A of the Education Act of 1989. Boards of trustees are also charged with a number of overall management functions in regard to effectively overcoming the barriers to learning. Thus guideline 1 of the NAGs requires that boards of trustees should ensure that the principal has the necessary resources to ensure that school programs adequately reflect the national curriculum statements. This includes support for learning programs, curriculum development, and the professional development of staff. In addition, it advocates that the planning processes of the school are adequate, that effective systems are in place to identify barriers to learning as well as access additional help, and that the school has the resources necessary to implement and monitor the strategies adopted to overcome such barriers.

While this is the official story of how schools in New Zealand are supposed to accommodate diversity in principle, the competing budgetary and financial priorities of self-managing schools make a school's actual commitments to all of these goals and objectives frequently less than ideal. What happens at the level of practice, in fact, is that many schools' commitments and respect for cultural difference remain largely a form of lip-service. In addition to the specifications and requirements enshrined in legislation as outlined above, a Habermasian resolution of the issue would seek to impose the conditions of the *ideal speech situation*, in the form of the consensus achieved through communicative rationality, on the parties so involved. This would constitute a political resolution at the level of the local school-community nexus. Such an approach would involve a customization of school practices—curriculum, assessment, pedagogy, and governance—in accord with minority group values and attitudes to avoid marginalization and ensure a commitment to diversity. Such a process could be institutionalized by requiring schools to negotiate forms of differentiated provision and assessment with each minority group represented in its population. Only if such structures of learning, assessment, pedagogy and governance are seen to be fair by the different groups involved can the marginalizing effects of "neutralism" be avoided.

Other studies also trace the effects of applying ostensibly neutral rules and universal standards to the education of refugee groups in New Zealand as they affect the norms and practices associated with teaching and learning. Still others examine issues to do with the management of the self in relation to matters concerning personal style and daily comportment as they intersect with organizational norms and procedures (see Bochner 1983; Cochrane, Lee and Lees 1993; Cummins 1988; Eckermann 1994; Harker and Connochie 1985; Humpage

1998; Jones 1991; Sharp 1997; Smith and Smith 1996; and Stockefel-Hoatson 1982).

CONCLUSION

Iris Young's concept of a "differentiated citizenship" provides an enriched and more powerful supplement to the conception of citizenship embodied in the social democratic sociology of Alfred Marshall. It is not that the traditional conception was worth nothing, for it did give equality before the law. While that may not amount to much practically when comparing a panel beater from Mangere to Fay-Richwhite, it did amount to something when arbitrating the rights of Polynesian women against National Women's Hospital. It is not, then, that Young's conception and Alfred Marshall's are mutually exclusive but that as complements they can extend our understanding of citizenship under a new welfare state.

There are of course remaining problems. Young's commitment to "differentiated citizenship" is based on the premise of a philosophy of difference and a rejection of the "logic of identity." In linguistics, Saussure (1988) uses a philosophy of difference to explain the complexity and functioning of language and representation. He claims that "language itself undermines and problematises the very identities it establishes." What difference entails is that an object's essential identity is not fixed within it but is established by its relations or connections to other objects. These relations are constitutive of a multiplicity revealing that any unity or essential identity is only an illusion. Hence it is argued that an analytic of difference consistently applied reveals the falsity of any supposed unity or totality.

If it is to be made to work, this conception of difference must effect a certain conception of the political, which I have called in previous papers "thin" communitarianism. Central to this perspective here is that the notion of difference must presuppose a "minimal universalism," which in turn necessitates a certain conception of community. This perspective is based on an analysis of the concept of difference in western ontology. Since the time of the Greeks, and certainly in Marxism and Hegelianism, difference has been articulated in relation to "unity." The central point here is that the ontological postulates of difference and unity have to be kept in balance, that is, the principle of difference cannot plausibly explain social relations on its own. This is why in classical philosophy the theme of otherness, which underpins difference, was always paired with that of unity or identity. To try to make one's philosophical orientation work solely on the grounds of difference neglects equally strong arguments for "unity," for to try to define objects solely in terms of their differences neglects equally compelling reasons for considering them as objects of certain *kinds*. Similarly, if—as the poststructuralist insists—a final synthesis is not possible to achieve, this doesn't mean, nor should it entail, that all unities or identities simply collapse into differences or that social life is simply a process of endless, vicious regress. In short, unless the theory of difference is to result in incoherence, there must be a minimal kind of unity.

To represent this argument in political terms, it can be said that pushing the principle of difference too far results in contradiction, for while Young wants to celebrate multiplicity and a decentered polis, the fundamental ambiguity results from the fact that the very possibility of respecting the autonomy of different groups—whether based on religion, race, gender, or ethnicity—is only possible within certain *common* bounds. Letting refugee groups set up their own education systems may result in a splintered, fragmented form of "apartheid" that undermines the very democratic values Young celebrates and upon which, in fact, the capacity for the society itself to survive depends.

Hence arguments for radical difference or pluralism cannot answer the objection that it is simply not possible in practice to allow unlimited difference within any territory. Andrew Sharp himself admits such a limit, and in this he may support my claim for a "thin" communitarianism over a pure philosophy of difference. For him, difference entails a situation where it is recognized that two parties constitute *ethne* worthy of equal respect. "In what way are the two parties equal?" he asks (p. 36). His answer is that "the equality between them is civic; the kind of equality that exists in well-organized societies." It is not based on "one person one vote" for this would simply create a "new kind of despotism" (as de Tocqueville said) based on a "tyranny of the majority" (Sharp 1990: 41). It requires that the parties be "equally in subjection to the same normative system, the same rules distinguishing right from wrong." Sharp continues, "Otherwise how could they—and the potentially enforcing Interested Parties (IPs)—agree that a wrong had been done, should be righted, and in virtue of what repayment remedy could be said to have been provided. The very idea of reparative justice can hardly be conceived outside a society which recognises common rules of right and wrong" (Sharp 1990: 36). Such equality also requires, he notes, (p. 36) that "each party has the actual ability to enforce the rights and duties of the agreed system." Sharp goes on to note Lucy Mair's (1982) account of relations among the Azende of North Africa and notes that if reparative justice is to be done, then "(a) they must share the same rules as defining right and wrong and appropriate reparations for wrongs and (b) it must be possible for force of arms to be brought to bear if satisfactory reparations are not forthcoming" (Sharp 1990: 36).

The real problem, then, relates to the issue of power and how to share it: that is, which practices can be tolerated in relation to difference, and which must be part of the common society?

NOTE

This chapter is based on an article that appeared in the journal *Educational Philosophy and Theory*. Permission has been received to reprint it here.

REFERENCES

AJHR. 1939. *Appendices to the Journals of the House of Representatives*. E-Report. Wellington: New Zealand Government Printer.

Bochner, S. 1983. "The Social Psychology of Cross-Cultural Relations." In *Cultures in Contact: Cross-Cultural Interaction*. Ed. S. Bochner. Oxford: Pergamon Press. 5–44.

Cochrane, N., Lee, A. and Lees, P. 1993. "Refugee Students with No Previous Schooling." *Many Voices: Journal of New Settlers and Multicultural Education Issues* 5 (May): 18–19.

Cummins, J. 1988. "From Multicultural to Anti-Racist Education: An Analysis of Programmes and Policies in Ontario." In *Minority Education: From Shame to Struggle*. Eds. J. Cummins and T. Skutnabb-Kangas. Clevedon: Multilingual Matters. 125–157.

Eckermann, A. 1994. *One Classroom, Many Cultures: Teaching Strategies for Culturally Different Children*. St Leonards, NSW, Australia: Allen and Unwin.

Education Review Office. 1995. *Barriers to Learning*. National Education Evaluation Report No. 9. Wellington: Education Review Office.

Gutmann, A. 1988. *Democratic Education*. Princeton, N.J.: Princeton University Press.

Harker, R. and Connochie, K. 1985. *Education as a Cultural Artifact: Studies in Māori and Aboriginal Education*. Palmerston North: Dunmore Press.

Humpage, L. 1998. *Refuge or Turmoil? Somali Adolescent Refugees in Christchurch Schools: Intercultural Struggle and the Practices of Exclusion*. Master's thesis, University of Canterbury.

Humpage, L. and Fleras, A. 2000. "Systemic Bias and the Marginalisation of Somali Refugee Adolescents within New Zealand Education." *New Zealand Sociology*.

Jones, A. 1991. *At School I've Got a Chance: Culture/Priviledge—Pacific Island and Pakeha Girls at School*. Palmerston North: Dunmore Press.

Mair, L. 1982. *Primitive Government*. Harmondsworth: Pelican.

Marshall, A. 1925. *Memorials of Alfred Marshall*. Ed. A.C. Pigou. London: Macmillan.

Marshall, T.H. 1997. "Citizenship and Social Class." In *Contemporary Political Philosophy*. Eds. Robert E. Goodin and Philip Pettit. Oxford: Blackwell.

Massey University College of Education. 1996. *A Guide to Writing Your EEO Programmes: For Boards of Trustees*. Palmerston North: Massey University College of Education.

Ministry of Education. 1993. *Health and Safety Code of Practice for State Primary, Composite and Secondary Schools*. Wellington: Learning Media.

Ministry of Education. 1993. *The New Zealand Curriculum Framework*. Wellington: Learning Media.

Ministry of Education. 1997. *Governing and Managing New Zealand Schools: A Guide for Boards of Trustees. Part One: The National Education Guidelines*. Wellington: Learning Media.

Saussure, F. 1988. *Course in General Linguistics*. Chicago, Illinois: Open Court Publishing Company.

Sharp, A. 1997. *Justice and the Māori: The Philosophy and Practice of Māori Claims in New Zealand since the 1970s*. 2nd ed. Auckland: Oxford University Press.

Smith, G.H. and Smith, L.T. 1996. "New Methodologies in Māori Education." In *Nga Patai: Racism and Ethnic Relations in Aotearoa/New Zealand*. Eds. P. Spoonley, C. McPherson and D. Pearson. Palmerston North: Dunmore Press. 217–234.

Stockfelt-Hoatson, B.-I. 1982. "Education and Socialisation of Migrants Children in Sweden with Special Reference to Bilingualism and Biculturalism." In *Uprooting and Surviving: Adaptation and Resettlement of Migrant Families and Children*. Ed. R. Nann. Dordrecht: D. Reidel. 72–77.

Young, I.M. 1997. "Polity and Group Difference: A Politics of Ideas or a Politics of Presence?" In *Contemporary Political Philosophy*. Eds. Robert E. Goodin and Philip Pettit. Oxford: Blackwell.

Young, I.M. 1986. "The Ideal of Community and the Politics of Difference." *Social Theory and Practice* 12 (1) spring: 1–26.

Young, I.M. 1990. *Justice and the Politics of Difference*. Princeton, N.J.: Princeton University Press.

Young, I.M. 1995. "Together in Difference: Transforming the Logic of Group Political Conflict." In *The Rights of Minority Cultures*. Ed. Will Kymlicka. Oxford: Oxford University Press. 155–178.

3

Experiential Learning, Social Literacy and the Curriculum

James Arthur and Jon Davison

An active citizen . . . is someone who not only believes in the concept of a democratic society but who is willing and able to translate that belief into action.

Education for Active Citizenship. 1989, p. 7. Australian Government.

INTRODUCTION

Since the nineteenth century, the concept of service has informed curricula aimed at the social development of pupils. The main purposes of such curricula were to develop habits and dispositions of thrift, prudence, and industry to preserve the social fabric and equip future workers with skills as well as qualities such as perseverance and humility. During the first half of the twentieth century, the construction of vocational and social education anchored in the workplace was based on the premise of inculcating in pupils a desire to be of service to the nation, or society. In the 1960s, however, the notion of individual needs in relation to citizenship was regarded as equally important. Such concerns slowly shaped policy. In the 1980s vocational and social education was primarily driven by a desire to develop libertarian citizens who would be able to operate successfully in a market economy. At the end of 1990s, however, this approach gave way to a commitment to the development of the social aspects of the curriculum founded on community service. The New Labour government in the United Kingdom stamped its ethical mark on the National Curriculum by placing an obligation on schools and teachers to promote social cohesion, community involvement, and inclusion together with a sense of social responsibility among young people. Citizenship education emphasizes a range of social skills and schools are to ensure that children will develop positive social dispositions through the curriculum.

Social literacy is concerned with the development of social skills, knowledge, and positive human values that engender in human beings the desire and ability to act positively and responsibly in a range of complex social settings. Many Commonwealth countries such as Canada, New Zealand, and Australia, as well as Scandinavian nations such as Sweden (Kerr 1999) have the development of the child in and through society as a foremost principle of education. The new Labour government's agenda for the social development of pupils is located within Personal, Social and Health Education and in the new curriculum area of citizenship education. In November 1997 the Advisory Group on Citizenship Education, chaired by professor Bernard Crick, was established to provide advice on effective education for citizenship in schools. The resultant "Crick Report" contains recommendations for the development of the knowledge, skills, understanding, and values necessary for "active citizenship" (Qualification and Curriculum Authority [QCA] 1998a: 10). The report highlights three "mutually-dependent" aspects believed to underpin an effective education for citizenship: "social and moral responsibility, community involvement and political literacy" (QCA 1998b: 11–13). In other words, citizenship education in the National Curriculum highlights the development of social literacy (Arthur, Davison and Stow, 2001).

This chapter explores the relationship between social literacy, citizenship education, and community involvement and argues the case for the centrality of experiential learning for the development of active citizenship.

SOCIAL LITERACY

The 1988 Education Reform Act effectively ended the development of social studies, which had developed during the 1970s (see, for example, Rennie et al. 1974 and Elliot and Pring 1975) in English schools through prescribing a range of traditional subjects and defining them in abstract academic terms. The social aspects of the curriculum were marginalized as academic subjects sought status in the hierarchy of academic credibility that underpinned the structure of the first National Curriculum statutory orders. Core and foundation subjects were not overtly concerned with the social and practical aspects of daily life. However, for the national curriculum to fulfill the intentions of the 1988 Act—the curricular aim, to fit pupils for life and the world of work—the teaching of the social component of the school curriculum needed to be integrated in a cross-curricular fashion. Consequently, a range of cross-curricular documentation relating to, among other things, citizenship, health education, economic and industrial understanding, was produced.

Elsewhere, during the 1980s in Australia and New Zealand, education for social literacy was developing. The term "social literacy" was first used within the context of multicultural education in Australia (Kalantzis and Cope 1983). Kalantzis and Cope extended the use of the term to include knowledge about, and particularly learning from, the social sciences as taught in schools. Subsequently, the New Zealand national curriculum spoke about children acquiring social literacy by means of a study of social studies through the social processes of enquiry, values exploration, and social decision-making. Here the term relates to the acquisition of knowledge and understanding linked to the promotion of responsible behavior and the development of appropriate social skills. During the 1990s, the "Emotional Intelligence and Social Literacy" movement developed in the United States (see, for example, Goleman 1996).

However, contrary to the direction of official government documentation in the 1990s, the Report of the National Commission on Education (1993), commissioned by the Paul Hamlyn Foundation, reasserts the importance of schools in the socialization of pupils. Further, it maintains that education is the conduit through which "society transmits its values from one generation to another" (ibid., 93). The Report exemplifies values that are not out of place in other approaches to developing social virtues. They include "truthfulness, respect for other people, a sense of the obligations due to the community in which we live . . . and a caring attitude towards others" (ibid., 93). A renewed emphasis has been given to the social dimension of the 1999 revision of the National Curriculum for England in its *Statement of Values, Aims and Purposes* (QCA 1999b). The statement includes the development of children's social responsibility, community involvement, the development of effective relationships, knowledge and understanding of society, participation in the affairs of society, respect for others, and children's contribution to the building up of the common good, including their development of independence and self-esteem. Indeed, since the election of the New Labour government in 1997, it has become clear that much of the content of educational policy has its roots in the 1993 National Commission Report.

Despite its acknowledgment that adults operate in a complex social world, the revised National Curriculum documentation ignores the complexity of the processes through which pupils' social literacy is developed. Unlike scientific or mathematical knowledge, which, in the main, may be developed in the school context, children's values, beliefs and attitudes are also developed within the home and in the wider community, where their socialization takes place. Indeed, some children's "home" values may be in direct opposition to those espoused by the school, as well as being at variance with those of other children. The "primary socialization" of the home may be based on values that are at variance with the "secondary socialization" of the school. The importance of home and school in the socialization of children is recognised by Lawton (1973). In all societies, primary socialization takes place predominantly within family groupings as a "process of inducting children into (the) rules, beliefs and values" (Ibid., 41). This is a mediated world view (a version of society's beliefs and values presented by someone with whom the child identifies), but for the child this is *the* world. Secondary socialization, on the other hand, "deals with the internalisation of *partial* realities" (emphases original author). Knowledge is now mediated by means of an institution, or by a functionary within the institution (work or school)" (Ibid., 41). A difficulty for schools lies in the fact that these beliefs and values may be markedly different from, or in direct opposition to, a child's primary socialization. In a pluralistic society, therefore, problems of knowledge and meaning are exacerbated by a multiplicity of groups holding different perspectives of the world and of knowledge (Ibid., 42). A limited model of citizenship education like the one presented in the revised National Curriculum will be insufficient to develop pupils' social literacy fully.

Bentley (1998) believes that "the practice of citizenship can best be described as a connection between the particular and the universal." While it is possible to accept the idea that an act of citizenship is always bounded by an interrelationship of self and other, Bentley's everyday use of the phrase "the practice of citizenship" ignores the fact that there are many versions of citizenship. National Curriculum guidance documents for Personal, Social, and Health education (QCA 1999b), which include Citizenship for Key Stages 1 and 2 (QCA 1999c), and Citizenship for Key Stages 3 and 4 (QCA 1999d) also present citizenship as monolithic. We would argue that such a position is untenable. We have argued elsewhere (Arthur and Davison 2000) that there are many versions of citizenship, some of which are diametrically opposed. Briefly, we propose four broad categories of citizenship: libertine, paleoconservative, libertarian, and communitarian. Each of these has its own values and discourses, which underpin the world view of its citizens. Clearly, models of citizenship education developed from different sets of values and beliefs are quite likely to lead to the construction of markedly different curricula.

In a chapter of this length any characterization of the beliefs and values of the various types of citizens will not be exhaustive and runs the risk of appearing reductive. We fully acknowledge that there are many other values, beliefs, and attitudes that might be attributed to the versions of citizenship education described below. Values have been ascribed with the sole intention of showing that it is too simplistic to refer to citizenship education as if it were not a debatable term. Similarly, the beliefs and values listed are not necessarily only confined to the particular version to which they have been ascribed. For example, the idea of *service* would naturally exist in both paleoconservative and communitarian versions of citizenship education, but the versions of service would be markedly different. For example, a paleoconservative acceptance of externally constructed and imposed rules is in opposition to a communitarian collective engagement in the construction of rules. Further, we offer these descriptions as a means to explore the concept of citizenship education and the values that underpin its varying forms, as they illustrate the differing values and beliefs that might be seen as characterizing types of citizenship.

Libertarian citizenship education would at best be about developing the child's competence to operate successfully within the capitalist system, to understand the rules, and develop the dispositions of utilitarian creativity and entrepreneurial drive. At worst, it could encourage the practice of deceit, fraud, and hypocrisy, which are destructive of community and lethal to democracy. Libertine citizenship education would be radically critical of concepts such as virtue, community, tradition, and its aim would not be to extend the common good. Instead, this type of citizenship education would engage in an on-going struggle to ensure the maximum freedom for each individual, with everything up for questioning and argument. At worst, this libertine approach could cause division, fragmentation, and strife within community. Citizenship education for the paleoconservative would mainly be about complying with various kinds of authority. At best this type of citizenship education would encourage qualities like respect, responsibility, and self-discipline; at worst, submission, conformity and docility. Finally, communitarian citizenship education would emphasize the role, depending on the ideological perspective, of "mediating" social institutions in addition to schools, in the belief that society as a whole is educative. At best, this would not restrict itself to the transmission of a set of social procedures, but aim to strengthen the democratic and participative spirit within each individual. At worst, it could become majoritarean in approach, insisting on the acceptance of the moral position of the majority in society. We would argue that the New Labour aspires to the best ideal of the communitarian citizen in its revision of the National Curriculum. (For a full discussion of these issues, see Arthur and Davison 2000: 23–37.)

Ultimately, the term "social literacy" is not unproblematic, for the means by which children acquire social literacy can privilege some over others. By using the "right" behavior and language in the "right way," that is, by entering the dominant discourse, socially literate citizens have avenues opened for them to the social goods and powers of society. The New Labour government in the United Kingdom seeks to use citizenship education in the school curriculum as a means to redress deficiencies in the prior social acquisition of children in the name of "inclusion." Fundamentally, the school is an agency of socialization that exerts pressures on those involved to accept its social values as their own. Successful engagement with learning through an induction into "educated discourse" (Mercer 1995: 84) will determine pupils' future acquisition of social "goods": for example, particular employment paths, further and higher education, and, ultimately, status and wealth.

However, the U.K. government's agenda goes further than the development of active, successful citizens by establishing citizenship education in the school curriculum. The government is also eager to reduce truancy and exclusion from schools together with reducing crime and reconviction among young people. The Social Exclusion Unit, based in the Cabinet Office, has sought to achieve these ends by means of a whole range of initiatives that involve interagency work with voluntary and community groups—another communitarian characteristic of government policy. With over three million children living in poverty and one in four living in inadequate housing, a Children and Young People's Unit has also been established to develop a national childcare strategy. This strategy will aim to increase the social literacy of children through interventions in socially disadvantaged areas of the country. It aims to develop confident children who are aware of their rights and responsibilities. The Policy Action Unit Team 11 published *Schools Plus: Building Learning Communities* (2001), a document that strongly advocates that schools in deprived areas should adopt a community focus and become centers of excellence in community involvement.

Essentially, the government wishes to build schools as learning communities that develop individuals who feel they have an active and full part to play in society, who feel they can cope with relationships with other people, who are sociable, and who are going to be good parents in the future. However, the school curriculum is not currently designed to facilitate this type of approach to education when the demand and emphasis is often that we simply make children literate and numerate. There is a real and growing tension between government policies that appear to advocate community learning and inclusion and others that aim to increase academic standards through competition between schools and encourage new forms of selection. It is perhaps why experiential learning in community was made mandatory in the new Citizenship Order.

EXPERIENTIAL LEARNING

Most school learning takes place in the classroom, and yet for citizenship education it is by no means an ideal learning environment. Indeed, the authors of the Crick report acknowledge that schools can "only do so much" (QCA 1998a: 9) in the development of active future citizens. Such development is not only the product of schooling, but is also the product of the complex interactions between children and their homes, and between children and the wider community in which they grow. This fact is acknowledged in the citizenship education curriculum as it recognizes that pupils should be offered opportunities to practice political and social responsibility in the community. Active citizenship implies and even requires *action* on the part of the citizen pupil. The ability to think and act on social and political concerns underpins effective citizenship education. Pupils therefore need to develop active, collaborative, and cooperative working patterns focused on real problems in a real community—what is variously called service learning, community-based learning, community participation, community education, or experiential learning. For the purposes of this chapter we will use the term "experiential learning" to cover most of the activities indicated by all the other terms listed above.

Dyson and Robson (1999) provide an excellent summary of the research and literature on school and community involvement, and clearly, experiential learning, of which community service is a type, has its roots in the writings of John Dewey. The most relevant of Dewey's works to our discussion are *How We*

Think (1933) and *Experience and Education* (1938). Aldous Huxley observed that experience does not happen to people; rather it is what people do with what has happened to them. Therefore, experience of itself need not result in learning. For Dewey, experience per se was not necessarily educative:

The belief that all genuine education comes about through experience does not mean that all experiences are genuinely or equally educative. Experience and education cannot be directly equated to each other. For some experiences are mis-educative. Any experience is mis-educative that has the effect of arresting or distorting the growth of further experience. An experience may be such as to engender callousness; it may produce lack of sensitivity and responsiveness. Then the possibilities of having richer experience in the future are restricted. (Dewey 1938; 25)

Dewey's comments are a salutary reminder that community learning experience is not unproblematic. For experience to become educative, an individual needs to engage in "reflective thinking," which Dewey defines as "active, persistent and careful consideration of any belief or supposed form of knowledge in the light of grounds that support it and the further conclusions to which it tends" (Dewey 1933: 9). Through engaging in reflective thinking practices, pupils will be enabled to begin to see and understand things about themselves, their peers, their school, their community and, ultimately, about the society in which they live.

Experiential learning can have an extremely broad or narrow definition depending on what the "experience" is. We define it as the knowledge, skills, and understanding acquired through observation, simulation, and/or participation by engaging the mind and/or body through activity, reflection, and application (Arthur and Wright 2001). It should facilitate pupils' affective and cognitive development. Experiential learning is therefore about doing something that integrates concrete experiences with reflective observations about the experience. Learning, the development of "knowledge, understandings, and beliefs is a synthesis of experiences" (Arthur, Davison, and Moss 1997: 77–78). The process of synthesizing enables pupils to focus, probe, and test and to begin to make sense of emergent attitudes, beliefs, and understandings of themselves, their peers, and the community. "Experiences" as described here will not only take the form of direct involvement, but may also result from reading, writing, or discussion with peers, teachers, community members, or others.

Director of Community Service Volunteers (CSV) Education for Citizenship, John Potter, calls experiential learning "active learning in the community" (ALC). He defines it as an educational method that offers concrete opportunities to pupils to learn new skills and to think critically. He believes it should be incremental, progressing from one year to the next, and integral to what is taught in the whole curriculum. Potter advocates a whole school approach that responds to the needs in the school and community. He also believes it should be assessed, accredited, and celebrated. ALC is clearly more than simply helping out in the community: there need to be outcomes, and pupil learning must result. There are also many benefits from such an approach including, among others, giving pupils a sense of purpose, independence, self-understanding, confidence, leadership skills, a sense of belonging, and positive personal values. In summary, Potter (1999: 10) defines experiential learning as "based on a methodology that brings together young people's activities that benefit others with structured curriculum-related opportunities to learn from the experience."

As such, this definition of effective community learning resonates well with communitarian conceptions of citizenship, which emphasize that identity and stability of character cannot be realized without the support of a community, and thus pupils need to make contributions to their community (Arthur 2000). The strongest advocates of "community service" programs have been American communitarians, who believe them to be an indispensable prerequisite for citizenship education. Etzioni (1995: 113) argues that community service programs are the "capstone of a student's educational experience" in school. Communitarians advocate mandatory community service programs in schools because they argue that volunteer programs only attract a minority of students. The issue of whether service learning should be required or voluntary has been debated for the last ten years in the United States. Service learning in the community has formed the basis of many programs in U.S. schools and colleges (see for example, Andersen 1998), but few states in the USA have made community service mandatory. In England, however, there is growing pressure on all schools to introduce some form of experiential community learning. The Crick report discussed whether "service learning or community involvement initiated by schools should be part of the new statutory Order for Citizenship Education," but it "concluded not to ask for their statutory inclusion" (QCA 1998a: 25). Nevertheless, it was given statutory status by the secretary of state for education in the citizenship order. Schools are, therefore, legally obliged to provide some form of community-based learning for every pupil.

Young (1999: 469) has outlined the main obstacles to experiential learning in the community:

• superiority of subject-based knowledge;
• undervaluing of practical knowledge;
• priority given to written knowledge as opposed to other forms of presenting knowledge;
• superiority of knowledge acquired by individuals over that developed by groups of pupils working together.

All these obstacles are located within the school curriculum. Young argues for an education that gives pupils a sense that they can act in the world, an education that helps create new knowledge, and for the relevance of school knowledge to everyday problems. Community participation on the part of pupils offers the possibility of fulfilling the vision outlined by Young. Garratt (2000) believes that community participation is predicated on an Aristotelian perspective, where the process of becoming habituated through experience in community leads to the development of a virtuous character. He argues that, both in and out of school, pupils should be exposed to as many experiences as possible that encourage positive behavior. Ruddock and Flutter (2000) also seek to "create a new order of experience for them [pupils] as active participants." They recognize that secondary schools offer less responsibility and autonomy than many pupils would be accustomed to in their lives outside of school. All of these educationalists, while recognizing the problems associated with experiential learning in community, believe that citizenship education offers, through its community dimension, opportunities to develop active citizens. Others, such as Tooley (2000), argue that citizenship education should be learned out of school. He believes that the state should not intervene in schooling by providing citizenship education, as this will lead to greater control over individuals. While recognizing that education alone cannot bring about the development of citizenship, we do not accept his arguments and refer readers to McLaughlin (2000) for a detailed rejection of Tooley's stance.

Hart (1992) offers us a way of understanding this process of becoming part of a community. He outlines a model of community participation that he calls the "participation ladder." It may be summarized as

(a) pupils understand the community project they are involved in and know its purpose;

(b) pupils know why they are involved;

(c) pupils have a meaningful role within the project;

(d) pupils have made a free choice to be so involved.

Hart concludes that (a), (b) and (c) are necessary before (d) can be reached. Holden and Clough (1998: 20) offer further clarification in detailing their idea of "action-competent." The action-competent pupil is able and ready to participate and can argue, reflect critically, and relate his or her opinions and actions to a values framework. Holden and Clough describe this as a values-based participation in community, but do not provide us with knowledge of how these values are formed in any depth.

A good community participation program will address the issue of academic relevance by connecting knowledge, skills, and concepts with accomplishing a meaningful purpose in the school and/or community. As such, experiential learning becomes an integral part of school improvement and contributes to this by ensuring that knowledge is gained by the pupil through guided interaction with the community and local environment. It should develop critical thinking skills that help pupils make evaluations and judgements so that they will also develop problem-solving skills, since community issues and problems cannot always be neatly defined and solved. This should in turn assist pupils to think across the boundaries of traditional curriculum subjects, which should help them become more adept at integrating and applying what they are learning. Experiential learning, well planned and executed, allows pupils from a variety of backgrounds and abilities to work together on real problems that provide unity and purpose beyond the classroom. This facilitates inclusion, promotes equity, and fosters appreciation of cultural diversity by assisting pupils to relate to others from a wide range of backgrounds and life situations. It will help pupils to value and understand the differences among individuals and communities. The school community itself will change by creating new relationships with the local community, which will increasingly be viewed as a positive learning environment that benefits the school. As all staff members and pupils become participants in the process of experiential learning, they develop a personal and collective stake in making something positive happen beyond the walls of the school.

NATIONAL CURRICULUM

The report of the National Advisory groups on Personal, Social and Health Education, *Preparing Young People for Adult Life* (Department for Education and Employment [DfEE] 1999) proposes that schools should provide pupils with opportunities for them "to play a positive part in the life of their school, neighbourhood and communities." In a paragraph reflecting Bentley (1998), the report notes that the learning environment goes beyond the school because the school "is part of the community and learning opportunities will be offered by the quality of the school's relationship with the wider community" (DfEE 1999: 2). The report identifies the roles of significant contributors to Personal, Social, and Health Education (PSHE), including parents, schools, governors, pupils, Further Education (FE) colleges, health services, and central government. From the community it cites such significant contributors as "the people living in the locality, the shops, the services and amenities which serve them, the churches and other religious groups they belong to and other cultural and ethnic groups with which they identify" (DfEE 1999: 19). Other local and national organizations, civic and voluntary bodies are mentioned as providing support for personal and social development "often in conjunction with businesses" (DfEE 1999: 20). Although there is mention of pupils working to be of service to the school in its pages, nowhere does the report exemplify the nature of service to, or in, the community. Therefore, any school beginning to develop a model of service learning in the community needs first to be clear about how it will construct its model.

Will the school develop a model based on:

- the community of the school?
- the community in the school? Or
- the school in the community?

What will be the underlying purposes of service learning? Will the school attempt to develop in pupils, understandings that will result from:

- learning for service?
- learning about service? Or
- learning from service?

However, the National Curriculum offers little in the way of answers to these questions. At the heart of the National Curriculum is the *Statement of Values by the National Forum for Values in Education and the Community* (QCA 1999a and b). The statement uses the refrain "On the basis of these values, we should" (QCA 1999a: 148). Although schools and teachers are assured that there is general agreement in society on these values, the "we" of the statement is never identified. "On the basis of these values," it is the responsibility of schools to develop in pupils the capacity to "understand and carry out our responsibilities as citizens"; "refuse to support values or actions that maybe harmful to individual communities"; "promote participation in the democratic processes by all sectors of the community" and "contribute to, as well as benefit from economic and cultural resources" (QCA 1999a: 147–149). Both *National Curriculum for England* documents (Key Stages 1 and 2 (QCA 1999a), Key Stages 3 and 4 (QCA 1999b)) are underpinned by a statement of values, aims, and purposes (see for example QCA 1999a: 10–12). In the preamble to the nonstatutory guidelines for PSHE and Citizenship at Key Stages 1 and 2, the authors state the importance of pupils finding out about "their rights and duties as individuals and members of communities" (QCA 1999a: 136). At Key Stage 1, opportunities for interaction with the wider community cited are "meet and talk with people (for example, with outside visitors such as religious leaders, police officers, the school nurse)" (QCA 1999a: 138). At Key Stage 2, the "Breadth of Opportunities" includes "meet and talk with people (for example, people who contribute to society through environmental pressure groups or international aid organizations, people who work in the school and the neighbourhood, such as religious leaders, community police officers)" (QCA 1999a: 141). The model of service learning exemplified in the National Curriculum at Key Stages 1 and 2 is based upon the community of the school (school nurse), *the community in the school* (visits by significant community members), and focuses upon opportunities for *learning about service*. These opportunities are, of course, at the passive end of community involvement and, as such, are unlikely to promote the active citizenship the National Curriculum espouses.

At Key Stage 3 the opportunities cited are similar but indicate a shift towards more active community involvement: "meet and work with people (for example, people who can give them reliable information about health and safety issues, such as school nurses)." This, of course, could be a passive activity based on the community of the school, learning about service. The example continues with "develop relationships (for example, by working together in a range of groups and social settings . . . by being responsible for a mini-enterprise scheme as part of a small group)"—*the community in the school, learning about service*—and "participate (for example, in an action research project designed to reduce crime and improve personal safety in their neighbourhood)" (QCA 1999b: 190). While such involvement is undoubtedly positive—with the possible exception of the action research project (see below)—it does not promote actual community service in a real sense as the engagement is more likely to be *academic* rather than *experiential*. Only at Key Stage 4 are pupils recommended to participate "in an initiative to improve their local community"—learning from service. Other recommendations refer to the traditional "work experience and industry days" (QCA 1999b: 193)—*learning for service?* Despite the fact that the revised National Curriculum for England is predicated on clearly articulated beliefs and values, much of what is proposed in relation to community service is consistent with "traditional" approaches to personal, social, and vocational development. The only mention of "community-based activities" in the programs of study for Citizenship at Key Stages 3 and 4 is the phrase, which is identical in each key stage, "negotiate, decide and take part responsibly in both school and community-based activities" (QCA 1999b: 184–186). On close inspection, however, this phrase is premised upon models of *the community of the school* and *the school in the community* as well as *learning from service*. From this brief analysis, it would appear that the dominant model proposing service learning in the National Curriculum, with the possible exception of some activities in Key Stage 4, is passive rather than active. Community service is mainly constructed on academic curricular experiences arising from models of *the community of the school* and *the community in the school*, which will promote *learning about service* rather than *learning from service*.

The Community Service Volunteers (CSV) organization has extensive experience in the area of community involvement and has listed five citizenship competencies for experiential learning that are worth listing here:

- Work in a variety of group settings.
- Identify and evaluate the values and ethics of self and others in the community.
- Recognize, appreciate, and support vital elements of the local community.
- Gather and evaluate data necessary to effect positive change.
- Implement effective decision-making and problem-solving strategies.

All of these competencies need to be integrated into the academic school curriculum. CSV also lists four components that must be present to provide a quality experience for pupils. First, *preparation* is concerned with orientating the pupils toward action. Second, *action* is hands-on experience. Third, *reflection* is developing critical skills. Finally, *celebration* is due recognition for pupils' efforts and learning (CSV 2000: 13).

PREPARATION

Community service projects may originate in a number of ways. Pupils conducting research on their community may identify community needs. This community might be the school itself, but such projects would carry the caveat above about the dangers of a model that focuses solely on the *community of the school*. Pupils might identify needs of the wider community in which the school is placed, either individually, jointly, or in collaboration with members of that community. It needs little reflection to appreciate that teacher-initiated, focused, and directed community projects are likely to reap fewest benefits. When pupils are engaging on a collaborative action research project, they will not only identify community needs, but will have to prioritize to identify areas of greatest need and make realistic judgments about the feasibility of their ability to meet those needs. At the same time, teachers will need to identify opportunities for learning within any proposed project: How does the project relate to other curriculum areas? What might pupils need to know, understand, or be able to do before the project? What might they need to be taught before the service learning experience? What might pupils know, understand, or be able to do after the project? What will they learn from the experience? How will this be logged, recorded, presented, and assessed? What opportunities will the service experience provide for oracy, literacy, numeracy, research, and problem solving? What affective outcomes might be reasonably expected—self-esteem, virtues, dispositions, habits, beliefs, and attitudes? Although this list of questions might begin to appear lengthy and perhaps a little daunting, it is in reality no different from preparation for any other teaching and learning experience. Central to preparation for service learning is the articulation of the points raised in this paragraph.

Action

Action as part of community service needs to be a learning experience. "Experience" as described here will not only take the form of direct involvement, but may also result from reading, writing, or discussion with peers, teachers, community members, or others. Pupils, therefore, need to be provided with opportunities for this range of experiences during service and, most importantly, they need to be provided with a means to record and document action. Pupils need to be supported in maintaining journals in which they record events, concerns, fears, pleasures, insights, doubts, critical questions relating to incidents, to people, and indeed to themselves.

Reflection

Arguably, for community service experience to be worthwhile, pupils need to see the connection between service and learning. The experience needs to be "made visible" to them. Data collected in service-experience journals, logs, and so forth will enable service learning experiences to become "texts" that may be studied by an individual pupil, groups of pupils, and others engaged in the project. In their early discussions/writings, it is quite likely that teachers will see pupils being what they believe to be more descriptive rather than reflective. However, we believe that this fact should not surprise us, nor does it invalidate the activity, for it is in the initial stages, in such articulation or description of some aspect of the service learning experience that may seem blindingly obvious to an adult, that learning and development takes place. Such description in these early stages can for the first time make visible the values, beliefs, attitudes present in the community.

McIntyre (1993: 44) identifies three levels of reflection: the technical level, which is concerned with the attainment of goals; the practical level, which is concerned with the "assumptions, predispositions, values and consequences with which actions are linked"; and the critical or emancipatory level, where concern ranges to wider social, political, and ethical issues that include "the institutional and societal forces which may constrain the individual's freedom of action or limit the efficacy of his or her actions." We would argue that pupils should be encouraged and supported in engaging in all levels of reflection.

What are the purposes of reflection? How will reflecting enable the social development of pupils? The following list (adapted from Frost 1993: 140) is by no means exhaustive, but it helps to provide answers to these questions. Reflection enables pupils to

- assess his or her own knowledge, understandings, and skills, and to improve them;
- evaluate the approach to their community service project in terms of its appropriateness;
- comprehend and, where appropriate, question their own assumptions and preconceptions and those embedded in aspects of the community/society they encounter;
- continue to examine and clarify their personal values and beliefs;
- continue to examine and clarify the values and beliefs they encounter in the community;
- theorize about the context of their service learning—that is, try to develop explanations for aspects of the community;
- examine the social and political dimensions of the issues that arise in their reflection on community service and provide a critique of the discourses in which they are located.

CELEBRATION

Finally, it is important that there is recognition not only of service, but also of the learning that has taken place. While the first may involve a public or community manifestation of recognition, or celebration of a successful project— a plaque, a newspaper report, a ceremony of some kind—the second may involve a more personal dialogue between pupil and teacher, groups of pupils or pupils and mentors. The second form of recognition may also involve community members, parents, siblings, and so forth, to recognize the school as a fully active member of the community. Pupils should be encouraged to develop a portfolio of community service or record of community involvement that might be used for assessment as appropriate, but might also be used as evidence for further work—voluntary, or paid on leaving school—as a tangible manifestation of the qualities of an individual pupil.

The processes above provide a useful starting point for beginning to construct an active version of community service, arising from a model of the school in the community that will promote learning from service. The essence of the benefits of effective service learning is mutuality. Instead of focussing primarily on meeting the needs of just one of the "stakeholders" in community service, effective service learning has benefits for each participant; the pupil, the school, and the community. Without doubt, the benefits to pupils are related to their academic, intellectual, personal, and social growth and development. Engagement in effective service learning will develop not only oracy, numeracy, and literacy skills, but will also involve them in higher-order thinking skills such as problem-solving, critical thinking, and learning skills such as inquiry, observation, and application. Most important, the pupils' capacities in relation to insight, judgment, and understanding will be developed, and pupils' self-esteem, personal efficacy, and sense of responsibility will be enhanced.

The benefits to schools are equally important. Effective community service encourages pupils to play a more active part in their schooling and to take more responsibility for their own learning. Increased pupil motivation and cooperative learning structures enhance the quality of work produced and the quality of classroom relationships. Teachers will become reflective practitioners engaged in curriculum enquiry and development. There will be increased benefits as a result of collaborative decision-making among school governors and managers, teachers, parents, pupils, and members of the community. Effective community service will not only enhance the ethos of the school, it is also likely to mean that the school will have access to community resources, both material and human, to support teaching and learning.

The benefits to the community can arise from the provision of service to meet real human, educational, social, health, or environmental needs. Positive school and community partnerships empower not only pupils and schools, but communities as well, through joint planning, negotiation, and resolution of community problems. Pupils are members of the community, and as a result of active and effective community service, they will become positive and effective members of the community as pupils and later as adults.

CONCLUSION

Community education is a term that is notoriously ambiguous and open to different interpretations. Many educationalists and teachers believe that experience in learning is as, if not more, important than the content of what is taught.

Active experiential learning aims to facilitate the acquisition of social, political, and personal skills that are essential to the practice as well as the understanding of citizenship. Experiential learning in the community provides pupils with concrete opportunities to participate with others in serving the public. It presents schools with a powerful way of enhancing their pupils' learning by developing an effective range of social skills. The progress of pupils in citizenship needs to be recorded through a variety of means, and they will need to learn how to gather their own evidence of progress. This means that teachers need to support pupils in reviewing and recording their own evidence. This information can be used by the teacher to compile the annual reports on citizenship that will be required. However, the circumstances for active community involvement need to be present in the local community for it to work. The school cannot create these itself, and they will only arise if local and national government truly encourage participation and involve the public in this process. Schools need to respond imaginatively to the new opportunities that experiential learning offers. Above all, schools will need to be committed and be able to adopt good principles for community involvement and participation that follow through into good practice.

Experiential learning cannot remain a peripheral activity of the school. It appears to us that this type of learning is often best addressed outside the formal structures of the school because the aims and values promoted are more congruent with the processes being learned. Many schools have successfully involved themselves in this area and found to their surprise that the community can also become the teacher. However, we know from the very limited studies that have been done that service learning or community involvement has not been a priority of many English schools (Unicef 2001: 8). Indeed, some believe that faith in community experiential learning schemes is perhaps overly optimistic for schools.

However, we believe that community experiential learning is more likely to inculcate and develop altruism, philanthropy, self-reliance, and personal social virtues than is a classroom-based, "delivered" course of citizenship education. The social dimension of the curriculum must be about acting and doing in real contexts—*learning from service*—not simply a cognitive activity, but *learning about service*. Opportunities for moral development and the development of virtues and social dispositions will arise as pupils take on new roles, identities, challenges and interests, and work collaboratively for the benefit of others. They will develop increased social responsibility and concern for others. Political and civic knowledge and understandings will also be developed. Ultimately, pupils will develop their appreciation of, and ability to relate to, a diverse range of situations with people from a variety of social backgrounds. Experiential learning in the community offers a tangible and valid way to develop pupils' social literacy that will actively involve, engage, and empower pupils.

REFERENCES

Andersen, V. 1998. "Community Service Learning and School Improvement." *Phi Delta Kappa* 72: 761–764.

Arthur, J. 1999. "Communitarianism: What Are the Implications for Education?" *Educational Studies* 24 (3): 353–368.

Arthur, J. 2000. *Schools and Community: The Communitarian Agenda in Education.* London: Falmer.

Arthur, J. and Davison J. 2000. "Social Literacy and Citizenship Education in the School Curriculum." *The Curriculum Journal* 11(1): 9–23.

Arthur, J., Davison, J. and Moss, J. 1997. *Subject Mentoring in the Secondary School.* London: Routledge.

Arthur, J., Davison, J. and Stow, W. 2001. *Social Literacy, Citizenship Education and the National Curriculum.* London: RoutledgeFalmer.

Arthur, J. and Wright, D. 2001. *Teaching Citizenship in the Secondary School.* London: David Fulton.

Bentley, T. 1998. *Learning Beyond the Classroom: Education for a Changing World.* London: DEMOS/Routledge.

Community Service Volunteers. 2000. *Discovering Citizenship through Active Learning in the Community: A Teaching Toolkit.* London: Community Service Volunteers.

Department for Education and Employment. 1999. Report of the National Advisory Groups on Personal, Social and Health Education. *Preparing Young People for Adult Life.* London: Department for Education and Employment.

Dewey, J. 1933. *How We Think.* London: D.C. Heath.

Dewey, J. 1938. *Experience and Education.* New York: Macmillan.

Dyson, A. and Robson, E. 1999. *School, Family and Community.* London: Roundtree Foundation.

Education for Active Citizenship. 1989. Australian government publication. Sydney.

Elliott, J. and Pring, R. 1975. *Social Education and Social Understanding.* London: University of London Press.

Etzioni, A. 1995. *The Spirit of Community.* New York: Basic Books.

Frost, D. 1993. "Reflective Mentoring and the New Partnership." In *Mentoring.* ed. D. McIntyre. London: Kogan Page.

Garratt, D. 2000. "Democratic Citizenship in the Curriculum: Some Problems and Possibilities." *Pedagogy, Culture and Society* 8 (3): 322–346.

Goleman, I. 1996. *Emotional Intelligence.* London: Bloomsbury.

Hart, R. 1992. *Children's Participation: From Tokenism to Citizenship.* Innocenti Essays no. 4. Florence: Unicef International Child Development Center.

Holden, C. and Clough, N. 1998. *Children as Citizens: Education for Participation.* London: Jessica Kingsley Publications.

Kalantzis, M. and Cope, B. 1983. *An Overview: The Teaching of Social Literacy.* Sydney: Common Ground.

Kerr, D. 1999. "The Citizenship Education Study." *International Review of Curriculum and Assessment Frameworks Project.* http://www.inca.org.uk/

Lawton, D. 1973. *Social Change, Educational Theory and Curriculum Planning.* London: Hodder and Stoughton.

McIntyre, D., ed. 1993. *Mentoring*. London: Kogan Page.

McLaughlin, T.H. 2000. "Citizenship Education in England: The Crick Report and Beyond." *Journal of Philosophy of Education* 34 (4): 541–570.

Mercer, N. 1995. *The Guided Construction of Knowledge*. Clevedon: Multilingual Matters.

National Commission on Education. 1993. *Learning to Succeed*. London: Paul Hamlyn Foundation.

Potter, J. 1999. *The Why and How of Citizenship Education: The Case for Active Learning in the Community*. London: CSV.

The Social Exclusion Unit Policy Action Unit Team 11. 2001. *Schools Plus: Building Learning Communities*. London: The Social Exclusion Unit Policy Action Unit Team.

Qualifications and Curriculum Authority (QCA). 1998a. *Education for Citizenship and the Teaching of Democracy in Schools: Final Report of the Advisory Group on Citizenship*. London: QCA.

QCA. 1998b. *Baseline Assessment Pack*. London: QCA/DfEE.

QCA. 1999a. *Early Learning Goals*. London: DfEE/QCA.

QCA. 1999b. *The National Curriculum*. London: DfEE/QCA.

QCA. 1999c. *Citizenship for Key Stages 1 and 2*. London: DfEE/QCA.

QCA. 1999d. *Citizenship for Key Stages 3*. London: DfEE/QCA.

Rennie, R. Lunzer, J.E.A. and Williams, W.T. 1974. "Social Education: An Experiment in Four Secondary Schools." Schools Council Working Paper 51. London: Evans/Methuen.

Richardson, R. 1998. "Inclusive Societies, Inclusive Schools—the Terms of Debate and Action." *Multicultural Teaching* 16 (2): 23–29.

Ruddock, J. and Flutter, J. 2000. "Pupil Participation and the Pupil Perspective: Carving a New Order of Experience." *Cambridge Journal of Education* 30 (1): 75–89.

Tooley, J. 2000. *Reclaiming Education*. London: Cassell.

UNICEF. 2001. *Citizenship in 400 Schools*. London: United Nations Children's Fund.

Young, M. 1999. "Knowledge, Learning and the Curriculum of the Future." *British Educational Research Journal*: 463–477.

4

Citizenship Education and Curriculum
Theory

Alistair Ross

A curriculum is not a neutral document. Any statement of what is to be learned is permeated with objectives and intentions. Outcomes, whether explicit or implicit, necessarily embody values, and the ways in which the projected consequences of learning are laid out predicate particular teaching styles and methods. If learning outcomes are closely defined, particularly in a climate in which political authorities have reservations about the efficiency of schools and teachers, it is both possible and likely that the achievement of those outcomes will be assessed and quantified. Manifest and palpable assessment goals—learning by objectives—inevitably lead to learning and teaching patterns that are dominated by the requirement to meet the defined and measurable objective.

This chapter will examine current and classical theories about the curriculum and relate these to models of citizenship education. Citizenship education can be defined in such a way that it fits several curriculum models, and can be seen as potentially falling into one of several different curriculum traditions. The English model that is emerging appears to be particularly instrumental in character. In particular, this chapter will examine how a behavioral objectives model with clearly defined learning outcomes might lead to citizenship education, which is at odds with the stated purposes of curriculum makers in this field, in the United Kingdom, and around the world. Before turning to models of the curriculum, however, it will be helpful to address a series of issues concerned with citizenship education. Firstly, what does citizenship mean in contemporary life? People used to be citizens *of* something—of a Greek city state, of a modern nation. I will argue that citizenship is no longer so tightly linked to that kind of identity. This change can be linked to the question, Why now? Why is there so much contemporary emphasis on citizenship education across much of Europe? Addressing these issues also calls into question what kind of "citizen" we want. There are various kinds of civic behavior on offer, and some of these may be less compatible with the desires of the curriculum masters than are others. This will lead to a consideration of curriculum models, and from this to an examination of the likely outcomes of current initiatives.

CITIZENSHIP OF WHAT? AND WHY NOW?

There have been citizenship education initiatives in a variety of European states and encouragement from the European Commission for Education for a form of European citizenship. One of the main reasons advanced by governments is to address the so-called democratic deficit: the evidence, through national and regional election results, of poor voter participation (Oevermann 2000). In only four European Union (E.U.) states did the turnout in the last national election exceed 75 percent, and in these four voting was, or had been until recently, compulsory. Most states have had election turnouts between 50 percent and 75 percent: two have had rates below 50 percent. The participation rates in European Assembly elections have been even lower. In almost every country that has been voting since 1979, the participation rate has been falling. In the last elections (1999), the overall rate for the European community as a whole fell below 50 percent participation, from a level of 64 percent in 1979. We can compare the difference between UK national levels of participation and European levels, and note that in every case the electoral turnout for Europe is lower, in seven cases more than 20 percent lower: this added European democratic deficit is alarming, and rising (European Consortium for Political Research [ECPR] News 1999).

Is this why interest in citizenship education has increased in so many states across Europe in the past decade? Initiatives are taking place that include revitalized approaches to traditional civics education, the introduction of new teaching approaches, the addition of new curricular content, and the reformulation of some traditional subjects such as history. Firstly, one must note that there are significant differences in what is meant by citizenship, or more precisely, the identity with which citizenship is to be associated. For several hundred years, citizenship has been indistinguishable from nationality. This is no longer quite so. Examining this may lead us to see where some of the new demands for citizenship education are coming from, and also understand some of the possible associations with concerns about "democratic deficits."

One new kind of citizenship is being suggested at the European level. The former E.U. Commissioner for Education and Youth, Edith Cresson, called for "the achievement of citizenship through the sharing of common values, and the development of a sense of belonging to a common social and cultural area . . . a broader-base understanding of citizenship founded on mutual understanding of the cultural diversities that constitute Europe's originality and richness" (Cresson 1997). This was the culmination of a decade of development at the European Commission level:

The European dimension in Education should . . . strengthen in young people a sense of European identity and make clear to them the value of European civilisation. (European Commission 1988)

Education systems should educate for citizenship; and here Europe is not a dimension which replaces others, but one that enhances them. . . . Education for citizenship should include experiencing the European dimension . . . and socialisation in a European context . . . because this enables each citizen to play a part on the European stage. . . . Teachers should develop a European perspective alongside national and regional allegiances; to make use of the shared cultural heritage; to overcome cultural and linguistic obstacles. (European Commission 1993)

The European programs make much of the idea of nested identities and seek to promote citizenship at the European level as part of a self-identity that includes national and regional elements. Some of the national programs are significantly different in their conception of citizenship: they are addressing the reinforcement of a simpler, national civic identity. In Estonia, for example, the problem of national identity is such that educational programs need to address citizenship for a school population that has a significant minority of pupils who do not speak the national language (and some of whom do not wish to learn it) (Vald-maa 1999). The French civic education has its roots in maintaining a French republican identity (Fumat 1999). On the other hand, the English (*qv*) citizenship education programs are perhaps understandably hazy: there is no real indication of which country one will be a citizen. England? The United Kingdom? No: pupils must learn "to participate in society as active citizens of our democracy." Swedish teachers try to make students internalize democratic values and ideology, but do so with a strong focus on "subject knowledge" of the political life of Sweden (Vernersson 2000).

These moves to educate for citizenship in different states and in Europe thus seem to have a range of ideas, at least at the political institution level, about identity. Some focus on a state identity, others on regions, unions, or principles of democracy. States themselves are not natural, but are recent social constructions that were forged at the beginning of the modern period. Linda Colley (1992) analyzed the way in which the United Kingdom defined itself in a similar way in *Britons: Forging the Nation 1707–1837*. She describes how the union of Scotland and England invented itself as a cohesive state: united in its differences from continental Europe; founded on Protestantism, mercantilist profits, on Empire—on not being the Other, not being continental Europe. The national identity that was forged in Britain in the eighteenth century was, she argues, precisely that: a forgery—an invented unity based on opposition. And as a phenomenon of modernism, it is perhaps unsurprising that, as the postmodernist age begins, the legitimacy of states comes into question—both the legitimacy of individual states and the legitimacy of states per se, which may be no more than imagined communities. There is a coherent literature that argues that states are simply recent creations of the past few hundred years, cemented together with myths and inventions. Anderson's (1991) *Imagined Communities* conceptualizes nations as dependent on unreal unities between its citizens. Hobsbawm and Ranger (1983) have written of the *Invention of Tradition*, which presents case studies from around the world showing how national traditions, often presented as symbols of national unity stemming from time immemorial, are often little more than creations of the recent past—practices "of a ritual or symbolic nature, which seek to inculcate certain values and norms of behaviour by repetition, which automatically imply continuity with the past." In Eastern Europe Hosking and Schöpflin (1997), in *Myths and Nationhood*, suggest "that democratic 'civil' societies appeared to rely on myths just as much as authoritarian 'ethnic' ones."

Artificial or not, why are there at least some indications that the idea of the nation is in decline? From where do integrationist ideas come? There are at least two major competing explanations that are current. The realist and neoliberal view of the relationship between states and their integration, as exemplified most recently by Greico (1988, 1993) has been countered by the neoliberalism of analysts such as Keohane (1986). While realists emphasize states as perpetuating national interests and identity through a traditional reliance on security systems, neoliberal explanations see international collaboration as inevitable and pragmatic in the face of current challenges to the supremacy and autonomy of the institution of the state. In the past fifty years—and particularly perhaps in the last ten—we have seen an erosion of the old national certainties. Political boundaries at the national level have weakened, and there have been other parallel major shifts in social structures:

- social mobility, as the old certainties of class have weakened, employment opportunities have moved from physical production to mental and electronic creativity and interconnectivity, the "middle class" has expanded, and educational opportunities have grown;
- population movements—migration, tourism, refugees—on a scale hitherto unimagined, which have defied national frontiers;
- a weakening of the traditional gender roles across European society: masculinity and femininity no longer closely define our own behavioral expectations or those imposed on us by others;
- enormously weakened ethnic distinctions: there are increasing numbers of marriages between ethnic groups, and, despite continuing racism and xenophobia, there are weakening distinctions in this area;
- the end of the European overseas empires, which has resulted in a new set of roles, less certain than before, between the states of the North and the South, and between the peoples of both;

- globalization and the growth of multinational business, which has left national states less able to defend their own close economic interests and enmeshed more and more firmly in the economic world system.

In a postmodern world, national states will survive in a different and attenuated form: our imagined communities may become make-believe fragments even more than they have been hitherto.

These changes may help explain some of the forces behind the decline in voter participation in the traditional political forms. In response to the question, Why the decline? the traditional answer of the politicians—perhaps the obvious answer for them—is that we have not had enough political education. Schools have let down the various nations (once again): make the schools tell the children about the virtues of democracy, and all will be well. Politicians are concerned that without popular endorsement at the polls they will lack authority, so getting people to believe in (and vote for) the existing political system might restore their legitimacy. But politicians have a much greater personal identity with the state (or the union) than do most other people. Their role depends on the political entity: ours does not. Questioning the existence of the nation state, the boundaries, and the rules of membership becomes a challenge to the identity and legitimacy of the politicians and the public service, but they do not challenge most of us in the same way. This may explain why there's both a "democratic deficit" (to some people the existing political entities may no longer "matter"), and why there is a demand from politicians for citizenship education (to them, political entities matter very much). Some nonpoliticians may also feel themselves particularly threatened by the erosion of the idea of the nation-state. Those who need the authority of a state, who choose to identify strongly with conceptions of "their race," their genetic stock, are undermined by questions that challenge the legitimacy of this institution: hence the resurgence of extreme right-wing parties across Europe. The political answer to such individuals is that they need more political education: the current rhetoric for citizenship education is, as noted earlier, interlaced with references about promoting social inclusion, about challenging xenophobia and racism.

WHAT KIND OF CITIZENSHIP EDUCATION? WHAT KIND OF CIVIC IDENTITY?

There is another group of problems with citizenship education. Education "for democracy" is particularly problematic. What does this mean? As Borhaug (1999) has pointed out, it rather depends on what kind of democracy. Traditional representative democracy puts its energies into ensuring the intermittent participation of the population in elections through political parties that stand for broad principles. The key actor is the informed voter. The classic 1960s study of *The Civic Culture* suggested that the ideal citizen was a careful mix of the active citizen and the passive subject (and suggested that the leading exponent of this tradition was Britain (Almond and Verba 1965)). But there are other kinds of democratic action, and many people over the past two decades have become involved in more specific political activities than simply supporting broad political parties. The growth of "single issue" politics has challenged traditional politicians, who have found electors deserting mass parties in favor of pressure groups such as Greenpeace, Drop the Debt, activism related to the World Trade Organization meetings, and the European coalitions of Greens. The old political parties have had their activities and compromises challenged by informed political activists. This is an alternative kind of democracy that is less concerned with the political structures and procedures than with the issues themselves. The key actor becomes the local activist.

But this is not what the politician and public servants want political education to be about. Their concerns are—quite naturally—with buttressing the systems and institutions that brought them into existence and maintaining them. For them, citizenship education is not just about the identity question, as I argued above, but arises more from concerns about the perceptions young people appear to have about civic duties and obligations, and the need to persuade them to participate in political processes, to understand the need for compromise, and to accept the decision-making processes. If future citizens can be told how fair the existing system is, how the machinery of government works in the interest of the citizen, how interest groups must (of course) be listened to, but balances struck between competing interests, then they will accept the legitimacy of the political processes and become part of *The Civic Culture*, the good citizen.

Postcommunist societies in Central and Eastern Europe have other problems with citizenship education and education for democracy. Pavel Vacek, writing from a Czech viewpoint, puts it this way in a forthcoming publication: the population in these countries have a

strong aversion to the use of terms that were discredited in the totalitarian period (seen as ideological contamination). Many terms used to describe widely accepted human values became discredited during the period of the totalitarian state, because of their misuse: a phenomenon known as ideological contamination. For example, if the term "democracy" was mentioned, the only correct way to use this was in "socialist democracy"; the word "morality" was always qualified as "communist morality," and in a similar manner, socialist patriotism and citizenship. Having rejected communist ideology, we have pushed aside issues of citizenship and ethics because of their previous associations and usage. To find ways of presenting topics such as these is particularly difficult for ordinary teachers in the schools. All the ideological discourse has been removed from schools, which is a good thing, but at the same time our schools have become apolitical, so that there is very little, if any, reflection on contemporary events—and this is *not* a good thing. Because of this, to talk about freedom, patriotism, love and pride in our own nation often seems to us pathetic and improper: it is as though we were ashamed of such feelings and attitudes. (Vacek, forthcoming)

Identities relate to the individual rather than the group, but we express our identities in terms of the groups to which we belong, or (not infrequently) to the groups to which we do not belong. Perhaps it used to be rather simple. Our identities were expressed in terms of, for example, our gender: such roles gave us firm positions where we had defined areas of authority, clear expectations of behaviour, and used our gender to "know" what we had to do. Social class gave us a further set of identities and roles, helping us "know our place." And our ethnicity gave us an added set of identities that marked our position: we fell into a particular place in the various sets. Each of these contributed to a prescriptive identity: the boundaries around them were firm and immutable, and they were omnipresent: identities were not contingent and fluid, but were a unitary package that we took with us into all social settings and situations. As remarked above, these sets of identities have become less firm, and the edges have become at least rather fuzzy.

There was another set of identities that was also firm and fixed: that of belonging to a place and the social institutions that were associated with it. These could be seen rather as a concentric set of identities: family, region, nation, and perhaps global citizen. We could belong to all of these at the same time. While mobility was low, there was little contingency in this: we did not switch sets. Any new notion of citizenship or identity based on the new Europe must be distinctly different from the old citizenships of the nation-states: less ethnocentric, more diverse, more inclusive, less wedded to nationalistic conceptions. Osler (1994), for example, urges caution and the "development of an inclusive rather than an exclusive understanding of identity and citizenship." Hladnik (1995) takes issue with those who argue that European citizenship should be confined to those falling within a tight legalistic definition: he raises the important point that refugees and others, such as migrants, should also be regarded as citizens, and that our definition needs to be broad, inclusive, and separated from historical definitions of citizenship by birth, ancestry, or naturalization.

Identities thus appear to be both contingent and situational in contemporary society: an individual will adopt and take on a particular identity when he or she is in a particular context. In the past, people met few different contexts in the passage of their lives and therefore had identities that were relatively immutable and fixed. Now it is possible to travel physically through space more easily, more quickly, and more often than ever before, and the individual needs therefore to assume different identities more frequently as the social context changes. Who I am in London is different from who I am in Budapest, which is again different from who I am in New York or Delhi. The globalization of aspects of our culture again forces new identities on us. And who am I when I surf in cyberspace? Will I behave differently when I am on a site provided by a Finnish ISP rather than an Hungarian ISP? Do my e-mails project a subtly different persona when I send a message to .it rather than .de?

The processes of education in general and the character of the school curriculum in particular are critical agents in the development of these identities. One can conceptualize the process as either developing a reflection of existing patterns, or as transformative. Durkheim characterized education as "the image and *reflection* [emphasis added] of society. It imitates and reproduces the latter in an abbreviated form; it does not create it" (1897: 372). For him, education was

the means by which society prepares, within the children, the essential conditions of its very existence. . . . the man whom education should realise in us is not man as nature has made him, but as the society wishes to be. . . . Society draws for us the portrait of the kind of man we should be, and in this portrait all the peculiarities of its organisation come to be *reflected* (1897: 64–65; emphasis added).

This functionalist view is still common: "all societies have the task of passing on to the next generation the knowledge and skills regarded as particularly worthwhile; . . . societies achieve this by means of . . . education" (Lawton and Gordon 1996: 10). Although Durkheim's model was not wholly static (1938), it emphasizes stability, and sees society as essentially homogeneous. The reflection is mirror-like and results in self-replication. We learn who we are to be: we are what we have learned to be: as Brillat-Savarin (1825) put it in a rather different context, "tell me what you eat: I will tell you who you are." In this model of the role of the curriculum, it is not that one's identity is learned so much as one's identity is what one has learned: as Lewis Carroll *almost* wrote: "Not the same thing a bit!" said the Hatter. "Why, you might as well say that 'I learn what I am' is the same as 'I am what I learn'!" (after Lewis Carroll, *Alice's Adventures in Wonderland*, ch. 7).

By contrast, John Dewey proposed a largely transformative model of education. The school processes should promote social equality, so that "each individual gets an opportunity to escape from the limitations of the social group in which he was born, and come into living contact with a broader environment" (1916: 20). Education also had a developmental role for the individual: "it creates a desire for continued growth and supplies the means for making the desire effective in fact" (50). These egalitarian and developmental functions partly derived from Dewey's view of knowledge as something to be constructed by the learner as an active experimenter, provoked into inquiry by the teacher. (Dewey's model can also be seen as reflective, reproducing his perception of American society—"mobile and full of channels for the distribution of change occurring anywhere" (Dewey 1900: 88).) More recently, John Rawls (1971:107) has similarly argued that education has such egalitarian and developmental functions: "resources for education are not to be allocated solely or necessarily mainly according to their return as estimated in producing trained abilities, but also according to their worth in enriching the personal and social life of citizens, including here the less favoured." But many observers have argued that, whatever the ambitions the egalitarians and liberals have for education to transform society, this has not happened. Raymond Williams (1961: 120) argued that "the common prescription of education, as the key to change, ignores the fact that the form and content of education are affected, and in some cases determined, by the actual systems of decision and maintenance": political (decision) and

Table 4.1
Curriculum Types

Content-driven	Objectives-driven	Process-driven	
preparatory	Elementary	developmental	Blyth, 1967 [Primary curriculum]
classical humanist	Reconstructionist	progressivist	Skilbeck, 1976
subject-centered/ knowledge-centered	society-centered	child-centered	Lawton et al (1978)
academic	Utilitarian	pedagogic	Goodson (1987)
liberal humanist	Technocratic	child-centered progressivism	Golby (1989)

economic (maintenance) structures tend to prescribe the composition of the curriculum and the systems by which it is delivered in ways that minimize the possibility of societal or economic change. Michael Apple (1990: 43) develops this further, concluding that schools contribute to inequality because they are intentionally organized to unequally distribute particular kinds of knowledge. Williams and Apple both hold that the educational systems in Britain and the United States, respectively, are designed to replicate social and economic inequalities.

CURRICULUM MODELS

One can argue that there are three distinct approaches to constructing a curriculum. Each has a different set of aims and ambitions, and each will determine a particular pedagogic style of implementation. It is unclear to which of these traditions citizenship education belongs: it depends on who is advocating such education, and why. Only when we understand the motives does it become clear what is meant by this term, and only then can we calculate how to approach the subject.

For the purpose of this chapter, these three will be called content-driven, objectives-driven, and process-driven curricula, but other writers have given different names to what is essentially the same division. As Goodson (1987: 26) points out, these three types are the "centres of gravity in the argument about styles of curriculum . . . representing three clear constellations of curriculum styles which recur in the history of school subjects." The argument that follows centers on analysis and descriptions of the U.K. curriculum, but it is not materially dissimilar from curricula theory worldwide. For a fuller account, see Ross (2000).

The *content-driven curriculum* has been the ground on which official pedagogic discourse has largely been fought, the area from which "a whole possible area of past and present, certain meanings and practices [have been] chosen for emphasis, [and] certain other meanings and practices . . . neglected and excluded" (Williams 1961: 205). This is a curriculum designed as a construction of formally delimited zones of subjects or disciplines, the dominant curriculum paradigm for most European education in the twentieth century. A traditional "A" level British Constitution course would undoubtedly have fallen into such a category. The slowness of curriculum change shows the enormous resilience of particular subjects. Bernstein's 1990 analysis suggests that this dominance is the consequence of a core of officials, consultants, and advisers, both educational and economic, who recontextualize the curriculum into disciplines (Bernstein 1990: 195–196). In "On the classification and framing of educational knowledge" (1971), Bernstein argues that the two key concepts of the code are classification and frame.

Classification describes the relationship between the contents of the curriculum. It is concerned with the existence and strength of the boundaries that are constructed and maintained between subjects. "Where classification is strong, contents are well insulated from each other by strong boundaries. Where classification is weak, there is reduced insulation between contents, for the boundaries between contents are weak or blurred. *Classification thus refers to the degree of boundary maintenance between contents*" [emphasis as in original] (ibid.: 88).

Frame, on the other hand, refers to the context in which knowledge is transmitted and received—the relationship between the teacher and the pupil. Frame refers to the strength of the boundary of what may or may not be taught; it "refers us to the range of options available to teacher and taught in the control of what is transmitted and received in the context of the pedagogic relationship. Strong framing entails reduced options; weak framing entails a range of options. *Thus frame refers to the degree of control teacher and pupil possess over the selection, organisation, pacing and timing of the knowledge transmitted and received in the pedagogic relationship*" [emphasis as in original] (ibid.: 88–89). The many qualifications about the delivery mechanisms for citizenship education in England might suggest a weak frame ("learning outcomes" rather than detailed programs of study, combination of citizenship with other subjects, and so forth (Crick 1998: 22)), but there are, equally, lists of essential concepts and basic knowledge and understanding (ibid.: 41–42), which suggest a rather stronger boundary.

The objectives-driven curriculum is rather different: it is essentially based on an instrumental view of schooling. The traditional humanist curriculum is presented to many children as utilitarian—both in the sense that there is a form of usefulness in acquiring credentials in such subjects because it brings access to careers and professions otherwise unavailable, and in the sense that most subjects can be portrayed in some way that demonstrates utility. While the end results may appear to be similar to the outcomes of the content-driven curriculum, the intentions and processes of the objectives-driven curriculum are rather different. Skilbeck calls this model reconstructionist and argues that "attempts to plan and organise individual and social experience in relation to agreed ends and using agreed social procedures," particularly through educational processes, will lead to "the deliberate cultivation of rationality, of problem-solving procedures, adaptability and flexibility and a generalised capacity to face up to the problems of practical life" (Skilbeck 1976: 12). Citizenship Education, as devised in England in the Advisory Group Report, seems to fit well with this model; "the statutory entitlement is established by setting out specific learning objectives . . . rather than detailed programmes of study" (Crick 1998: § 4.2). And, as has been set out earlier, there are particularly compelling societal pressures for developing some form of informed citizenry, at least when seen from certain perspectives.

In these objectives-driven curricula, whether reconstructionist or otherwise, objectives that meet specific needs for competencies—of society, of the economy, or of the individual—are specified in advance, and a curriculum is drawn up to achieve these. Abilities and capabilities necessary to meet the needs of contemporary life are specified and used to justify the collection of subjects that constitute the curriculum. The justification depends not on the academic worthiness or otherwise of the subject, but on its ability to deliver the particular skills that are judged necessary. It is not essential that subjects have strict boundaries, so the classification code could, in theory, be weak. The frame, however, necessarily remains strong, because the dominant pedagogic model remains one of transmission from the expert teacher to the novice pupil.

Ralph Tyler (1949) was one of the principal exponents of managing the curriculum by setting objectives that were capable of evaluation. His analysis was deceptively simple: define the desired outcomes of education clearly, and do so in terms of the specific desired behavior that is expected after the educational process is completed. Then, the curriculum that will be the means to achieve that end will also be defined. The most technically apposite way to achieve these behavioral changes will be the "best" curriculum. The means are determined by the ends. Objectives-driven models assume that one can predetermine the shape to which a learner will be moulded: an analysis of the very carefully defined learning outcomes for citizenship in England (Crick 1998: 46–52) shows the kind of society that is to be created.

The third variant, the *process-driven curriculum*, has variously been described as the pedagogic curriculum in secondary schools (Goodson 1987), the developmental curriculum in primary schools (Blyth 1967)—sometimes described as the child-centered curriculum (Lawton et al. 1978; Golby 1989), and also as the progressive curriculum (Skilbeck 1976; Golby 1989). Its distinguishing characteristic seems to be that it is principally concerned with, or guided by, the *processes* of learning. It can often be sharply distinguished from the traditional academic/classical humanist curriculum, and was therefore often aligned with the utilitarian curriculum. The two sometimes formed an uneasy alliance in the secondary modern schooling system and in many comprehensive schools: a simple dualism made categorization and description easier. Thus Shipman (1971: 101–102) could write of "a schools system that is still clearly divided into two sections, one geared to a system of external examinations, the other less con-strained. . . . It is the consequence of innovation into these two separate sections rather than the curricula themselves which may be producing a new means of sustaining old traditions." On one hand was the content-driven tradition, which was "planted in revered academic tradition, adapted to teaching from a pool of factual knowledge and has clearly defined, if often irrelevant subject boundaries" and on the other hand was an experiential area that "focuses on contemporary problems, groups subjects together and rejects formal teaching methods" (ibid.: 104). Aspects of the English citizenship curriculum can also be seen in this process-driven model because there is a strong and persistent focus on the proc-ess of learning and, in many cases, an emphasis on the individual and his or her needs.

The three models of curriculum have other distinguishing characteristics. For example, the content-driven tradition sees knowledge as a distinct body of data, hierarchically arranged, which needs to be acquired. The process-driven tradition is that education is a process: rather than knowing *what*, one should know *how*— and in particular, learning how to learn (about knowledge) is more important than acquiring knowledge itself. For the objectives-driven curriculum, knowl-edge simply becomes a commodity.

Each type has its own particular characteristics, and they tend to be regarded in some ways as polar types. That is, many of those engaged in curricular discussion treat one or other of the types as desirable, and everything else as undifferentiated and undesirable (or one of the types as undesirable, and every-thing else as undifferentiated and desirable). Thus, for example, there is an "academic-nonacademic" axis for debate, in which groups form from those advocating a classical-humanist style curriculum and from those who are against it.

CHARACTERIZING CITIZENSHIP EDUCATION WITHIN THIS DEBATE

Citizenship education does not appear to fit simply into one of these three types: confusingly, it can be variously described to meet any one of them. In this paragraph, some of the examples have been drawn from the final report of the Advisory Group on the Teaching of Citizenship in England (Crick 1998), and these are indicated in italics. It can be seen as a body of knowledge: the pupil can be asked to *know about local government, general elections, taxation* and *the welfare state*, and so on. Such knowledge can be tested and graded, and will be of high esteem. Or the activity can be classed instrumentally, within the objectives-driven curricula. Such education will be presented as useful to the individual and socially desirable. It can be presented to the pupil as a way to develop useful skills—such as *taking part in a formal debate*, or *researching an issue of significance*—(in the *Civic Culture* form, this would be portrayed as "how you become a good citizen and vote"; while in the local activist form it would be described as "how you make political action work"). It is presented by politicians as both ensuring participation and securing acquiescence to political decisions, thus achieving legitimacy. Finally, citizenship education can be presented in a process-driven way. This will nurture the development of the individual's value system, will enable reflective and critical participation (or nonparticipation) on a reasoned, personally validated basis, such as *expressing a personal opinion relevant to an issue*, or being *able to reflect critically on working with others on a challenge of shared significance.*

Disentangling statements about citizenship education in different states may also help us see how intentions differ (Kerr 1999). Unsurprisingly, three broad sets of statements emerge, corresponding to the three curricula types. First, there are statements that pupils should know about and understand society and its institutions. Many curricula once fell in this content-driven category: for example, in Portugal and Greece in the early twentieth century (Chelmis 1999; De Freitas 1999). But often interwoven with civic education are threads of determining national identity and establishing a civic culture and pride, which suggests elements of an objectives-led curriculum. Some of the newer programs in the Eastern and Central European states understandably include such aspects: Estonia is a case in point (Valdmaa 1999). Hungary has some similar elements, but as Le Métais (1997) puts it, the Hungarian curriculum combines "the reassertion of national identity after political upheaval" with "national assertiveness within an international framework" (see also Gocsal 1999). The German curriculum values have also been revised to reestablish unity following reunification by some stress on the teaching of political and organizational information (Le Métais 1997). Sometimes it appears that the curriculum is not explicit about content in the sense that the objectives are written in terms of attitudes, values and behavior, but the details of what is to be taught focus on information about political institutions (contemporary Greece may be such a case; Chelmis 1999). In other situations, the teachers themselves may stress political institutional content over values and instrumental norms, despite its absence from the formal curriculum documents (for example, in Sweden; Vernersson 2000).

Second, there are statements that pupils should develop the capacity to act as "good" citizens and members of society. Although these may tend to be described in terms of empowerment of the individual—providing them with skills to make informed choices and to act—it may be that in at least some instances, what is meant by a "good citizen" is one who is "good" for the state: participating at the required instances of elections, acceptant of the legitimacy and authority that the process offers, and little more. Good citizens are those who fulfill their civic obligations, accept their duties, and perhaps make little use of their rights. It is necessary for the preservation of existing societies and institutions that citizens participate to the extent of accepting: such arguments are instrumental in nature. Some states describe aims for education that reveal these tendencies. For example, the French curriculum seeks "to prepare students for work, not just for qualifications." The English curriculum is even more explicit as to who will be the beneficiary: "to prepare young people for the opportunities, responsibilities and experiences of adult life and to increase the relevance of student achievement to the world of work so as to enhance the nation's international competitiveness" (in Le Métais 1997).

Third, there are statements that pupils should become reflective and critical participants. The emphasis here is clearly on process. Thus an educational aim in Sweden is "to instill those values on which society is based [an objectives-driven element] and to help students develop the ability to critically examine facts and relationships and appreciate the consequences of the various alternatives facing them [clearly process-driven]." Sweden also refers to enabling young people "to keep their bearings in a complex reality, with a vast flow of information and rapid change." Spain refers to the "promotion of progressive independence" (Le Métais 1997).

AN OBJECTIVES-DRIVEN CURRICULUM FOR CITIZENSHIP AND THE TEACHING OF DEMOCRACY

The motivation for citizenship education in England appears to be inspired by social considerations, rather than by concerns for the individual's self-development or for the hegemony of the subject-knowledge. In her forward to the Advisory Group Report (1998: 3), Betty Boothroyd, at the time Speaker of the House of Commons, referred to the lack of impact of citizenship education as "a blot on the landscape of public life . . . with unfortunate consequences for the future of our democratic processes." The group itself defines the area as "so important both for schools and for the life of the nation that there must be a statutory requirement on schools," for only this will provide an adequate basis "for animating the idea of a common citizenship with democratic values" (§1.1). The objective of their proposals, they claim, is "a change in the political culture of this country" (§1.5). The democratic deficit is more than implicit in references to "worrying levels of apathy, ignorance and cynicism about public life." This is an instrumental view of this kind of education: it is education for planned social change. There are references to other curricular forms; for example, to teaching "the knowledge, skills and values relevant to the nature and practices of participatory democracy" (§4.4), and to the "entitlement" that will "empower [individuals] . . . to participate in society effectively as active, informed and critical" members (§1.10), but these can be seen as no more than ritual genuflection to, respectively, the content-driven and the process-driven forms of the curriculum, necessary to appease proponents of these traditions.

The proposals are explicitly driven by objectives: "setting out specific learning outcomes for each key stage" (§4.2), "tightly enough defined so that standards and objectivity can be inspected" (§4.3). There are some particular and specific difficulties that follow when learning objectives are defined for practices, beliefs, and attitudes that might be loosely grouped under the umbrella of "life-skills." There are a number of socially important behavioral patterns, beliefs, and social constructions, which it is important that societies pass on to their new members. Environmentally responsive behavior and knowledge, economic and financial literacy, a concern with one's own health, civic and socially minded behavior, some sort of understanding of the need for personal endeavour to support oneself as far as one is able and to contribute to the common good as much as one can: these are broadly held current values of society. They change in nature and in emphasis, but are (at the moment) aspects of personal behavior that mediate with the behavior of the societies of which we are part. Contemporary society needs to ensure that its newest members develop behavioral patterns that will sustain social practice (which term is intended to include sustaining the possibility of social change). But we can't assess the achievement of these objectives in the same way we can assess more simple learning outcomes or skills.

It is (relatively) easy to define the achievement of a content-driven curriculum based on knowledge. "Can conjugate the present tense of *Amo*"; "can identify seven principal rivers in England and Wales." These outcomes are more or less objectively assessable in everyday terms. Some are absolutes, some may depend on a degree of judgement (such as what exactly a "principal river" might be), and some are matters of debate. Many skills can also be assessed in a straightforward way in a school situation: "being able to swim," for example, may need some definition—how far, within what time, in what particular manner—but it is assessable, and with some degree of confidence that the skill will still be there if the pupil is assessed next week, or even next year.

Behavior that relates to "life skills," however, is less easy to test directly. Like assessing swimming ability, we cannot see how well learners will behave until they meet the real situation. The assessment tasks that are set can only be proxies for what may arise later. The objectives that are set in citizenship education are measures that stand in for the real demonstration of political literacy. They are likely to remain subjective evaluations of how the child might behave when an adult and when placed in a situation where a real choice might be made.

In a situation where teachers and schools feel that their competencies are being challenged and that they are constantly being measured, compared, and ranked, it is inevitable that teachers will teach toward the test. It is necessary that their pupils' progress can be calibrated. If the assessment task is real—as in demonstrating the ability to swim, or the ability to speak French, or read information from a map—this may cause the teaching to move towards achieving the testable items, but at least what is tested is a real competence. But if the assessment task is artificial, a proxy for the real thing, then what is being taught is toward the achievement of performance of something that is not a real accomplishment of political/civic competency.

Assessment and teaching also tend to migrate from focusing on the ability to act toward an emphasis on the ability to recall facts and describe structures: toward a content-determined curriculum. The citizenship curriculum is thus likely in practice to reinforce emphases on subject knowledge, and this in turn raises the prospect of some students becoming "failed citizens" at the end of their schooling. This is not what was intended.

NOTES

This chapter is based on a paper given to a conference, "Diverse Citizenships?" at the University of North London in April 2001. I am grateful for the comments made by participants and also those made by my colleague, Dr. Merryn Hutchings. The responsibility for this chapter remains mine alone.

REFERENCES

Almond, G. and Verba, S. 1965. *The Civic Culture: Political Attitudes and Democracy in Five Nations*. Boston: Little, Brown.

Anderson, B. 1991. *Imagined Communities: Reflections in the Origins and Spread of Nationalism*. 2nd ed. London: Verso.

Apple, M.W. 1990. *Ideology and the Curriculum*. 2nd ed. London: Routledge.

Bernstein, B. 1971. "On the Classification and Framing of Educational Knowledge." In *Knowledge and Control: New Directions in the Sociology of Education*. ed. M.F.D. Young. London: Collier-Macmillan.

Bernstein, B. 1975. *Class, Codes and Control. Vol. 3: Towards a Theory of Educational Transmission*. 2nd ed. London: Routledge and Kegan Paul.

Bernstein, B. 1990. *Class, Codes and Control. Vol. 4: The Structuring of Pedagogic Discourse*. London: Routledge.

Blyth, W.A.L. 1967. *English Primary Education, Vol 1*. 2nd ed. London: Routledge and Kegan Paul.

Borhaug, K. 1999. "Education for Democracy." In *Young Citizens in Europe*. ed. A. Ross London: Children's Identity and Citizenship in Europe. TNP. 37–44.

Bourdieu, P. and Passeron, J.-C. 1990. *Reproduction in Education, Society and Culture*. 2nd ed. trans. R. Nice. London: Sage.

Brillat-Savarin, J.-A. 1825. *Physiologie de Goût*. Paris.

Chelmis, S. 1999. "Citizenship Values and Political Education in Greek Primary Schools: An Historical Perspective." In *Young Citizens in Europe*. ed. A. Ross. London: CiCe TNP. 65–71.

Colley, L. 1992. *Britons: Forging the Nation 1707–1837*. London: Yale University Press.

Cresson, E. 1997. *Towards a Europe of Knowledge*. COM 97 (563) final. 11 November 1997. Brussels: European Commission.

Crick, B. 1998. *Education for Citizenship and the Teaching of Democracy in Schools*. Final report of the advisory group on citizenship, 22 September 1998. London: QCA.

De Freitas, M.L. 1999. "Civic Education, Social and Personal Development and Citizenship Education: Changes in Portugal through the 20th Century." In *Young Citizens in Europe*. ed. A. Ross. London: CiCe TNP. 85–90.

Dewey, J. 1900. *The School and Society*. Chicago: University of Chicago Press.

Dewey, J. 1916. *Democracy and Education*. New York: Macmillan.

Durkheim, E. [1897] 1970. *Suicide: A Study in Sociology*. London: Routledge and Kegan Paul.

Durkheim, E. 1938. *L'evolution pedagogique en France*. Paris: Acan. 1977. [*The Evolution of Educational Thought: Lectures on the Formation and Development of Secondary Education in France.*] trans. P. Collins. London: Routledge.

ECPR News. 1999. *The 1999 European Parliamentary Elections*. Special issue 11 (1). Colchester: European Consortium for Political Research. www.essex.ac.uk/ecpr/ publications/ecprnews/autumn1999/elections.htm

European Commission. 1988. Resolution of the Council and Ministers of Education meeting within the Council of 24 May 1988 on the European Dimension in Education. In *Official Journal of the European Communities* C177-7 (June 1988: 5–7. Luxembourg: Office for Official Publications of the European Communities.

European Commission. 1993. *Green Paper on the European Dimension of Education*. 29 September 1993 (COM(93) 457) 7. Luxembourg: Office for Official Publications of the European Communities.

Fumat, Y. 1999. "School and Citizenship." In *Young Citizens in Europe*. ed. A. Ross. London: CiCe TNP. 107–112.

Gocsal, A. 1999. "Prospects of Civic Education in Teaching and in Teacher Training: The Experience of Hungary." In *Young Citizens in Europe*. ed. A. Ross. London: CiCe TNP. 101–106.

Golby, M. 1989. "Curriculum Traditions," In *Policies for the Curriculum*. eds. B. Moon, P. Murphy, and J. Raynor. London: Hodder and Stoughton.

Goodson, I. 1987. *School Subjects and Curriculum Change: Studies in Curriculum History*. rev ed. London: Falmer.

Goodson, I. 1988. *The Making of Curriculum: Collected Essays*. London: Falmer.

Greico, J. 1988. "Anarchy and the Limits of Cooperation: A Realist Critique of the Newest Liberal Institutionalism." *International Organisation* 42: 485–507.

Greico, J. 1993. "Understanding the Problems of International Cooperation: The Limits of Neoliberal Institutionalism and the Future of Realist Theory." In *Neorealism and Neoliberalism: The Contemporary Debate*. ed. D. Baldwin. New York: Columbia University Press.

Hirst, P. 1965. "Liberal Education and the Nature of Knowledge." In *Philosophical Analysis and Education*. ed. R. Archanbauld. London: Routledge.

Hladnik, M. 1995. "All Different—All Equal: Who Defines Education for Citizenship in a New Europe?" In *Teaching for Citizenship in Education*. eds. A. Osler, H.-F. Rathenow and H. Starkey. Stoke on Trent: Trentham.

Hobsbawm, E. and Ranger, T., eds. 1983. *The Invention of Tradition*. Cambridge: Cambridge University Press.

Hosking, G. and Schöpflin, G., eds. 1997. *Myths and Nationhood*. London: Hurst/SEES.

Keohane, R. 1986. *Neoliberalism and Its Critics*. New York: Columbia University Press.

Kerr, D. 1999. *Citizenship Education: An International Perspective*. International Review of Curriculum and Assessment Frameworks, Paper 4. London: QCA.

Lawton, D. et al. 1978. *Theory and Practice of Curriculum Studies*. London: Routledge and Kegan Paul.

Lawton, D. and Gordon, P. 1996. *Dictionary of Education*. 2nd ed. London: Hodder and Stoughton.

Le Métais, J. 1997. *Values and Aims in Curriculum and Assessment Frameworks*. International Review of Curriculum and Assessment Frameworks, Paper 1. London: School Curriculum and Assessment Authority.

Oevermann, U. 2000. "The Analytical Difference between Community ("Gemeinschaft") and Society ("Gesellschaft") and Its Consequences for the Conceptualisation of an Education for European citizenship." In *Developing Identities in Europe: Citizenship Education and Higher Education.* ed. A. Ross. London: CiCe TNP.

Osler, A. 1994. "Education for Development: Redefining Citizenship in a Pluralist Society." In *Development Education: Global Perspectives in Education.* ed. A. Osler. London: Cassell.

QCA. 1999. *Citizenship Education.* London: QCA.

Rawls, J. 1971. *A Theory of Justice.* Oxford: Oxford University Press.

Ross, A. 2000. *Curriculum: Construction and Critique.* London: Falmer.

Shipman, M. 1971. "Curriculum for Inequality." In *The Curriculum: Context, Design and Development.* ed. R. Hooper. Edinburgh: Oliver and Boyd.

Skilbeck, M. 1976. "Three Educational Ideologies." In *Curriculum Design and Development: Ideologies and Values.* Buckingham: Open University Press.

Tyler, R. 1949. *Basic Principles of Curriculum and Instruction.* Chicago: Chicago University Press.

Vacek, P. "On the Development of Education for Democracy and Citizenship in the Czech Republic." In *Children's Understanding in the New Europe.* eds. E. Nasman and A. Ross. Stoke on Trent: Trentham. Forthcoming.

Valdmaa, S. 1999. "Identities in Estonia—Challenges to Citizenship Education." In *Young Citizens in Europe.* ed. A. Ross. London: CiCe TNP. 95–99.

Vernersson, F. 2000. "Teachers' Didactic Work: Compulsory School Teacher's Conceptions of Their Own Civics Teaching." *Children's Social and Economics Education* 4 (1): 11–21.

Williams, R. 1961. *The Long Revolution.* London: Chatto and Windus.

5

Citizenship Education and the Strengthening of Democracy: Is Race on the Agenda?

Audrey Osler

INTRODUCTION

The British government, along with its European partners, is developing policies that emphasize the importance of education as a means of ensuring social inclusion and preventing social exclusion. A key challenge facing the education service is how to raise the achievement of all students and make schools, colleges, and universities fairer and more inclusive communities. In 1999 the British government passed an Order to introduce citizenship education into schools in England by 2002, with the explicit aim of strengthening democracy and enabling the greater participation of young people (QCA 1999). In her foreword to the report of the advisory group on *Education for Citizenship and the Teaching of Democracy in Schools* (the Crick report), which prepared the ground for the order, the then speaker, Betty Boothroyd, claimed that the lack of adequate citizenship education in schools "has been a blot on the landscape of public life for too long, with unfortunate consequences for the democratic process" (QCA 1998: 3). At the time of the report's publication, education secretary David Blunkett was also widely quoted as saying, "Education for citizenship is vital to revive and sustain an active democratic society in the new century" (*Express, Daily Mail, Birmingham Post* 23 September 1998).

In February 1999 the report of the Stephen Lawrence Inquiry (Macpherson et al. 1999) identified institutional racism as a major cause of social exclusion in Britain. Senior politicians from a range of political parties went on record to acknowledge institutional racism in British society, and the government pledged itself to a program to eradicate racism. The government's response to the Stephen Lawrence Inquiry's recommendations (Home Office 1999) identified citizenship education as a key means by which schools would address and prevent racism and encourage young people to value cultural diversity. In this chapter I explore the degree to which the British government's broad policy aim of promoting race equality is reflected in education policy and, particularly, in the plans for citizenship education.

GOVERNMENT POLICY, RACE EQUALITY, AND SOCIAL EXCLUSION

Since 1997 the Labour government has taken a number of steps to promote race equality. In setting up the Stephen Lawrence Inquiry and accepting its finding of institutional racism, it acknowledged the importance of political leadership in challenging racism and in creating a climate in which race equality is seen as the responsibility of all. As Home Secretary Jack Straw stated, when presenting the report to the House of Commons, "The report does not place a responsibility on someone else; it places a responsibility on each of us. We must make racial equality a reality. The vision is clear: we must create a society in which every individual, regardless of colour, creed or race, has the same opportunities and respect as his or her neighbour" (*Hansard*, 24 February 1999). The report of the Stephen Lawrence Inquiry defined institutional racism as

the collective failure of an organisation to provide an appropriate and professional service to people because of their colour, culture, or ethnic origin. It can be detected in processes, attitudes and behaviour which amount to discrimination through unwitting prejudice, ignorance, thoughtlessness and racist stereotyping which disadvantage minority ethnic people. It persists because of the failure of the organisation openly and adequately to recognise and address its existence and causes by policy, example and leadership. Without recognition and action to eliminate such racism, it can prevail as part of the ethos or culture of the organisation. It is a corrosive disease. (Macpherson et al. 1999: ¶ 6.34)

The report drew attention to institutional racism in the police force, but it did much more than that. It effectively made clear to white British people something about which black British people had known for years, namely that institutional racism is endemic in British society. The prime minister and the home secretary responded by pledging themselves to eradicating institutional racism. The Home Secretary explained that "any long-established, white dominated organisation is liable to have procedures, practices and a culture which tend to exclude or disadvantage non-white people. The police service in this respect is little different from other parts of the criminal justice system, or from government departments . . . and many other institutions" (Straw, *Hansard*, 24 February 1999). In making this statement the home secretary stressed that institutional racism is not confined to the police force and criminal justice system but has a profound impact across society, affecting everyone. Educational institutions are not exempt from the pernicious effects of racism. Nevertheless, the report recommended that education, and in particular schools, have an important role in enabling the development of greater racial justice.

Although schools are implicated in institutional racism they are also seen as part of the solution and are required to address and prevent racism. Of the Stephen Lawrence Inquiry report's seventy recommendations, three address education. As well as proposing amendments to the National Curriculum so that schools might more effectively value cultural diversity and prevent racism, the inquiry recommended that local education authorities (LEAs) and school governors take a lead in ensuring that racist incidents be recorded and reported. It recommended that schools monitor exclusions by ethnicity and that the school inspection agency, Office for Standards in Education (OFSTED), be given a lead role in monitoring how schools are addressing and preventing racism.

The government made the links between racial discrimination and social exclusion explicit in the report *Minority Ethnic Issues in Social Exclusion and Neighbourhood Renewal* (Social Exclusion Unit 2000). The report highlighted how people from minority communities are more likely than others to:

- live in deprived areas and poor housing;
- be poor and unemployed;
- suffer from ill health.

This Social Exclusion Unit report also identified educational disadvantage: children from some minority communities are likely to do less well at school and to be excluded from school in disproportionate numbers. The report concluded that members of minority ethnic communities are likely to suffer a double disadvantage since they are disproportionately concentrated in deprived areas and experience all the problems that affect others who live there, but also suffer from the consequences of racial discrimination. They are likely to be the victims of racial harassment and racial crime, both of which are widespread. Some services fail to reach them or meet their needs, and they may experience language and cultural barriers to accessing information and services. All these factors serve to limit individuals' citizenship rights. Among the actions proposed in the report are:

- Monitoring the outcomes of mainstream services by ethnicity;
- Involving minority ethnic users in service design and delivery;
- Developing program specifically targeted to meet minority ethnic needs;
- Tackling racist crime and harassment;
- Improving information about these communities.

In 1999 the Department for Education and Employment (DfEE) introduced the Ethnic Minority Achievement Grant (EMAG), which replaced the former section 11 arrangements, administered by the home office, as the main funding mechanism for addressing the specific educational needs of children from minority communities. The EMAG budget is over £150 million per year. The section 11 arrangements had been seriously criticized by inspectors as providing inadequate and short-term funding, which led to difficulties in recruiting and retaining specialist teachers, with the quality of the teaching being "variable" (OFSTED 1999b: 21). Nevertheless, educational arrangements under the old section 11 funding mechanism had never been evaluated. Evidence submitted to the Commission on the Future of Multi-Ethnic Britain suggests that although much of the thinking behind the new arrangements is sound, many of the criticisms of section 11 still apply, and that "it appears unlikely that the grant will have substantial impact on the patterns of underachievement" identified by the commission (Parekh 2000: 150).

The 2001 DfEE White Paper, *Schools: Building on Success*, claims that "targeted measures will include a rigorous approach to monitoring the progress of ethnic minority pupils and to setting targets for underachieving groups of pupils, aided by the increasing effectiveness of national and local level data analysis" (DfEE 2001: 58, ¶ 4.62). Yet a preliminary analysis of LEA plans indicated that some authorities were, in fact, setting targets for the improvement of various ethnic groups, which, if achieved, would widen the gap in performance and increase inequality. In these authorities the target percentage increase for those groups whose average performance was lowest was smaller than the target percentage increase for the highest achieving group (Gillborn and Mirza 2000). When EMAG was introduced, the government made an assurance that the grant would be independently evaluated. Without an effective evaluation of EMAG it will be difficult for the government to guarantee "a rigorous approach to monitoring the progress of ethnic minority pupils." In particular, it will be difficult to establish which approaches and projects have been most effective, and why.

The British government published an equality statement in November 1999 that stressed its commitment to building an "inclusive and prosperous" society, and outlined its plans to extend discrimination law and to support progress through nonlegislative means (Home Office 2001). An important element of the British government's policy on race equality is the passing of the Race Relations Amendment Act 2000. The Act places a positive duty on public bodies, including schools, to promote race equality. It is no longer sufficient for public bodies simply to avoid discrimination; the Act requires them to introduce policies and practices that actively promote race equality.

The realization of a multicultural society in which all individuals and communities are able to participate freely and where institutional racism is eradicated will require more than legal changes; it will also require a change in public culture. The law can, of course, make a substantial contribution to such a culture. The 1976 Race Relations Act, which outlawed both direct and indirect racial discrimination and gave powers to the Commission for Racial Equality, has contributed to a climate of improved race relations in Britain (Parekh 1991b; Blackstone, Parekh and Sanders 1998). Despite its limitations, the law has contributed over a period of 25 years to a climate in which public manifestations of racism are condemned, and direct discrimination is no longer a regular feature of daily life.

The absence of discrimination is a prerequisite if individuals and communities are to flourish within a multicultural society, but it is insufficient to guarantee the full participation of all citizens within such a society. Diversity also needs to be "given public status and dignity." Politicians need to work together with other citizens to "develop a new social and cultural policy capable of nurturing ethnic identities" (Parekh 1991a: 197). As Figueroa puts it, " 'British' must be seen as fully including the ethnic minority communities. But the minority communities being seen as British does not imply their denying their 'ethnic' origins and identity" (2000: 59–60). In other words, what is needed is a vision of multiculturalism that recognizes that each individual has multiple identities. This new multiculturalism needs to be founded on human rights and must be inclusive of all, including white communities (Osler and Starkey 2000).

A NEW MULTICULTURAL VISION?

Modern Britain is often referred to as a multicultural society. What this usually means is that the processes of postwar immigration have led to the development of "visible" minority communities. The term "multicultural" is often used synonymously with "ethnic minority" or "nonwhite," so that communities or neighborhoods which are referred to as multicultural are usually assumed to have significant numbers of African, Caribbean, or Asian residents. The concept of multiculturalism is often exclusive of white communities, which may mistakenly be assumed to be culturally homogeneous.

Recent constitutional reform, including the establishment of a Scottish parliament and Welsh assembly and the development of a new settlement between Britain and Northern Ireland, have led to increased interest and debate on what it means to be British and how citizenship is related to national and regional identities. So, for example, what does it mean to be British and Scottish? Meanings of nationality and national identity are being reexamined and redefined.

It is within this new political and constitutional context that a new vision of multicultural Britain will be forged. Certainly, politicians highlight the positive features of our multicultural society. The prime minister, addressing an international convention on Sikhism in Birmingham, stated:

The Sikh community is a vital part of British life. In every walk of life, in business, culture, the legal profession, you are adding to the strength of Britain. . . . In Britain it is our ambition to create a modern civic society for today's world, to renew the bonds of community that bind us together. That society is based on shared values: rights and duties which go together; tolerance and respect for diversity. . . . We stand up for our racial and cultural diversity; we fight against discrimination and violence; we value our differences and respect each other's background, ethnic and religious. (Tony Blair, 5 May 1999)

At a Diwali celebration later the same year he spoke of his "vision of Britain of the 21st century" as being "a society which gives everyone a chance to fulfil their potential, which looks forward, is suited to the future in which we will live and work, and above all else offers opportunity and hope to people regardless of their background, or their culture, or their religion, or their race" (Tony Blair, 4 November 1999). However, such speeches affirming the value of multiculturalism are generally reserved for black and ethnic minorities, rather than predominantly white audiences. A review of speeches on the 10 Downing Street website (www.number-10.gov.uk) between January 1999 and April 2001 identified just five by the prime minister that refer to racial equality or to the multicultural nature of Britain. They include those quoted, to Sikh and Hindu audiences; an address to an international audience at London's First Global Network; another to a black and ethnic minority network of civil servants; and a speech marking the first U.K. Holocaust Memorial Day in 2001.

In spite of the introduction of the Race Relations Amendment Act 2001, British government initiatives to promote a vision of a multicultural society have been less in evidence. Policies, with some exceptions, tend to focus more broadly on reversing social exclusion, rather than directly addressing racial inequalities (Alibhai-Brown 1999: 7). So, for example, targets were set to cut the overall number of permanent exclusions from school by one third by 2002. The targets failed to address the disproportionate number of exclusions of pupils from particular communities, notably African Caribbean boys and girls. The policy failed to take into consideration the research evidence, which suggests that when schools and LEAs are successful in cutting exclusions, they do so across the board. Without specific targets and strategies for particular groups, such groups will remain disproportionately vulnerable to exclusion (Osler and Hill 1999).

Racism is recognized across Europe as a barrier to the full participation and inclusion of minorities. In other words, racism serves to undermine democracy and therefore needs to be addressed as part of policies and practices that promote and support citizenship and social inclusion. It also needs to be addressed through programs in schools and in teacher education. At the Council of Europe Vienna summit held in 1993, heads of state and government, persuaded that "manifestations of intolerance threaten democratic societies and their basic values," called for a "broad European Youth Campaign to mobilise the public in favour of a tolerant society based on the equal dignity of all its members and against manifestations of racism, xenophobia, antisemitism and intolerance" (Council of Europe 1993). However, in Britain there is little evidence of this being a government priority during the 1990s. Following the election of a Labour government in 1997, there were mixed messages from ministers concerning racism and antiracism. A number of commentators argued that certain government policies addressing the needs of refugees and asylum seekers—such as the distribution of vouchers for food and other essentials, and particularly some statements by government ministers—served to undermine the status of these groups and fuel racism. On the other hand, certain government ministers made powerful statements stressing the need to adopt antiracist policies and practices. The following example is from a home office minister.

Anti-racism is not about helping black and Asian people; it is about our future—white and black. We all live in a multicultural society and we all have a choice: either we make a success of multicultural Britain or we do not. If we fail to address those issues, our children—white and black—will pay the price of that failure. That is why all of us, white and black, have a vested interest in the [Race Relations Amendment] Bill and in anti-racism. We must make Britain a success as a multicultural society. (Mike O'Brien, *Hansard*, 9 March 2000, col. 1281)

However, despite the acceptance of the need for schools to prevent and address racism through their curriculum and ethos, no British education minister has yet made a positive statement arguing that schools have a key role to play in challenging racism in society. Nor has any education minister acknowledged the existence of institutional racism in the education service. Bernard Crick, the chair of the government's *Advisory Group on Education for Citizenship and the Teaching of Democracy in Schools*, suggests that those home office ministers who have endorsed antiracism in schools are "perhaps not wholly conversant . . . with good practice in actual classroom teaching" (Crick 2000: 134). He argues that education ministers are wiser in not adopting an explicit antiracist position.

CITIZENSHIP EDUCATION FOR A PLURAL SOCIETY

Citizenship does not depend solely on legal status; it also requires a sense of belonging. Thus, within any program of learning for citizenship, it is necessary to address the cultural and personal aspects of citizenship, focusing on issues of identity as well as addressing structural and political issues (Osler and Starkey 1996). Schools can and should play an important role in supporting and extending the identities of their students, enabling all of them, including white students, to feel a part of a multicultural society, and enabling all to participate in the future development of our democracy.

As explained above, the Lawrence Inquiry report proposed changes to the National Curriculum "aimed at valuing cultural diversity and preventing racism" (Macpherson et al. 1999). The government's response was to argue that its plans for citizenship education, which were already outlined in the Crick report, would meet that need. Yet the Crick report makes no reference to racism. The Crick report is also patronizing in its references to minorities and has at times a somewhat colonial flavor (see Osler 2000 and Osler and Starkey 2000 for a more detailed analysis). It does, however, seem to support a recommendation that "an explicit idea of multicultural citizenship needs to be formulated for Britain" (QCA 1998: 17; Modood and Berthoud 1997).

Crick himself advocates "multiculturalism" rather than antiracism. He fears that "head-on" opposition to racism in schools will simply provide fuel for racist youth. He prefers instead a more subtle, indirect "multicultural" approach where the very word "race" is avoided, and young people learn instead about the legal and human rights underpinning society and the longstanding national, regional, religious, and ethnic identities within the United Kingdom. Through understanding history, Crick believes it will "be easier to bring the racially prejudiced, firstly into tolerance, then into acceptance and finally, hopefully into mutual respect" (Crick 2000: 131). It is not clear how he expects prejudiced young people to move along this path towards mutual respect without any opportunity to address issues of racism, power, and inequality in their own communities and society.

In arguing this line, Crick overlooks some of the realities facing schools. Within the community of the school it is important to create an environment where all students feel secure and are free from racial harassment. This is likely to require explicit policies and teaching programs that support those policies. Some students will experience racial harassment and discrimination outside of school that serve to restrict their citizenship rights. If citizenship programs fail to address such matters, they will quickly be seen as irrelevant. While young people need to have a historical understanding of citizenship within a plural society, this is unlikely to be sufficient. They also need to have an opportunity to explore questions of human rights, justice, and injustice in their own lives and communities (Osler et al. 1996). As Figueroa (2000) argues, historical analysis needs to be complemented by a social analysis in which young people are given the opportunity to explore questions of diversity, inequality, racism in contemporary society, and to see citizenship in the context of globalization. For teachers seeking practical guidance, Dadzie (2000) suggests ways of introducing sensitive, real-life issues into the classroom. This approach is totally compatible with Crick's concept of "political literacy," which underpins the citizenship curriculum for England.

An understanding of human rights is essential, since they provide the basic principles and a framework within which differences of opinion and perspective can be resolved (Osler and Starkey 1996; Spencer 2000). In Britain antiracism is often simply seen as the opposite of racism, rather than a set of values or beliefs that is part of a human rights discourse (Lloyd 1998). If multiculturalism and antiracism are to be inclusive of all and to appear relevant to all, then students need to understand the links between various forms of injustice, to recognize the need for solidarity, and to understand how, in practice, racism may combine with other forms of discrimination. It is only through understanding the complex ways in which racism may operate to exclude that we can begin to find effective ways of challenging it.

Some advocates of human rights education tend to overlook the impact of racism on the lives of learners, and is possible to find human rights education materials that do not explicitly make the links between human rights and racial justice. Richardson (2000: 86–87) suggests we need to engage in "the politics of conjunctions," bringing together "human rights and racial justice." He reminds us that that such an approach will have implications for curriculum planning and school organization. Such an approach is certainly in the spirit of the Universal Declaration of Human Rights 1948 (UDHR), which was developed in response to the abuses perpetrated by the Nazi regime and stresses the importance of education as a central part of the project to secure human rights:

The General Assembly proclaims this Universal Declaration of Human Rights as a common standard of achievement for all peoples and all nations, to the end that every individual and every organ of society, keeping this Declaration constantly in mind, shall strive by teaching and education to promote respect for these rights and freedoms and by progressive measures, national and international, to secure their universal and effective recognition and observance. (UDHR 1948: preamble)

RACIAL JUSTICE, SCHOOL SELF-EVALUATION, AND INSPECTION

If educators are to work towards genuine racial equality in education they will need to apply the definition of institutional racism to the education service and examine its implications. Richardson and Wood (1999) provide a useful working definition of racism in education, exploring how it can become institutionalized:

In the education system there are laws, customs and practices which systematically reflect and reproduce racial inequalities. . . . If racist consequences accrue to institutional laws, customs and practices, a school or a local education authority or a national education system is racist whether or not individual teachers, inspectors, officers, civil servants and elected politicians have racist intentions. . . . Educational institutions may systematically treat or tend to treat pupils and students differently in respect of race, ethnicity or religion. The differential treatment lies within an institution's ethos and organisation rather than in the attitudes, beliefs and intentions of individual members of staff. The production of differential treatment is "institutionalised" in the way the institution operates. (Richardson and Wood 1999: 33)

Table 5.1 highlights examples of racial inequality in the education system in Britain, drawing on the research evidence. To avoid discrimination and promote racial equality, schools need to develop self-evaluation tools that enable them to monitor their performance by ethnicity. In doing so they will need to monitor attainment, access to particular subjects, courses, examinations, and the use of specific rewards and punishments, to assess whether there are any differentials between ethnic groups. Where disadvantage, discrimination, or exclusion are

Table 5.1
Racial Inequality in Schools

Dimensions of inequality	Examples of inequality in the education system
OUTCOMES White people receive more benefits than black, and racial inequality is therefore perpetuated. Black people receive negative results more than do white people and in this way too, inequality is perpetuated.	White pupils leave school at 16 or 18 with substantially better paper qualifications than African Caribbean pupils (Gillborn & Gipps 1996; Richardson & Wood 1999). African Caribbean pupils experience punishments, particularly permanent and fixed term exclusions, more than white pupils (Osler 1997a).
STRUCTURE In senior decision-making and policy-making positions there are proportionately more white people than black, and in consequence black interests and perspectives are inadequately represented.	There are few black and ethnic minority headteachers or deputy heads, and few black education officers, inspectors, teacher trainers and text book writers (Osler 1997b).
CULTURE AND ATTITUDES In the occupational culture there are assumptions, expectations and generalizations that are more negative about black people than about white.	Black pupils are more likely than white pupils to be seen as trouble-makers, and to be criticised and controlled (Gillborn 1995; Sewell 1997).
RULES AND PROCEDURES Customary rules, regulations, and practices work more to the advantage of white people than black.	The national curriculum reflects white interests, concerns and outlooks and neglects or marginalises black experience (e.g. Figueroa 1993).
STAFF TRAINING Staff have not received training on race and racism issues, and on ways they can avoid indirect discrimination.	Neither initial nor continuing professional development pays sufficient attention to race and racism issues (Siraj-Blatchford 1993; Osler 1997).
FACE-TO-FACE INTERACTION Staff are less effective in communication with and listening to black people than they are in interaction with white people.	Encounters between white staff and black pupils frequently escalate into needless confrontation (Wright 1992; Sewell 1997).

Adapted from Richardson and Wood (1999).

identified, schools may need to redirect resources to address any inequality. Since racism operates in many indirect and complex ways it is important that monitoring includes gender as well as self-defined ethnic background. For similar reasons it may be important to collect data on religious affiliation.

From 2002 the Department for Education and Employment (DfEE) will include ethnic monitoring among the data it requires from schools as part of the annual school census. The Commission on British Muslims and Islamophobia expressed concerns that there are no plans to include religious monitoring, although the DfEE is happy for local authorities to collect this data. The DfEE told the Commission it is reluctant to pose an additional burden on schools.

Final decisions have yet to be taken, but Ministers are concerned to keep demands on schools to an absolute minimum. . . . We do not presently collect information on religious identity and an additional exercise of the scale required would be a considerable extra demand on schools. . . . This is not in any way to diminish the importance that individuals and faith organisations place in their religious identity or the respect that schools should have for a child's language, cultural background or religious belief. (DfEE response, quoted in Commission on British Muslims and Islamophobia, 2001)

The inclusion of an optional question on religious affiliation in the U.K. census 2001 signalled government recognition of the need for such data in policy development and planning. The home office has commissioned research in an attempt to assess the scale and nature of religious discrimination in society and the degree to which it overlaps with racial discrimination in Britain (Home Office 2001: 35). There is already some evidence of underachievement among certain groups of Muslim pupils in England, notably those of Pakistani and Bangladeshi descent (Gillborn and Mirza 2000). The decision not to collect such data means it is impossible to investigate whether there is any systematic disadvantage experienced by children of a particular faith group. If members of any faith community are systematically treated in a way that serves to disadvantage the group, then the government's commitment to overcome social exclusion and raise educational standards for all is undermined.

The collection of data is, in itself, insufficient, and needs to be accompanied by discussion and consultation with faith communities so that coherent policies and practices can be developed in relation to issues such as dress code, school meals, collective acts of worship, religious holidays, and other observances. Such a dialogue will need to recognize children's "multiple identities and belongings" (Runnymede Trust 1997: 46). This does not assume that all who identify with a particular faith group do so in exactly the same way.

School self-evaluation and monitoring processes are complemented by external inspection, as part of a policy initiative towards race equality. As noted above, the Stephen Lawrence Inquiry recommended that the Office for Standards in Education (OFSTED), the school inspection agency, take a leading role in monitoring how schools are preventing and addressing racism. OFSTED, as a nonministerial government department, is among the public authorities that were made subject to the duty to promote race equality, under the Race Relations Amendment Act 2000 (Home Office 2001: 23). An analysis of the school inspection framework and its implementation, conducted on behalf of the U.K. Commission for Racial Equality, found that although the inspection framework is sound, inspection reports were inadequate, inconsistent, and incomplete in addressing race equality concerns (Osler and Morrison 2000).

Banton (1999) suggests that the government used the momentum generated by the findings of the Lawrence Inquiry—which provoked considerable public sympathy and positive media coverage—to carry through aspects of its policy agenda that were already planned. An examination of education policy would seem to support Banton's assertion. The citizenship curriculum was put forward as a response to one of the Lawrence Inquiry recommendations, yet the groundwork for citizenship was already complete, and subsequent guidance to teachers fails to address racism or antiracism (QCA 2000). Similarly, the OFSTED school inspection framework (OFSTED 1999a), which was already being prepared, was put forward as a means of monitoring race equality initiatives. Nevertheless, Her Majesty's chief inspector of schools (HMCI) saw no need to inform either inspectors or schools of OFSTED'S designated responsibility to monitor how schools were preventing and addressing racism. This inaction suggests that he failed to recognize it as a key government policy initiative or priority. Indeed, when questioned as to how headteachers or inspectors were to learn about OFSTED's new role, he simply declared, "We do not rely on paper communication in OFSTED" (Osler and Morrison 2000: 38, 167).

Researchers, working on behalf of the U.K. Commission for Racial Equality, found members of the OFSTED senior management team ill at ease in discussing race equality matters. On occasion they were dismissive, with one inspector asserting that "race equality is not a priority. Our priority is underachieving white boys" (Osler and Morrison 2000: 58). HMCI later admitted that of the 3647 school inspections carried out between the publication of the Stephen Lawrence Inquiry report and July 2000 only four included race equality issues among the key action points (Woodhead 2000).

In November 2000 HMCI was questioned closely by the House of Commons Select Committee on Education on the findings of this research. The chair of the Select Committee criticized HMCI for his failure to cooperate with the researchers, declaring that his professional judgement was "flawed" (House of Commons 2000). HMCI resigned two days later. OFSTED has since revised its training plans on "educational inclusion" to emphasize racial equality much more strongly. This training is now mandatory for all inspectors who are contracted to OFSTED. It would appear that this particular aspect of the British government's plans for race equality in education was enacted only when pressure was brought to bear by the Commission for Racial Equality and members of parliament.

CITIZENSHIP EDUCATION: WHOLE SCHOOL
APPROACHES

Guidance to schools on implementing the citizenship curriculum stresses the importance of taking a whole-school approach (QCA 2000), recognizing that there needs to be congruence between what students are considering within citizenship and what is taking place within the wider school community. There is a statutory inclusion statement in each subject in the National Curriculum for England, including citizenship. The statement outlines three principles of inclusion:

- setting suitable learning challenges;
- responding to pupils' diverse needs;
- overcoming potential barriers to learning and assessment (QCA 1999).

Although the statement makes reference to the need for teachers to set high expectations and provide opportunities for "pupils from all social and cultural backgrounds, pupils of different ethnic groups including travellers, refugees and asylum seekers, and those with diverse linguistic backgrounds" (QCA 1999: 19), and to ensure that pupils learn to appreciate differences arising from race, gender, ability or disability, the statement avoids any direct reference to racism as a barrier to learning or citizenship, either in schools or society. Teachers are reminded that they should be familiar with the requirements of equal opportunities legislation relating to race, gender, and disability.

The formulation of a statutory inclusion statement is an important symbolic step toward realizing inclusive schools. Nevertheless, if schools are to address and prevent racism in line with the government's response to the Lawrence Inquiry, then it is curious that the inclusion statement makes no reference to this. Citizenship education is highlighted again and again by the British government as the main curricular vehicle by which race equality will be promoted, but there is no specific guidance on how this can be achieved. Race is sidelined in the education policy agenda and virtually absent when it is translated into practical guidance for teachers and schools.

The National Healthy School Standard (DfEE 1999) sets out a whole-school approach to equalities issues in school, addressing race equality within a broader equalities framework. It is this document, published by the DfEE, which provides schools with the strongest official practical guidance on promoting equalities through their ethos and organization. It is not mandatory that schools incorporate the standard into their curriculum and organization, but it was envisaged that by March 2002 all LEAs would be involved in an accredited education and health partnership and that the majority of schools would be involved (DfEE 1999). The Commission for Racial Equality (CRE) has also published a useful checklist for schools seeking to minimize exclusions and develop a genuinely inclusive community (CRE 1997), and has provided guidance for schools on promoting race equality (CRE 1999).

One of the proposals of the Social Exclusion Unit's (SEU) report on ethnic minorities (SEU 2000) is to involve users from minority communities in service design and delivery. If the government's agenda to tackle social exclusion and promote race equality is to be realized in the education service, then consideration might be given to the implications of this for schools. Gittens (2000), in a study of the roles and experiences of black school governors, highlights the distinctive contribution they can make to both the processes of curriculum development and the wider processes of school decision making. "By examining black people's perceptions of their roles and responsibilities it is possible not only to gain insights into their priorities and concerns about education but also to begin to gain a broader understanding of their perception of their roles as citizens within the local community" (Gittens 2000: 177–178).

Schools' engagement with local communities, and particularly their engagement with those individuals and groups who come from backgrounds and communities that are represented in the school community, but less likely to be represented among the teaching staff, provide a range of opportunities for development. Black school governors, as Gittens demonstrates, have insights into the relationship between social inclusion, race equality, and citizenship to which schools might not otherwise have access. They can also inform the process of curriculum planning for citizenship by enabling schools to understand more fully the sites of learning for citizenship that students draw on beyond the school. Consultation with parents from minority communities is also vitally important. Carolan's (2000) study of parents' understandings of human rights and human rights education in an inner city primary school found that they stressed the importance of making equalities issues, justice, and fairness part of the curriculum from the reception class onwards. For these parents, human rights education implied antiracism and an opportunity for children to learn, not only about their rights and responsibilities, but the actions open to them if their rights are infringed. "Parents were concerned that schools were not simply paying lip-service to antiracist education. They saw race equality as a central feature of education, rather than an optional extra. They continually stressed how crucial it was for schools to be actively promoting, prioritising and teaching within an antiracist framework" (Carolan 2000: 187).

It is important in considering the views of "user groups" not to overlook students' viewpoints when planning a curriculum, particularly when planning for citizenship. Research into exclusion from school and racial equality, which sought the viewpoints of both primary and secondary school students, highlighted children's concerns about bullying and racial harassment. The young people argued that school was likely to be a more secure and just environment if they were involved in decision-making. The evidence suggests that a more democratic school ethos, where there is provision for a school council or other mechanisms to listen to students' perspectives, is likely to promote greater inclusion and racial justice and a better disciplined school (Osler 2000).

CONCLUSION

Citizenship education has been promoted as a way of strengthening democracy. It has also been proposed as a means by which schools can address and prevent racism through education. The British government has acknowledged the pernicious effects of institutional racism in society and introduced some broad policy initiatives to promote greater racial justice. A number of government statements indicate that racial equality is recognized as an essential foundation for a successful multicultural society. It is seen as more than a moral imperative; it is also recognized as essential for the social and economic well-being of all. Despite formal equality, various groups continue to encounter barriers to claiming their citizenship rights as a result of disadvantage and/or discrimination. In other words, racism may operate with or alongside other factors to create an environment where certain individuals and groups are excluded from full participation in the public sphere and from political processes.

Schools have a key role to play in the development of a new multicultural vision of Britain where there is genuine equality and respect for diversity, and in helping transform this vision into a reality. In response to the Lawrence Inquiry, the new curriculum subject of citizenship was highlighted as a means by which schools can address racism. Nevertheless, citizenship, education policy documents do not acknowledge racism as a barrier to citizenship, and racial equality issues are sidelined within these documents. "Racism" and "antiracism" remain uncomfortable terms, particularly for those responsible for developing education policy. If antiracism is mainstreamed within the education service, and government highlights racial equality as a central aspect of its educational inclusion agenda, then schools can confidently develop citizenship programs that challenge racism as an antidemocratic force. Government statements of commitment to racial equality issued by the Home Office will need to be taken on board by the Department for Education and Employment and translated into education policy documents and practical curriculum guidance for schools. As part of the process of mainstreaming antiracism in education, policy makers and schools will need to consult more fully with particular "user groups," namely minority ethnic communities and young people themselves. Such consultation, and the developments that arise from it, will enable more inclusive schools and a more inclusive society, in which young people themselves are able to exercize their citizenship rights and work for greater racial justice.

REFERENCES

Alibhai-Brown, Y. 1999. *True Colours: Public Attitudes to Multiculturalism and the Role of the Government*. London: Institute of Public Policy Research.

Banton, M. 1999. "What Follows Confrontation?" *The Runnymede Trust Bulletin*, September.

Birmingham Post. 1998. Editorial. Birmingham: *Birmingham Post-Herald*, 23 September.

Blackstone, T., Parekh, B. and Sanders, P. 1998. *Race Relations in Britain: A Developing Agenda.* London: Routledge.

Carolan, S. 2000. "Parents, Human Rights and Racial Justice." In *Citizenship and Democracy in Schools: Diversity, Identity, Equality.* ed. A. Osler. Stoke on Trent: Trentham.

Commission for Racial Equality. 1997. *Exclusion from School and Racial Equality: Good Practice Guide.* London: CRE.

Commission for Racial Equality. 1999. *Learning for All: Race Equality Standard for Schools.* London: CRE.

Commission on British Muslims and Islamophobia. 2001. *Ethnic and Religious Monitoring in the Education System: Some Current Issues.* London: Commission for British Muslims and Islamophobia.

Council of Europe. 1993. *Vienna Declaration.* 9 October. Strasbourg: Council of Europe.

Crick, B. 2000. *Essays on Citizenship.* London: Continuum.

Dadzie, S. 2000. *Toolkit for Tackling Racism in Schools.* Stoke on Trent: Trentham.

Daily Express. 1998. Editorial. London: Express Newspapers, 23 September.

Daily Mail. 1998. Editorial. London: Daily Mail and General Trust PLC, 23 September.

Department for Education and Employment. 1999. *National Healthy School Standard: Guidance.* London: DfEE.

Department for Education and Employment. 2001. *Schools: Building on Success.* White Paper, Cm 5050. London: Stationery Office.

Figueroa, P. 1993. "History: Policy Issues." In *Cultural Diversity and the Curriculum*, vol. 1. eds. P.D. Pumfrey and G.K. Verma. London: Falmer.

Figueroa, P. 2000. "Citizenship Education for a Plural Society." In *Citizenship and Democracy in Schools: Diversity, Identity, Equality.* ed. A. Osler. Stoke on Trent: Trentham.

Gillborn, D. 1995. *Racism and Antiracism in Real Schools.* Buckingham: Open University Press.

Gillborn, D. and Gipps, C. 1996. *Recent Research on the Achievements of Ethnic Minority Pupils.* London: Stationery Office.

Gillborn, D. and Mirza, H.S. 2000. *Educational Inequality: Mapping Race, Class and Gender, a Synthesis of Research Evidence.* London: Office for Standards in Education.

Gittens, I. 2000. "The Role of Black Governors." In *Citizenship and Democracy in Schools: Diversity, Identity, Equality.* ed. A. Osler. Stoke on Trent: Trentham.

Hansard. 1999. London: House of Commons Information Service, 23 February.

Hansard. 1999. London: House of Commons Information Service, 24 February.

Hansard. 2000. London: House of Commons Information Service, 9 March.

Home Office. 1999. *Stephen Lawrence Inquiry: Home Secretary's Action Plan.* London: Home Office.

Home Office. 2001. Race Relations (Amendment) Act. New Laws for a Successful Multi-Racial Britain: Proposals for Implementation. London: Home Office. www.homeoffice.gov.uk/raceact/welcome.htm

House of Commons. 2000. Education and Employment Committee Second Report: OFSTED Corporate Plan 2000, together with the Proceedings of the Committee and the Education Sub-Committee relating to the Report, Minutes of Evidence and Appendices to the Minutes of Evidence. 12 December. London: Stationery Office.

Lloyd, C. 1998. *Discourses of Antiracism in France*. Aldershot: Ashgate.

Macpherson, W. et al. 1999. *The Stephen Lawrence Inquiry*. London: Stationery Office.

Modood, T. and Berthoud, R. 1997. *Ethnic Minorities in Britain: Diversity and Disadvantage*. London: Policy Studies Institute.

Office for Standards in Education. 1999a. *Inspecting Schools: The Framework*. London: Stationery Office.

Office for Standards in Education. 1999b. *Raising the Attainment of Minority Ethnic Pupils: School and LEA Responses*. London: OFSTED Publications Centre, March.

Osler, A. 1997a. *Exclusion from School: Research Report*. London: CRE.

Osler, A. 1997b. *The Education and Careers of Black Teachers: Changing Identities, Changing Lives*. Buckingham: Open University Press.

Osler, A. 2000. "Children's Rights, Responsibilities and Understandings of School Discipline." *Research Papers in Education* 15 (1): 49–67.

Osler, A. 2000. "The Crick Report: Difference, Equality and Racial Justice." *The Curriculum Journal* 11 (1): 25–37.

Osler, A. and Hill, J. 1999. "Exclusion from School and Racial Equality: An Examination of Government Proposals in the Light of Recent Research Evidence." *Cambridge Journal of Education* 29 (1): 33–62.

Osler, A. and Morrison, M. 2000. *Inspecting Schools for Race Equality: OFSTED's Strengths and Weaknesses*. Stoke on Trent: Trentham, for the Commission for Racial Equality.

Osler, A. and Starkey, H. 1996. *Teacher Education and Human Rights*. London: David Fulton.

Osler, A. and Starkey, H. 2000. "Citizenship, Human Rights and Cultural Diversity." In *Citizenship and Democracy in Schools: Diversity, Identity, Equality*. ed. A. Osler. Stoke on Trent: Trentham.

Osler, A. et al. 1996. *Learning to Participate: Human Rights, Citizenship and Development in the Local Community*. Birmingham: Development Education Centre.

Parekh, B. 1991a. "British Citizenship and Cultural Difference." In *Citizenship*. ed. G. Andrews. London: Lawrence and Wishart.

Parekh, B. 1991b. "Law Torn." *New Statesman and Society* (14 June).

Parekh, B. 2000. *The Future of Multi-Ethnic Britain*. Report of the Commission on the Future of Multi-Ethnic Britain. London: Runnymede Trust.

QCA. 1998. *Education for Citizenship and the Teaching of Democracy in Schools* (Crick Report). London: QCA.

QCA. 1999. *The National Curriculum for England: Citizenship Key Stages 3–4*. London: DfEE/QCA.

QCA. 2000. *Citizenship at Key Stages 3 and 4: Initial Guidance for Schools*. London: QCA.

Richardson, R. 2000. "Human Rights and Racial Justice: Connections and Contrasts." In *Citizenship and Democracy in Schools: Diversity, Identity, Equality*. ed. A. Osler. Stoke on Trent: Trentham.

Richardson, R. and Wood, A. 1999. *Inclusive Schools, Inclusive Society: Race and Identity on the Agenda*. Stoke on Trent: Trentham.

Runnymede Trust. 1997. *Islamophobia: a Challenge for Us All*. London: The Runnymede Trust.

Sewell, T. 1997. *Black Masculinities and Schooling: How Black Boys Survive Modern Schooling*. Stoke on Trent: Trentham Books.

Siraj-Blatchford, I., ed. 1993. *"Race," Gender and the Education of Teachers*. Buckingham: Open University Press.

Social Exclusion Unit. 2000. *Minority Ethnic Issues in Social Exclusion and Neighbourhood Renewal*. London: Cabinet Office.

Spencer, S. 2000. "The Implications for the Human Rights Act for Citizenship Education." In *Citizenship and Democracy in Schools: Diversity, Identity, Equality*. ed. A. Osler. Stoke on Trent: Trentham.

Universal Declaration of Human Rights. 1948. New York: United Nations Department of Public Information.

Woodhead, C. 2000. Letter in Response to parliamentary questions by Phyllis Starkey MP. 27 July. House of Commons Library.

Wright, C. 1992. *Race Relations in the Primary School*. London: David Fulton.

6

Differentiated Civics Curriculum and Patterns of Citizenship Education: Vocational and Academic Programs in Israel

Orit Ichilov

INTRODUCTION

The idea that citizens *qua* citizens are equal without any achieved or ascribed qualifications is echoed again and again in modern political thought (for ex-.ample, Callan 1997; Heater 1990; Gutmann 1987; Dahrendorf 1994; Marshall 1977). According to Young (1995), the universality of citizenship transcends particularity and difference. Whatever the social or group differences among citizens, whatever their qualities of wealth, status, and power in the everyday activities of civil society, citizenship gives everyone the same status as peers in the political sphere.

Democratic societies assign schools a prominent role in the development of citizenship virtues, values, and skills. Niemi and Junn (1998: 2–3) maintain that "schools, along with their teachers and curricula, have long been identified as the critical link between education and citizenship, as the locus from which democratic citizens emerge." Converse (1972) characterizes formal education as the "universal solvent" that explains more aspects of democratic citizenship than any other factor (p. 324). The first moral obligation of schools in democracy is, therefore, "to give all children an education adequate to take advantage of their political status as citizens" (Gutmann 1987: 288). The question that will be addressed in the present chapter is, Do schools meet these societal expectations and equally prepare all students to become citizens?

Bernstein (1971: 47) maintains that "formal education knowledge is considered to be realized through three message systems: curriculum, pedagogy, and evaluation. Curriculum defines what counts as valid knowledge, pedagogy defines what counts as a valid transmission of knowledge, and evaluation defines what counts as a valid realization of knowledge on the part of the taught." In this chapter, I will focus on one component only of citizenship education: the contents of civics as a school subject within Israeli vocational and academic high schools. The central issue that will concern us is, Is the projected citizen role that is imparted to students indeed universal, or does the differentiated civics curriculum socialize students into dissimilar citizenship roles? In other words, are students on the academic track encouraged to develop critical awareness and active citizenship, while vocational school students are initiated into an uncritical, conforming, and "domesticated" citizenship role?

Three types of content documents will be analyzed concerning civics as a school subject. The first of these is the civics curriculum displaying the official educational policy of the Ministry of Education, as well as the goals that should be achieved in each type of school and the pedagogical means that should be employed. The second is two textbooks, one designed for students in academic high schools, and one prepared for students in vocational programs. The third is teachers' guides that accompany the textbooks.

I will start by examining how schooling in general is related to the development of citizenship orientations, and focus especially on educational stratification and on the differentiated civics curriculum as components of citizenship education. Sociologists attribute schooling effects to two distinct yet interrelated processes: socialization and allocation. The allocation tradition has been greatly overlooked by scholars who studied the effects of schooling on the development of citizenship. My argument is that the allocative perspective provides important insights and clues about how schooling so profoundly affects the development of citizenship orientations. For one, it demonstrates that citizenship education is not as universal as had been suggested, and that differentiated educational experiences produce dissimilar citizenship roles: leadership versus followership. I will then proceed to analyze civics curriculum documents prepared for Israeli high school students in vocational and academic programs. The structure and content of the documents as well as the entailed pedagogical apparatus will be examined. The main purpose of this inquiry is to discover whether students in vocational and academic tracks are guided into similar or dissimilar patterns of citizenship.

SCHOOLING, DIFFERENTIATED CURRICULUM, AND CITIZENSHIP EDUCATION

The paradox about schooling and democracy is that while there is abundant evidence for the existence of a strong positive relationship between educational attainment and a variety of civic orientations and behaviors (Almond and Verba 1963; Barnes and Kaase 1979; Dalton 1988; Kamens 1988; Nie, Powell and Prewitt 1969; Verba, Nie and Kim 1978; Delli Caprini and Keeter 1996), how schooling does it remains an enigma, and the causal connection between formal education and democratic citizenship is in effect an undeciphered "black box" (Torney-Purta 1997). My argument is that a differentiated civics curriculum is one component of schooling that has been greatly overlooked, yet may provide important insights about the development of citizenship orientations.

Sociologists attribute schooling effects in general to mainly two distinct but interrelated processes: socialization and allocation. In a socialization approach, schools are engaged in deliberate instruction and education of students. This is both their social mandate and their expertise. Differential outcomes are considered a consequence of the types, quality, and quantity of experiences that schools provide, holding students' abilities and motivations constant. This leads to the expectation that students whose schools provided richer curricular and extra-curricular experiences, and who were tutored by highly qualified teachers, will be more knowledgeable about politics and manifest greater commitment to democracy than students whose schooling experiences were less favorable. Political socialization and citizenship education research has been dominated by the socialization approach. Taken together, studies reveal that variables related to the formal instruction of civics, such as civic curriculum and teachers' qualifications, yield at best only moderate, and immediate, effects on youngsters' citizenship orientations and knowledge (Jennings and Niemi 1968, 1974; Diamond 1960; Litt 1963; Tapp 1971; Education Commission of the States 1973; Kohlberg and Lockwood 1970; Patrick 1977; Delli Carpini and Keeter 1996).

From an allocation outlook, schools, as social institutions, do far more than impart knowledge, skills, traditions, and values to students. Through the form and substance of the educative process, schools also operate as "sorting machines" that select and certify individuals for adult roles at particular levels of the social hierarchy. The allocative perspective proposes that through schooling students accumulate "cultural capital." Symbolized by certificates, cultural capital becomes fixed assets by which individuals are assigned social positions and are initiated into class-related life-styles (Bourdieu 1971; Collins 1979). Nie, Junn and Stehlik-Barry (1996) propose that by allocating scarce social and political ranks, formal education places individuals in their adult life either closer or further from the center of critical social and political networks. This, in turn, affects adult levels of political engagement. Citizenship orientations and behaviors are clearly an important component of status-related lifestyles, as indicated by studies that show a relationship between individuals' socioeconomic status and their voting behavior, sense of political efficacy, and involvement in public affairs (Himmelweit et al. 1981; Lane 1959; Easton 1965; Lipset 1960; Milbrath 1965; Stouffer 1955; Kohn 1969). Studies have shown that youth from working-class families are generally uninterested in politics (Bhavnani 1991; Bynner and Ashford 1994; Torney-Purta 1990). This could reflect the influence of both their family and community, as well as their educational placement.

Educational institutions convey to students normative descriptions of society and of their anticipated place in society as adults (Kamens 1981). My argument is that the development of status-related citizenship orientations is linked to individuals' placement in schools, and that such orientations begin to emerge in the course of schooling. Already in school, students experience being placed closer or further away from the center where meaningful social assets are allocated. Educational stratification is related to the development of citizenship patterns through two distinct, yet interrelated processes: placement of students in differentiated social networks (this will not be discussed in this chapter), and exposure of students to differentiated curricular and extracurricular schooling experiences (Ichilov 1991, 2001).

The most powerful manifestation of educational stratification is the separation of students into different schools, programs, and tracks on the basis of their ability, career aspirations, and socioeconomic backgrounds. Schools and educational programs enjoy dissimilar levels of esteem. This separation, therefore, symbolizes students' present status as well as future prospects. Thus, for example, students in academic tracks enjoy greater prestige among their peers, teachers, and in the community outside school than do students in vocational tracks, and the same holds true for students in the upper and lower ability groups (Oakes, Gamoran and Page 1992; Oakes 1985; Keddie 1971; Rist 1977; Dewey 1966). Furthermore, educational stratification closely corresponds to social stratification in society. This means that students from better-established families are often overrepresented in the more prestigious academic programs, while students belonging to minority groups and those representing lower socioeconomic echelons of society form the majority in the least prestigious programs (Ichilov 1991; Oakes 1985; Keddie 1971). In other words, students representing marginal segments of society are often marginalized in schools as well.

Not only students are stratified and processed in schools. Knowledge too is stratified, and high prestige knowledge is available almost exclusively to students in the high-status programs and tracks (Young 1971; Bernstein 1971; Apple 1990). Indeed, civic virtues such as critical thinking, problem solving, drawing conclusions, making generalizations, evaluating or synthesizing knowledge, and acting deliberatively in a pluralistic world, are intimately related to high-stratified knowledge, notably to literacy, and access to such knowledge is unevenly allocated in schools. Students' uneven access to socially meaningful knowledge and educational experiences in school significantly determines their placement in the social hierarchy (Hargreaves 1967; Rist 1970; Keddie 1971; Spring 1980; Bowles and Gintis 1976; Bowles 1977; Sarup 1978; Collins 1979; Carnoy and Levin 1985; Oakes 1985). Furthermore, the way teachers observe, classify, and react to socioeconomic and cultural differences in children affects the implementation of the curriculum in classrooms and evidently results in differentiated learning experiences and opportunities (Keddie 1971; Oakes 1985; Davies, Gregory and Riley 1999). In schools dominated by academic curricula, a teacher's reputation is often determined by teaching in high status programs that cater to the "ablest" students (Young 1971). In a study of Israeli high school teachers, Ichilov (1989) found that those who teach in academic programs and in schools that cater to well-established students are more open to discussing controversial issues and conflict situations and to exposing students to criticism and pluralism than teachers who teach in schools with a majority of disadvantaged students. Thus, educational stratification results in differentiated curricular and extracurricular experiences for students.

The division between academic and vocational programs is of special significance in this respect. In England, for example, citizenship education is considered "practical" and, therefore, inferior to academic education grounded in liberal humanist conceptions of culture. Consequently, overt education for citizenship was designated largely for children of the working class. Such low status citizenship courses were intended to foster "quietism," "domestication," and uncritical, conforming citizens (Whitty 1985: 279). Dewey (1966) expressed similar concerns about academic and vocational programs in the United States:

The separation of liberal education from professional and industrial education goes back to the time of the Greeks, and was formulated expressly on the basis of a division of classes into those who had to labor for a living and those who were relieved from this necessity. . . . [Such distinctions] effected a division between a liberal education, having to do with the self-sufficient life of leisure devoted to knowing for its own sake, and a useful, practical training for mechanical occupations, devoid of intellectual and aesthetic content. . . . The problem of education in a democratic society is to do away with the dualism and to construct a course of studies which makes thought a guide of free practice for all. . . . This movement [toward vocational training] would continue the traditional liberal or cultural education for the few economically able to enjoy it, and would give to the masses a narrow technical trade education for specialized calling, carried under the control of others. This scheme denoted, of course, simply a perpetuation of the older social division . . . under conditions where it has much less justification for existence. (Dewey 1966: 250, 261, 319)

The assignment of students to vocational and academic programs is an established form of curriculum differentiation (Ichilov 1991; Oakes 1983). The academic curriculum is related to the vocations of the upper and professional classes, while school subjects that are related to majority vocations are persistently viewed as low status (Goodson 1987). Ayalon (1994) reports that academic school subjects enjoy high prestige within Israeli high schools and are offered less often at an advanced curricular level in schools dominated by students representing underprivileged Jewish ethnic groups. She concludes that curricular decisions that are based on matching school subjects with the assumed capacities and interests of students lead to the monopolization of highly valued knowledge by privileged social groups.

There is growing evidence that school placement affects individuals' value orientations (Ichilov, Haymann, and Shapira 1990; Sullivan, Marcus, and Minns 1975; Travers 1983). Ichilov (1991) reports that program placement—academic or vocational—had a differential effect on students' expressed interest in politics, media use, willingness to become actively involved, discussion of politics with others, support of freedom of speech, and sense of political efficacy. Overall, the positive effect of academic programs, reinforcing a variety of civic orientations, was greater than that of vocational programs where zero or negative effects more often prevailed. Ichilov (1991) concludes that academic programs offer not only richer curricular and extracurricular experiences, but also interaction with peers representing upper social echelons and prospects for future upward mobility. This combination of factors may reinforce democratic civic orientations that are typically associated with upper socioeconomic echelons. Evidence for the importance of an anticipated future for the formation of citizenship orientations and knowledge can be found in several studies. The report of the International Civic Education Study (Torney-Purta, Lehmann, Oswald and Schutz 2001) reveals that "expected years of further education" had the strongest effect on civic knowledge among 14-year-old students in twenty-eight countries, stronger than "home literacy resources" and "open classroom climate." A similar variable was an important predictor of civic knowledge in both the 1971 IEA Civic Education Study (Torney, Oppenhein, and Farnen 1975) and in Niemi and Junn's (1998) analysis of the National Assessment of Civics in the United States. Educational placement could, thus, result in the preparation of students for dissimilar citizenship roles: students in high status programs are initiated into a leadership role, while the "followership" role is reserved for the less advantageous students (Apple 1990).

The idea that citizenship education is imparted in schools equally to all students seems to prevail among scholars and could be the reason for the fairly common neglect of allocation processes in relation to citizenship education. Even neo-Marxist scholars share this view and claim that schools are engaged in the production of opposites: workers for the capitalist workplace, and democratic citizens. Schools are, thus, coping with the perpetual tension between two contradicting imperatives: respond to the needs of unequal hierarchies associated with the capitalist workplace, and respond to the democratic values and expectations associated with equality of access to citizen rights and opportunities (Carnoy and Levin 1985; Spring 1980).

The issue of a differentiated civics curriculum was relatively neglected. This was because the consequences of curricular differentiation were studied mainly with reference to high-prestige knowledge such as English and mathematics, whereas civics is a marginal school subject in many countries (Torney-Purta, Lehmann, Oswald and Schulz 2001; Torney-Purta, Schwille and Amadeo 1999). Also, unlike high-prestige school subjects, civics is typically taught in heterogeneous classrooms without separating students by levels of achievement or ability.

Dewey (1966) considers "equal opportunity to receive and to take from others . . . [and the exposure to] . . . shared undertakings and experiences," a hallmark of democratic education. "Otherwise, the influences which educate some into masters, educate others into slaves" (p. 84). Do schools fulfill these expectations? Are processes producing workers and citizens contradictory or complimentary? Are students in vocational and academic programs guided into universal citizenship patterns or into status-determined, dissimilar citizenship roles?

The present study can offer only a limited response to these queries. Only one component of the educational process will be examined here, namely, the prescribed, official, and authoritative civics curriculum as it unfolds in textbooks and teacher guides that are designed for academic and vocational programs in Israeli high schools.

ACADEMIC AND VOCATIONAL HIGH SCHOOL PROGRAMS IN ISRAEL

The purpose of this section is to give readers who are unfamiliar with the Israeli educational system information about vocational and academic programs in Israeli high schools. In Israel, placement in academic or vocational programs that are offered within both separate schools and comprehensive schools clearly reflects students' degree of present success as well as future prospects. Academic programs prepare students for a matriculation certificate—a requisite for college entry and a wide range of semiprofessional training programs as well as occupational positions. Vocational programs, on the other hand, with the exception of some highly selective programs that provide graduates with both a matriculation certificate and technological training, have become alternative educational frameworks for low achievers who were rejected by academic schools (Ichilov 1991; Kahane and Starr 1984). The diploma that graduates receive does not qualify them for university candidacy. Vocational programs prepare for low-prestige occupations and produce certified semiskilled workers. There are also differences among academic and vocational programs in the ethnic and socioeconomic make-up of the student population. While students from middle and upper socioeconomic groups and of Ashkenazi (Western) origin form the majority in academic programs, students from lower socioeconomic echelons and of Sephardic (Eastern) origin are overrepresented in vocational programs (Ichilov 1991).

ANALYSIS OF CURRICULUM DOCUMENTS: METHODOLOGICAL CONSIDERATIONS

Three types of curriculum documents will be discussed and analyzed in the present study: the curriculum, textbooks, and the teachers' guides that accompany the textbooks. Curriculum documents embody important ideas concerning the contents, organization and transmission of knowledge in several ways:

- Such documents prescribe a selection of what is worthy of transmission in school. By implication, what is omitted is considered less worthy or unworthy.
- Such documents reflect ideas about the acquisition of knowledge.

- Such documents contain ideas concerning the organization of knowledge: how different areas of knowledge—both within and across subjects—are related to one another. In other words, they may (implicitly or explicitly) contain ideas about the relationship of various school subjects to one another.

- They reflect ideas about the educational aims that go beyond the transmission of narrowly conceived knowledge to include the development of attitudes toward self and others (Schrag 1992; 277).

I will start by briefly describing the documents that will be analyzed. A more detailed description will be provided in the analysis itself. I will then proceed to describe the methods by which the curriculum documents were analyzed. Special attention will be given to the content categories that were employed in the content analysis of the textbooks. More detailed information about research procedures will be provided as part of the presentation and analysis of the research data.

THE CURRICULUM DOCUMENTS

The *Civics Curriculum* refers to the official program or blueprint for civics as a school subject, prepared by the ministry of education, specifying the goals of civic education and its organization and contents. The vocational program includes sixteen pages and the academic program consists of twenty-nine pages.

Textbooks will get the most attention in the present study. Textbooks are only one component of political education in the schools; nevertheless, they are a central one. For teachers, they serve as an important source of preparation for various subsequent curricular and extracurricular activities (Ichilov 2000). Students spend a great deal of time reading, summarizing, and discussing topics included in textbooks. Textbooks are educational tools specially designed to represent the central values, norms, knowledge, and skills within a particular culture and society. Their content is often perceived as an authoritative statement about the state of the art. Venezky (1992: 436) maintains that "for the public, textbooks are visible manifestation of the school's beliefs and intentions." It is, therefore, important to examine what textbooks communicate to Israeli students about the nature of citizenship and democracy. Two textbooks, one for academic and one for vocational programs, will be analyzed. Venezky (1992: 437) sees a correspondence between curriculum and textbooks: "A curriculum is an abstraction, an amalgamation of goals and aspirations. From a single set of curriculum guidelines an infinite number of textbooks could be built, each with its own interpretation of the intent of the guidelines. Amount of coverage for specific topics, difficulty level, language of explanation, and the like, could differ." In this case, both books have been explicitly developed to meet the requirements of the official civics curriculum. A textbook is considered to be an instruction manual for a particular subject. This implies selectivity of content, sequencing, and presentation. The centrality of textbooks in mediating knowledge may differ by subject matter. In the arts (music and literature, for example) students interact directly with the artists' works, and textbooks play a secondary role. In contrast, history, philosophy, the social sciences, and civics, are typically taught with textbooks (Venezky 1992).

The *Teacher Guides* provide teaching suggestions and highlight the central concepts and ideas that should be imparted to students through the designated textbooks. The *Guide for Vocational School Teachers* has 367 pages. It is a source book for teachers that includes state documents, newspaper articles, academic articles, poems, and a short bibliography. It also includes teaching suggestions for each subject and what ideas should be emphasized. The academic guide is still in preparation, and the present temporary guide has 149 pages. However, all civics teachers participated in training programs that were specially designed to familiarize them with the new curriculum, textbook, and form of the civics matriculation examination. These are summarized in the temporary teachers' guide.

METHODOLOGY AND PROCEDURES

According to Venezky (1992), textbooks typically contain a manifest curriculum, a latent or hidden curriculum, and a pedagogical apparatus. The manifest curriculum is what is most evident, both in the table of contents and in the index. It is also found in the difficulty level of the material presented (number of variables in graphical presentation, for example). The latent curriculum is a series of secondary messages, transmitted on top of the manifest curriculum through commission and omission. It is not intentionally defined in either the table of contents or the index but can sometimes be inferred from these. The number of pages dedicated to various topics, for example, may indicate the differential measure of importance assigned to each. The pedagogical apparatus of a textbook is reflected in its arrangement of topics and its didactic mechanisms: quizzes, practices, diagrams, teaching suggestions. Textbooks may include teaching suggestions for teachers, or offer suggestions for study techniques and self-evaluation for students. The intention is to explore the overt structure of the textbooks, the pedagogical apparatus, and the latent messages. The analysis of the overt curriculum will focus on the topics that are common to both books and on those that are unique to each of them, on the amount of pages dedicated to each topic, the number of assignments for students in each book, and the amount of instructional materials that are included in each textbook (such as tables, newspaper excerpts, state documents, photos, and illustrations). This implies a descriptive and quantitative approach. More details concerning the procedures that were adopted in this respect will be provided in the analysis itself.

It is important, however, to go beyond the structure of the textbooks and analyze their contents. The major objective was to see what dimensions and role patterns of citizenship emerge when the contents of the textbooks are analyzed.

Content analysis of the two textbooks was carried out using categories, which were based on Ichilov's (1990) taxonomy of dimensions and role patterns of citizenship in democracy. Ichilov (1990) identifies ten dimensions of citizenship that can be clustered to form numerous profiles of citizenship in democracy. Included are types of citizenship behavior—active participation versus passive compliance; types of value orientations—particularistic versus universalistic; arenas of citizenship—local versus international and political versus civic. Also included are types of attitudinal orientations—affective versus cognitive and evaluative; motivational orientations—external/obligatory versus internal/voluntary; participatory means—expression of consent versus expression of dissent; and participatory means—conventional versus unconventional. These will be explained here only briefly.

The active/passive dimension discriminates between activities directed toward the manipulation of the sociopolitical environment and activities that have results mainly for the individual. Voting, for example, was classified as active behavior, whereas the view of a citizen as one who regularly reads newspapers was classified as passive behavior. It is true that an informed citizen may decide to become active, but information seeking in itself is more like consumption.

A particularistic orientation is specific to a given society and reflects its unique history, culture, national values, symbols and institutions. A universalistic orientation represents values such as freedom and equality, which are frequently shared by democratic societies regardless of their particular heritage. These two sets of orientations may often be inconsistent and even conflict with one another.

Citizenship may be perceived as involvement in activities and issues that pertain to one's country only, or be more broadly perceived as global awareness—expressing interest and taking a stand on issues in other countries and regions. Citizens may be expected to operate as citizens in the political domain only, as voters or candidates for political office, for example. They may also be expected to act as citizens in the various civic social domains, for example, the family, the school, and religious institutions.

The distinction between affective versus cognitive and evaluative attitudes assumes that affection represents a less sophisticated approach than cognition and evaluation. Furthermore, democratic citizenship implies that rationality should prevail over emotionality. Evaluation can reflect emotions and cognitions simultaneously, but critical thinking is given priority.

The external/obligatory versus internal/voluntary identifies two distinct sources of motivation for civic action. Democratic theory assumes that citizens should act mainly voluntarily and out of convictions, rather than in response to outside pressures. And finally, citizens may express dissent, not just consent, by conventional and by unconventional participatory means. The classification of specific civic actions as conventional or unconventional may vary from one period to another and from one society to another.

Ichilov (1990) demonstrates that a great variety of citizenship profiles can be drawn using the classification of various citizenship objects (such as knowledge, actions, attitudes, and symbols). Such profiles may range between two poles of a continuum, one representing a narrow view of citizenship, and the other representing a broad view of the citizenship role. The narrow profile of citizenship is based primarily on affection, and actions are guided by obligatory, passive, and particularistic orientations. Citizens express consent by conventional means and perceive citizenship as related to objects exclusively in the political domain and within the national arena. The broad profile is based primarily on cognition and evaluation and actions are guided by voluntary and active orientations. It reflects a more equal balance between universalistic and particularistic orientations and may include the expression of dissent via unconventional methods. Citizenship is related to a plurality of civic/social domains, including the national and transnational arenas.

CIVICS IN THE ISRAELI ACADEMIC AND VOCATIONAL HIGH SCHOOL PROGRAMS: RESEARCH RESULTS

There is a fair amount of overlap among the three types of curriculum documents. For example, a detailed list of topics that should be discussed, suggestions for teaching methods, assignments, and preparation of instructional materials, together with statements concerning the purposes that the programs wish to accomplish, are included in all the documents. In order to avoid repetitions these common elements will be discussed as part of the analysis of the textbooks that were specially designed to implement the planned curriculum.

According to Bernstein (1971) the status of a specific school subject is manifested through several features, such as the amount of time accorded to teaching the specific subject, whether the subject is compulsory or optional, whether students are evaluated by means of an external or internal examination, whether the school subject represents specialized or nonspecialized knowledge, and what the significance of the subject is in a given educational career. By these criteria, civics is a marginal school subject in both academic and vocational high school programs, but much more so in vocational schools, as can be inferred from the analysis of academic and vocational curricula.

By "civics curriculum" I refer to the official civics program or outline prepared by the Israeli ministry of education, specifying the goals of civic education, its organization and contents, and recommendations concerning the instruction of civics. A differentiated civics curriculum was developed, for academic programs in 1994 and for vocational programs in 1990. Both curricula were prepared by a program committee consisting of representation by officials of the ministry of education, educators, and experts from universities. The personal composition of the two program committees, however, was not identical.

Analysis of the documents that the program committees produced suggests that the point of departure of each committee was different. In vocational schools civics did not exist as a distinct school subject. It formed a section only within the study of history of the Jewish people and the state of Israel, a school subject that was not universally taught in all vocational schools. Civics textbooks for vocational schools were nonexistent as were training programs for civics teachers. Consequently, only a few vocational school students had a chance to study civics.

What alerted the ministry to the condition of civics in vocational programs were the results of studies examining students' knowledge and perceptions of democracy, which revealed great ignorance and intolerance among vocational program students (notably, Semach and Zin 1987). The ministry's conclusion was that "education for citizenship and democracy in the technological tracks must be invigorated" (Ministry of Education and Culture 1990: 5). The committee made the following recommendations. First, civics should become a distinct and autonomous school subject that would be offered in either the eleventh or twelfth grade. Sixty annual hours would be dedicated to the teaching of civics, of which forty hours would be assigned to an obligatory core entitled "my state: basic values and government in Israel," and twenty additional hours to an elective topic. The electives include "basic economic concepts," "basic issues in the economy of Israel," "economy and employment in Israel," and "Israel's relations with Arab neighboring countries." Three out of the four optional topics deal with economy and employment, presumably catering to the needs of future workers. Secondly, the final civics examination should no longer constitute part of the history examination, and a grade in civics would be entered in the high school diploma. The committee also recommended the preparation of suitable textbooks and the provision of training programs for civics teachers in vocational schools. Thus, the 1990 civics curriculum represents the first (and so far the only) endeavor to establish civics as an independent school subject in vocational schools.

The civics curriculum for academic high schools, which the program committee was dealing with, was prepared in the early 1970s and has been updated several times since then. The Israeli educational system consists of regular (non-religious) Hebrew schools, religious Hebrew state schools, and Arab state schools. There is no common civics curriculum for all state schools, and only partial overlap existed. The civics curriculum for Hebrew schools consisted of seven sections. Teaching "The Israeli political system" was required, and two more topics were left to the choice of the school principals. The elective topics included "Basic issues concerning Israeli economy"; "The Arab citizens of Israel"; "Labor and work relations in Israel"; "Social inequality, social problems and welfare policy"; "The Arab-Israeli conflict"; and "Religion, society, and state" (for state religious schools only). "Israel and the diaspora" was recently added as an additional elective topic. A comparable curriculum was developed for Arab schools. However, because teaching materials in Arabic were not prepared, many Arab schools continued to implement a curriculum that was developed in the 1960s.

The new civics curriculum was developed because of the need to reform the old program and to weave the separate sections together into a coherent concept of citizenship and democracy. The committee saw no justification for having diverse civics curricula within the Israeli educational system, and developed a common core curriculum that would be universally implemented in all academic Hebrew and Arab state schools. Vocational schools, however, were not included as part of the target population.

Civics is taught at the eleventh or twelfth grade, and ninety annual hours are dedicated to the teaching of civics. Seventy hours are allotted to the teaching of the core curriculum, and twenty additional hours to one out of four elective topics. The elective topics seem be designed to fit the particularistic nature of schools. Thus, "Religion, society, and state" is suitable as an elective in state religious schools; "the Arab or Druz citizens of Israel" is most likely to appeal to Arab and Druz state schools, while "National security" and "Social and economic policy in Israel" are probably attractive in regular state schools.

In conclusion, the time allotted to the teaching of the core curriculum in academic programs (70 hours) is almost twice the amount of time allocated in vocational programs (40 hours), but an identical amount of time is dedicated to the elective topics in both types of programs. However, schools' major efforts and emphasis are focussed on the implementation of the obligatory part of the curriculum. The optional topics remain marginal and are not even included in the textbooks. Another important difference is that students in vocational schools take an internal final examination, while students in academic schools take the national matriculation examination in civics. By these criteria, it can be concluded that civics is a more marginal school subject in vocational than in academic high schools. Compared, however, with the time allotted to the teaching of high-prestige school subjects, civics is marginal in the academic programs as well. Another sign of its marginality in academic tracks is that civics, unlike prestigious school subjects, is offered uniformly only at a basic level and cannot be studied at an advanced curricular level.

The elective subjects are not included in the textbooks and will, therefore, be analyzed here. In the academic curriculum the electives are designed to "provide an opportunity for a broader and deeper analysis of issues that have been discussed in the core curriculum" (Ministry of Education, Culture and Sports 1995: 6). Examination of the vocational curriculum reveals that the optional topics are not included in the obligatory part of the curriculum and provide an opportunity to acquire additional knowledge. I chose to examine a topic common to both the academic and vocational program. The vocational curriculum lists three electives that deal with social and economic issues, while the academic curriculum lists only one. The curriculum stipulates that in academic programs, the study of "economic and social policy in Israel" should be based on concepts derived from economy, sociology, and political science that are indispensable for gaining understanding. No similar recommendations are made, however, in the vocational curriculum. Students in academic programs should be introduced to issues concerning the modern welfare state, such as the liberal and socialist views on liberty and equality and on state intervention in the various social spheres. They should become familiar with debates concerning the development of the welfare state in the 1990s and with the variety of means proposed for achieving the goals that welfare states have set. Students are expected to learn about the place of geopolitical, demographic, and social considerations in determining the socioeconomic policy of the government, and to understand the effects of direct and indirect governmental interventions in the various social spheres.

"Society and social policy in Israel" should impart to vocational program students the recognition that Israel is a heterogeneous society consisting of various ethnic, religious, and national groups and cultural traditions, as well as different forms of settlement (such as kibbutz and development towns). Next, students are introduced to the idea that social and welfare policy is rooted in the Jewish tradition of charity and social justice, as well as in the Western idea of the welfare state. The welfare state, however, is only briefly mentioned and is left undiscussed. The purpose of social and welfare policy is described as providing basic economic security, improving the standard of living, and decreasing social gaps. Students learn about state welfare services and about services provided through nongovernmental organizations. The list of basic concepts that should be acquired includes different forms of settlements (such as kibbutz and development towns), "poverty line," stereotypes, charity, rehabilitation, types of families (nuclear and extended families, for example; single-parent or same-gender families are not mentioned), and the Social Security Institute. "Economy and work in Israel" starts with information about the labor force in Israel and about the central role that the government plays in taxation, research and development, as well as in formulating wage and employment policy. The section on "Man at work" is especially revealing. Students learn about the value of work for the individual and society and about considerations that should guide the selection of a vocation, place of work, and training and retraining programs. Students acquire "basic principles for appropriate work relations and professional success: working habits, human relations, etc." (Ministry of Education and Culture 1990: 14). Students learn about labor unions, labor laws, and procedures for settling labor disputes. "Basic economic concepts," as the title suggests, familiarizes students with concepts such as means of production, supply and demand, division of labor, expenditure and income, import and export, different types of taxes (direct, indirect, progressive), exchange rate, savings, investment, and budget.

Overall, it seems that while students in the academic programs are expected to develop a broad and interdisciplinary view of the welfare state and social issues, and learn to approach current issues through a multifaceted perspective, students in vocational programs receive mainly practical knowledge concerning work and welfare services, as well as basic knowledge and concepts that they should accept uncritically.

THE TEXTBOOKS

The distinct points of departure of the program committees, which were mentioned above—namely, the need to strengthen democratic knowledge and the support for democratic values and behaviors in vocational schools and to create a common curriculum for students representing various segments within Israeli society in academic schools—are reflected in the contents and emphases of the civics curricula.

Israeli society is greatly heterogeneous and deeply divided. Israel, as its Declaration of Independence states, was established as a Jewish nation-state and a democracy. This in itself is a source of conflict. Major rifts exist, for example, between religiously observant and nonobservant Jews and between Israeli-Arabs and Israeli-Jews. While observant Jews wish to see more religious practices implemented in public life, many nonobservant Jews support the democratic and Israeli components more strongly than the Jewish component and consider the observation of a religious way of life a private matter. The national symbols of the State of Israel that represent Jewish themes (such as the Star of David in the Israeli flag) are not an acceptable form of Israeli identity for the Arab minority. Many Israeli-Arabs seek to transform Israel from a Jewish state into "a state of all its citizens," and this is one source of tension between Arabs and Jews (Ichilov 1999).

Educating the younger generation for citizenship where little consensus exists regarding what the character of society should be, and what binds citizens together, is an extremely difficult task (Ichilov 1999; Byrne 1997). However, the ministry of education was determined to formulate a common core curriculum for all academic state schools: Arab and Druz, regular state schools, and religious state schools. The supreme goal of such a curriculum is to help students become "autonomous and conscious citizens, capable of critical thinking, of analyzing, evaluating, and forming an independent opinion, playing by the rules of democracy, and being 'immune' to demagogical influences" (Ministry of Education 2001: 10). The central goals that such a curriculum should achieve are stated in the teacher guide as "to inculcate a common Israeli civic identity, together with the development of distinct national identities, and to impart to students the values of pluralism and tolerance, educate students to accept the diversity that exists within Israeli society, and to respect those who are different from oneself" (ibid.: 10). The core curriculum should thus provide Arab and Jewish students alike with "a thorough examination of the values on which Israel and its government are founded, given that Israel is simultaneously a Jewish and democratic state. The analysis should reveal, on the one hand, how the Jewish and democratic components are connected, and on the other, the fact that tensions may arise between them. Examination of the social reality in Israel should be related to these two sets of values" (Ministry of Education, Culture, and Sports 1994: 6). The structural rationale of the academic textbook can be described best by Figure 6.1. It starts with the Declaration of Independence, in

Figure 6.1
The Layout of the Academic Textbook

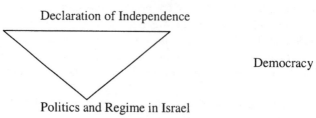

Democracy

Politics and Regime in Israel

which Israel is defined as a Jewish and a democratic state. These two elements, a Jewish state and democracy, are then discussed separately, followed by a discussion of what issues arise when these two foundations are implemented and converge.

The strategy that was adopted for academic programs is clearly analytical and problem oriented. The affective aspect of "developing attachment and commitment to the [Israeli] state and society" (Ministry of Education 2001: 10) is marginalized in comparison with the centrality of the cognitive elements in the curriculum. This approach is already evident in the title of the academic textbook: *To Be Citizens in Israel: A Jewish and Democratic State.*

Examination of the civics curriculum for vocational programs reveals some similarities to the curriculum that was developed for academic programs. The underlying premises that are advanced include "a justification of democracy as the best political regime, and a belief in the right of Israel to exist as a Jewish state" (Ministry of Education and Culture 1990: 6). The need "to develop understanding of the complexity of the social and political systems in a democracy, especially in Israel as a young state that is coping with existential problems" is listed as an objective for civics. Also mentioned is the development of awareness of tensions that may arise "between universalistic ideals and national values and goals; between public and private interests; between majority rights and protection of minorities; and between obeying the law and criticism and aspirations for change" (ibid.: 6). Half the teaching time of the compulsory part of the curriculum (20 annual hours) is allotted to democracy, and the other half to Israel as a Jewish and democratic state (ibid.: 10–13). However, the textbook and teacher guide clearly give priority to democracy, and little attention is given to the Jewish character of Israel. A closer look at the proposed curriculum reveals that students are introduced to democracy in general and to the Israeli situation in a very unsophisticated fashion, and are expected to accept uncritically basic information about democracy and about the structure and procedures of Israeli political institutions. The curriculum lists cognitive and affective objectives. The cognitive objectives of the curriculum consist mainly of "making students familiar with," while "developing an understanding of" is rarely mentioned. One of the cognitive objectives is to make students familiar with the

Israeli economy, stressing the value of work and the competencies that students should acquire through civics, including "the development of proper work habits" (ibid.: 8). The "affective objectives" are emphasized to a greater extent in the vocational than in the academic curriculum, and include, for example: "development of a sense of personal responsibility; developing a positive attitude toward democracy and the rule of law; and development of a feeling of partnership and responsibility in defending the country, while believing in peace and striving to achieve peace" (ibid.: 7). The title of the textbook, *My State*, may imply an attempt to attract vocational school students to the study of civics via emotional attachment more than through intellectual curiosity.

It is important now to examine the structure of the two textbooks and the overt and covert messages that can be inferred. In Table 6.1 the main parts of each textbook are presented, as well as the number of chapters that are dedicated to each part. The number and percentage of pages devoted to each part are also shown. Table 6.1 reveals that the civics textbook for academic programs includes 604 pages: 593 pages of the textbook itself, 6 pages of glossary, and a 5-page bibliography. The textbook for vocational schools contains 305 pages and includes neither a glossary nor a bibliography.

All three parts of the vocational textbook deal with democracy from various vantage points, although the fact that Israel is also a Jewish state is acknowledged. Part 1, "Man and Society, Citizen and State" deals with the rights and obligations of the individual as a member of society and as a citizen within a state. Part 2 deals with democracy in general, and part 3 deals with Israeli democracy. The sequence of discussion, as shown in Figure 6.2, goes from the individual to society and then to the state.

Forty annual lessons are dedicated to the teaching of the compulsory part of the vocational civics curriculum, and the textbook subsequently consists of forty chapters (or "lessons," as they are labeled). The academic textbook, in contrast, holds twenty-five chapters, although seventy annual hours are allocated to the teaching of the core curriculum. The purpose is to allow academic schools flexibility in the implementation of the curriculum. Although no topic can be skipped, "there is a possibility to expand or to limit the discussion of specific topics and sections according to the decision of the teachers or the schools" (Ministry of Education, Culture, and Sports 1994: 6). More pages are dedicated to democracy then to the Jewish component, and the encounter between these two components of the Israeli regime occupies about sixty percent of the textbook.

The vocational curriculum and textbook, in contrast, are structured very tightly, allowing teachers and schools no flexibility. A possible explanation is that because civics was newly introduced in vocational schools, civics teachers are considered less experienced compared with their colleagues in academic programs. In a similar vein, students in vocational programs are perceived as less capable of independent study, and can thus find it easier to follow a structured textbook specially tailored for each class.

Table 6.1
Structure of Textbooks

Part	Subject	Academic Textbook Chapters N	%	Pages N	%	Vocational Textbook Subject	Chapters N	%	Pages N	%
Preface	Declaration of Independence – Foundation of Government in the State of Israel	1	4	10	1.68	-	-	-	-	-
Part One	What is a Jewish State?	5	20	64	10.79	Individual and Society, Citizen and State	8	20	52	17.04
Part Two	What is Democracy?	7	28	158	26.64	Principles of Democratic Government	15	37.5	103	33.77
Part Three	Government and Politics in Israel	12	48	355	59.86	The Democratic State of Israel	17	42.5	147	48.19
	Glossary			6	0.9		-	-	-	-
	Bibliography			5	0.8		-	-	-	-
Total Chapters/Pages		25	100	604	100		40	100	305	100

Figure 6.2
The Layout of the Vocational Textbook

The academic textbook opens with an "introduction," addressing the students and explaining to them that the purpose of the joint curriculum is to form a common civic denominator for all students and to demonstrate the relevance of civics for all future citizens. Students are informed that the textbook includes diverse opinions and political views, as well as Islamic, Christian, and Jewish sources that support democratic ideas. Students are also informed about the structure of the textbook and what they may expect to learn. In the vocational textbook, a brief introduction is provided for each of the three parts of the book, and in addition, each chapter begins with an "introduction" and ends with a "summary." This practice is described in the teacher guide as a pedagogical strategy: "The introduction and summary make students aware of the learning process. This awareness facilitates both learning, and the assimilation of ideas and values" (Ministry of Education and Culture, 1995: 4). This seems to reflect the notion that students in vocational programs need tight guidance and supervision over each step they take and are more comfortable when the learning context is familiar, repetitious, and structured.

As was mentioned earlier, no glossary is provided in the vocational civics textbook. However, footnotes can frequently be found at the bottom of each page, to provide explanation and definitions of concepts, explanation of Hebrew words that are considered difficult for vocational program students, and pieces of information, for example, about authors who are cited in the text. A concept in the text that is considered difficult is explained in the footnotes over and over again. Many of the concepts that are explained in footnotes are taken for granted as known to students in the academic tracks. For example, following the idea in the text that "all men are born equal," a footnote explains to vocational program students that "equality" does not mean that all men look alike or are similar in their character and inclinations, but rather, that they share equal duties and rights. Both the glossary and footnotes are ways to assist students. However, using a glossary requires a competence that students in vocational schools presumably have not acquired. Thus, assistance is made more promptly accessible to users of the vocational textbook in the form of footnotes. Similarly, the perception of the writers of the textbook is apparently that vocational program students will not benefit from the inclusion of a bibliography.

Subjects that are presented in both textbooks were then identified. The results are shown in Table 6.2. Table 6.2 reveals that democracy forms 50.20 percent of the total number of pages dedicated to similar topics in the vocational textbook, while the state of Israel has a priority in the academic textbook (53.57% of the total number of pages). In both textbooks the democratic component gets

Table 6.2
Common Subjects in Textbooks

Subject	Pages		Pages	
Declaration of Independence	10	2.38%	10	4.01%
The Jewish Aspect	37	8.80%	21	8.43%
The Democratic Aspect	148	35.23%	125	50.20%
State of Israel	225	53.57%	93	37.34%
Common Total	420	100.0%	249	100.0%

more attention than the Jewish character of Israel, and a substantial part of the vocational textbook is dedicated to the state of Israel. However, a closer look reveals that these apparent similarities are misleading. The analysis reveals that the discussion of the various topics in the two books is qualitatively different. The various concepts and issues are presented in the academic textbook in a sophisticated and analytical manner, and not as a matter of fact. Students learn that social phenomena evolve and do not merely emerge out of nowhere, and how various social, political, and cultural factors may explain such occurrences. They learn to analyze issues from a plurality of vantage points, and become aware of the fact that individuals and groups may interpret similar events differently. There is no hesitation in dealing with controversial issues over which Israeli society is deeply divided. The multifaceted and problem-oriented approach is also evident in the subjects that are unique to the academic civics textbook. These include, for example, a discussion of issues related to nationality and nation states; issues related to national, ethnic, and cultural identities; various definitions and forms of democracy; and a discussion of social rifts within Israeli society. The vocational textbook, in contrast, presents phenomena as given, offers a standard definition of concepts, and avoids the discussion of controversial issues and plurality of points of view. For example, the discussion of the rule of law concludes "the law is stable and supreme . . . all citizens must obey the law, cannot 'take the law into their own hands' but must find solutions within the frame of law" (Ministry of Education and Culture 1993: 76). In contrast, in the academic textbook, students deal with distinctions concerning illegal behaviors and moral issues. For example, delinquency, corruption of public officials, and dissent are discussed. Students learn about the right and obligation of citizens to express dissent and about the moral obligation to disobey certain laws, notably a law that violates human rights. The topics unique to the vocational textbook include observations such as man is a social being, a central government is a requisite for the maintenance of law and order, and that the essence of democratic citizenship is to accept responsibility for one's actions. Students learn that bureaucracy can sometimes cause delays and inefficiency in decision-making processes. Students also learn "what . . . the actions [are] that citizens must take in order to be eligible to vote" (ibid.: 182). Overall, then, the vocational textbook provides basic knowledge about democracy and about the structure and function of Israeli governmental institutions that students should accept uncritically, as well as practical suggestions and some behavioral guidance.

Both textbooks include assignments. These assignments are clearly part of the pedagogical apparatus. In the academic textbook all assignments appear under the heading of "exercise." An exercise typically includes several assignments. The vocational textbook includes three types of assignments in each chapter: "task," "conversation," and "homework." Each of these may include several assignments. Tasks and conversations are typically classroom activities carried out jointly by all students or by groups of students with the guidance of a teacher. "Homework" is sometimes omitted and is clearly marginal in comparison with "task" and "conversation."

In order to examine the assignment, the number of individual tasks included under the various headings were counted. These were then classified into nine categories, according to the specific demands they make. In Table 6.3 the number of assignments in each category is shown, and the percentage out of the total number of assignments in each textbook. The categories have been ordered in Table 6.3 from the simplest to the more sophisticated tasks: from reading and reading comprehension, which are considered basic competencies, to evaluation and critical thinking, which require greater sophistication.

Table 6.3 reveals that reading and reading comprehension are required in about one third of the assignments in each textbook. Students are typically asked to read an excerpt of a newspaper article, state documents, literature, religious sources, and so forth, which are provided in the textbook. However, a closer analysis of the passages that are included as reading material in each textbook shows that the quantitative similarity is misleading. The citations in the academic textbook are longer, while in the vocational textbook excerpts are very short and appear in an adapted linguistic form rather than in the original. The second category—examples and information—is more prevalent in the vocational textbook. Here again, while students in academic tracks are encouraged to explore additional sources of information such as encyclopedias, internet sites, and libraries, students in vocational tracks are requested to collect information from friends, parents, or other adults. For example, they are instructed to ask people about different roles that they perform, how they feel about these roles, whether their job is a paid job or a voluntary one, etc., or they are required to ask an adult about his organizational affiliations: work place, charity or political or-

Table 6.3
Types of Assignments (N, %)

Textbook/ Type of Tasks	Academic Textbook		Vocational Textbook	
	N	%	N	%
Reading / Reading Comprehension	115	35.49	114	32.29
Examples / Information	18	5.55	43	12.18
Role Play	0	0	42	11.89
Conversation	0	0	23	6.51
Formation / Expression of Opinion	40	12.34	31	8.78
Synthesis of Knowledge	45	13.88	33	9.34
Drawing Conclusions	54	13.58	24	6.79
Evaluation / Critical Thinking	47	14.50	32	9.06
Other	5	1.54	11	9.63
Total	324	100.0	353	100.0

ganization, religious organization, recreational organization (Ministry of Education and Culture 1993: 29, 31). The "role play" category is unique to the vocational textbook. Students are requested to establish a state, be members of parliament, be a spaceship crew, and so forth. The purpose is to make abstract ideas more concrete and to develop empathy with political institutions, processes, and officials. The "conversation" category is also unique to the vocational textbook. Students are asked "to talk about" various issues, but such discussions are typically rather vague and shallow. In the academic textbooks there are fewer direct requests for a discussion of a specific matter, but the textbook implicitly requires a thorough and comprehensive discussion of complex issues. The more demanding categories—formation and expression of opinion, synthesis of knowledge, drawing conclusions, and evaluation and critical thinking—are more common in the academic textbook. Here, again, the demands are noticeably different, as can be inferred from the two following examples. The "exercise" pertaining to the chapter on nationality and nation-states in the academic textbook requires students to do the following:

• Read (the documents are included in the textbook) parts of the American Bill of Rights and Israel's declaration of Independence, and explain how differences between Israel and the United States concerning nationality and the characteristics of nation-states are reflected in the two documents.

• Explain the difficulties associated with the implementation of nations' right for self-determination.

Table 6.4
Nontext Learning Materials (N and % of pages)

Textbooks/ Type of Tasks	Academic Textbook		Vocational Textbook	
	N	%	N	%
Pictures	70	11.58	31	10.16
Illustrations	39	6.45	59	19.34
Tables (not part of tasks)	6	0.99	3	0.98
Maps	6	0.99	4	1.31
Graphs	15	2.48	2	0.65

• Respond to two questions that refer to part of an article (included in the textbook). The questions are related to the ethnic and political characteristics of nation-states, and students are asked to justify and explain their answers. (Ministry of Education 2000: 26, 27)

In the vocational textbook students are introduced to the difference between patience (defined as self-control, deferment of gratifications) and tolerance (defined as recognition of the existence of diverse opinions, beliefs, customs, manners, etc.). Five events are then presented, and students are asked to identify which events are associated with patience, and which manifest tolerance. One of the affairs describes the behavior of a girl who waits a long while in line in the bank "without pushing or sneaking ahead of others." Another case tells about a boy whose friends include Israeli born children, newly arrived immigrants, and foreign citizens, as well as wealthy and poor, educated and uneducated children. When students have completed the task, they are requested to "talk about" their responses in class. Teachers closely supervise students' individual or group work and must be constantly available to assist students and make sure that all students actively participate in the various assignments. During classroom discussions, teachers must exemplify by their own behavior how civilized civic discourse is carried out. They must also insist that students listen to one another and tolerate views that they oppose (Ministry of Education and Culture 1995: 4, 5).

The pedagogical apparatus also includes nontext materials such as photographs, illustrations, tables, maps, and graphs. Table 6.4 shows the number of pages that include nontext information in each textbook. In the academic textbook, nontext information is included in about one third of the textbook pages, and in the vocational textbook it forms about a quarter of the textbook pages. Pictures and illustrations are most frequently used in both textbooks, while tables, maps, and graphs are rare. However, graphs are more frequently used in the academic textbooks, and illustrations are more common in the vocational textbook. The graphs and tables in the academic textbook are taken out of official documents such as the Israel Statistical Abstract (for example: Ministry of Education 2000: 321, 325), while those included in the vocational textbook are typically taken out of daily newspapers (for example: Ministry of Education and Culture 1993: 195). In other words, the tables and graphs in the academic textbook provide more elaborate and sophisticated information. The illustrations in both books are fairly unsophisticated. In the vocational textbook, illustrations provide an oversimplistic visual expression for complex processes and concepts. For example, people with plates in their hands are waiting in line to get a slice of a pie—the budget pie—or an illustration of a coalition government showing a worker, an orthodox Jew, and a woman holding hands (Ministry of Education and Culture 1993: 98, 222).

CONCLUSION AND DISCUSSION

The idea that citizenship education is imparted in school equally to all students has been challenged in this chapter. In all the curriculum documents that were analyzed, there is ample evidence that those who produced them were aware of the differences in levels of knowledge, ability and learning skills between students in the academic schools and those in vocational schools. A distinction must be made, however, between awareness of such differences and the explicit or implicit consequences that such awareness may have for civic education. In other words, it is clearly the duty of educators to be attuned to any learning difficulties and deficiencies that students may have. What matters, however, is how educators react to such differences. Educators may attempt to guide students to similar ends, using differentiated pedagogical means. Or they may aim at differential, predetermined ends that are considered appropriate for specific groups of students, based on the assumed capacities and interests of students. Under these circumstances, underprivileged students are often denied the opportunity to try and cope with highly valued knowledge. Our analysis reveals that the Israeli Ministry of Education adopted a policy of differentiated civics curriculum for academic and vocational schools. Civics was introduced into the vocational curriculum only in 1990. When a decision to develop a common civics core curriculum for all types of academic high schools was made in 1994 "to inculcate a common civic identity" (Ministry of Education 2001: 10), vocational high schools were left out. An alternative solution that would not exclude vocational program students could have been adopted. For example, an identical curriculum could have been developed for vocational schools, producing a more simply written textbook similar in content to the academic one, and spreading the teaching of civics over two or three years of high school instead of condensing it into one academic year.

Table 6.5
Citizenship Orientations in Civics Curriculum Documents

Type of Orientation	Academic	Vocational
Attitudinal Orientation	Cognitive/evaluative	Affective
Motivational Orientation	Internal/voluntary	External obligatory
Action Orientation	Active	Passive
Value Orientation	Universalistic/particularistic	Universalistic
Participatory Objective	Expression of consent/dissent	Expression of consent
Participatory Means	Conventional/unconventional	Conventional
Domains of Citizenship	Political	Social
Arenas of Citizenship	National	National

The analysis of the curriculum materials designed for vocational and academic high schools has shown that the differentiated curriculum guides students into dissimilar citizenship roles. Academic school students are expected to acquire the capacity to perceive citizenship issues through a broad, interdisciplinary, and multifaceted prism. Students in vocational schools, in contrast, are initiated into an unsophisticated and uncritical pattern of citizenship.

Using Ichilov's taxonomy of citizenship dimensions (Ichilov 1990), the prevailing patterns of citizenship that unfold in curriculum documents designed for vocational and academic schools are summarized in Table 6.5. The profile of citizenship in vocational civics curriculum document is a narrow one. Citizenship is based primarily on affection, and civic actions are guided by obligatory and passive orientations. Students learn to express consent by conventional means. In contrast, academic high school students are guided into a broad profile of citizenship. Citizenship is based primarily on cognition and evaluation, and civic actions are guided by voluntary and active orientations. Students learn to express dissent, not only consent, via conventional and less conventional means. While the vocational curriculum focuses mainly on the universalistic aspects of democracy, the academic curriculum reflects a more equal balance between universalistic and particularistic orientations. Global awareness and concerns are lacking in both curricula, and citizenship focuses solely on the national arena. The academic curriculum mainly highlights the political dimension of citizenship, while the vocational curriculum deals with the relationships of individual-society and citizen-state.

A caveat must be mentioned, however. Curriculum documents are only one component of citizenship education in schools and thus provide only partial information about citizenship education. To obtain a more comprehensive view of the consequences of the differentiated curriculum, additional factors must be examined. These would include, for example, the implemented curriculum, the school climate, the various curricular and extracurricular activities, as well as teachers' behavior, expectations, and attitudes.

THE CURRICULUM DOCUMENTS THAT WERE ANALYZED

Ministry of Education and Culture, Curriculum Department. 1993. *My State: Chapters in Civics for Technological Tracks (general and religious)*. Jerusalem. (In Hebrew).

Ministry of Education and Culture, Curriculum Department. 1995. *My State: Chapters in Civics for Technological Tracks (general and religious)*. Teacher's guide. Jerusalem. (In Hebrew).

Ministry of Education, Culture, and Sports, Curriculum Department. 1994. *Citizenship: [Academic] High School Curriculum for Jewish (general and religious), Arab, and Druz Schools*. 1st ed. Jerusalem. (In Hebrew).

Ministry of Education, Curriculum Department. 1990. *Citizenship: High School Curriculum for the Lower Vocational Tracks in General and Religious Jewish Technological High Schools*. Jerusalem. (In Hebrew).

Ministry of Education, Curriculum Department. 2000. *To Be Citizens in Israel: A Jewish and Democratic State*. Jerusalem. (In Hebrew).

Ministry of Education, Curriculum Department. 2001. *Leaflet for Civics Teachers*, no. 16. [Teacher's guide for academic high schools]. Jerusalem. (In Hebrew).

REFERENCES

Almond, G.A. and Verba, S. 1963. *The Civic Culture: Political Attitudes and Democracy in Five Nations*. Princeton: Princeton University Press.

Apple, M.W. 1990. *Ideology and Curriculum*. 2nd ed. New York: Routledge.

Ayalon, H. 1994. "Monopolizing Knowledge? The Ethnic Composition and Curriculum of Israeli High Schools." *Sociology of Education* 67: 264–278.

Barnes, S.H. and Kaase, M. 1979. *Political Action: Mass Participation in Five Western Democracies*. Beverly Hills, CA: Sage.

Bernstein, B. 1971. "On the Classification and Framing of Educational Knowledge." In *Knowledge and Control*. ed. M.F.D. Young. London: Collier-Macmillan. 47–70.

Bhavnani, K.K. 1991. *Talking Politics: A Psychological Framing of Views from Youth in Britain*. Cambridge: Cambridge University Press.

Bourdieu, P. 1971. "Systems of Education and Systems of Thought." In *Knowledge and Control*. ed. M.F.D. Young. London: Collier.

Bowles, S. and Gintis, H. 1976. *Schooling in Capitalist America*. New York: Basic Books.

Bowles, S. 1977. "Unequal Education and the Reproduction of the Social Division of Labor." In *Power and Ideology in Education*. ed. J. Karabel and A.H. Halsey. New York: Oxford University Press. 137–153.

Bynner, J. and Ashford, S. 1994. "Politics and Participation: Some Antecedents of Young People's Attitude to the Political System and Political Activity." *European Journal of Social Psychology* 24: 223–236.

Byrne, S. 1997. *Growing Up in a Divided Society*. Teaneck, N.J.: Fairleigh Dickinson University Press, Associated University Presses.

Callan, E. 1997. *Creating Citizens*. Oxford: Clarendon Press.

Carnoy, M. and Levin, H.M. 1985. *Schooling and Work in the Democratic State*. Stanford: Stanford University Press.

Collins, R. 1979. *The Credential Society*. New York: Academic Press.

Converse, P.E. 1972. "A Change in the American Electorate." In *The Human Meaning of Social Change*. eds. A. Campbell and P.E. Converse. New York: Russell Sage Foundation.

Dahrendorf, R. 1994. "The Changing Quality of Citizenship." In *The Condition of Citizenship*. ed. B. van Steenberger. London: Sage. 10–19.

Dalton, R.J. 1988. *Citizen Politics in Western Democracies*. Chatham, NJ: Chatham House.

Davies, I., Gregory, I. and Riley, S.C. 1999. *Good Citizenship and Educational Provision*. London: Falmer Press.

Delli Carpini, M.X. and Keeter, S. 1996. *What Americans Know About Politics and Why It Matters*. New Haven: Yale University Press.

Dewey, J. [1916] 1966. *Democracy and Education*. New York: Free Press.

Diamond, S. 1960. "Studies and Projects in Citizenship Education." In *The Adolescent Citizen*. ed. F. Patterson. New York: Free Press.

Easton, D. 1965. *A Framework for Political Analysis*. Englewood Cliffs, NJ: Prentice-Hall.

Education Commission of the States. 1973. *National Assessment of Educational Progress: Political Knowledge and Attitudes*. Washington, DC: Government Printing Office.

Goodson, I. 1987. *School Subjects and Curriculum Change*. London: Falmer.

Gutmann, A. 1987. *Democratic Education*. Princeton: Princeton University Press.

Hargreaves, D. 1967. *Social Relations in a Secondary School*. London: Routledge and Kegan Paul.

Heater, D. 1990. *Citizenship: The Civic Ideal in World History*. London: Longman.

Himmelweit, H.T., Humphreys, P., Jaeger, M. and Katz, M. 1981. *How Voters Decide*. London: Academic.

Ichilov, O. 1989. "Perceptions and Attitudes of Israeli High School Civic Education Teachers Concerning Citizenship in Democracy." *Studies in Education* 48: 69–89. (In Hebrew).

Ichilov, O. 1990. "Dimensions and Role Patterns of Citizenship in Democracy." In *Political Socialization, Citizenship Education, and Democracy*. ed. O. Ichilov. New York: Teachers College Press, Columbia University. 11–25.

Ichilov, O. 1991. "Political Socialization and Schooling Effects among Israeli Adolescents." *Comparative Education Review* 35 (3): 430–447.

Ichilov, O. 1999. "Citizenship Education in a Divided Society: The Case of Israel." In *Civic Education across Countries: Twenty-four National Case Studies from the IEA Civic Education Project*. eds. J. Torney-Putra, J. Schwille, and J.A. Amadeo. Amsterdam: International Education Association, 371–395.

Ichilov, O. 2000. *Citizenship Orientations of 11th Grade Students and Teachers in the Israeli Hebrew and Arab High Schools*. Research report, submitted to the steering committee of the IEA Civic Education Study and to the Israeli Ministry of Education.

Ichilov, O. 2002. "Education and Democratic Citizenship in a Changing World." In *Handbook of Political Psychology*. eds. D. Sears, L. Huddy and R.L. Jervis. New York: Oxford University Press.

Ichilov, O., Haymann, F. and Shapira, R. 1990. "Social and Moral Integration and At-
   tachment to the Nation-state: A Case Study of Israeli Adolescents." *Urban Education* 25 (2): 143–157.
Jennings, K.M. and Niemi R.G. 1968. "Patterns of Political Learning." *Harvard Edu-
   cational Review* 38 (3): 443–468.
Jennings, K.M. and Niemi R.G. 1974. *The Political Character of Adolescence*. Princeton:
   Princeton University Press.
Kahane, R. and Starr, L. 1984. *Education and Work: Vocational Socialization Processes
   in Israel*. Jerusalem: Magnes. (In Hebrew).
Kamens, D.H. 1981. "Organizational and Institutional Socialization in Education." *Re-
   search in Sociology of Education and Socialization* 2: 208–219.
Kamens, D.H. 1988. "Education and Democracy: A Comparative Institutional Analysis."
   Sociology of Education 61: 114–127.
Keddie, N. 1971. "Classroom Knowledge." In *Knowledge and Control*. ed. Michael F.D.
   Young. New York: Collier-Macmillan.
Kohlberg, L. and Lockwood, A. 1970. *The Cognitive Developmental Psychology and
   Political Education: Progress in the Sixties*. Cambridge, MA: Harvard Moral
   Development Project.
Kohn, M. 1969. *Class and Conformity: A Study in Values*. Homewood, IL: Dorsey.
Lane, R.E. 1959. *Political Life*. New York: Free Press.
Lipset, S.M. 1960. *Political Man*. New York: Doubleday.
Litt, E. 1963. "Civic Education, Community Norms, and Political Indoctrination." *Amer-
   ican Sociological Review* 28: 69–75.
Marshall, T.H. 1977. *Class, Citizenship and Social Development*. Chicago: University of
   Chicago Press.
Milbrath, L.W. 1965. *Political Participation*. Chicago: Rand McNally.
Nie, N.H., Powell, B. and Prewitt, K. 1969. "Social Structure and Political Participation."
   American Political Science Review 63: 361–378.
Nie, N.H., Junn, J. and Stehlik-Barry, K. 1996. *Education and Democratic Citizenship
   in America*. Chicago: University of Chicago Press.
Niemi, R.G. and Junn, J. 1998. *Civic Education: What Makes Students Learn*. New
   Haven: Yale University Press.
Oakes, J. 1983. "Limiting Opportunity: Student Race and Curricular Differences in Sec-
   ondary Vocational Education." *American Journal of Education* 91 (3): 328–355.
Oakes, J. 1985. *Keeping Track: How Schools Structure Inequality*. New Haven: Yale
   University Press.
Oakes, J., Gamoran, A. and Page, R.N. 1992. "Curriculum Differentiation: Opportunities,
   Outcomes, and Meanings." In *Handbook of Research on Curriculum*. ed. P.W.
   Jackson. New York: Macmillan. 570–626.
Patrick, J.J. 1977. "Political Socialization and Political Education in Schools." In *Hand-
   book of Political Socialization*. ed. S.A. Renshon. New York: The Free Press.
   190–223.
Rist, R.C. 1970. "Student Social Class and Teacher Expectations: The Self-fulfilling
   Prophecy in Ghetto Education." *Harvard Educational Review* 40: 411–451.
Rist, R.C. 1977. "On Understanding the Processes of Schooling: The Contributions of
   Labeling Theory." In *Power and Ideology in Education*. eds. J. Karabel and A.H.
   Halsey. New York: Oxford University Press. 292–313.
Sarup, M. 1978. *Marxism and Education*. London: Routledge and Kegan Paul.

Schrag, F. 1992. "Conceptions of Knowledge." In *Handbook of Research on Curriculum*. ed. P.W. Jackson. New York: MacMillan Library Reference. 268–302.

Spring, J. 1980. *Educating the Worker-Citizen*. New York: Longman.

Stouffer, S.A. 1955. *Communism, Conformity and Civil Liberties*. Garden City, NJ: Doubleday.

Sullivan, J., Marcus, G. and Minns, D. 1975. "The Development of Political Ideology: Some Empirical Findings." *Youth and Society* 7: 148–170.

Tapp, J.L. 1971. "Developing a Sense of Law and Legal Justice." *Journal of Social Issues* 27 (2): 65–91.

Torney, J.V., Oppenhiem, A.N. and Farnen, R.F. 1975. *Civic Education in Ten Countries: An Empirical Study*. New York: John Wiley and Sons.

Torney-Purta, J. 1990. "Youth in Relation to Social Institutions." In *At the Threshold: The Developing Adolescent*. eds. S.S. Feldman and G.R. Elliott. Cambridge, MA: Harvard University Press. 457–478.

Torney-Purta, J. 1997. "Links and Missing Links between Education, Political Knowledge, and Citizenship." *American Journal of Education* 105: 447–457.

Torney-Purta, J., Lehmann, R., Oswald, H. and Schulz, W. 2001. *Citizenship and Education in Twenty-eight Countries*. Amsterdam: IEA.

Torney-Purta, J., Schwille, J. and Amado, J.A. 1999. *Civic Education across Countries: Twenty-four National Case Studies from the IEA Civic Education Project*. Amsterdam: IEA.

Travers, E. 1983. "The Role of School in Political Socialization Reconsidered." *Youth and Society* 14 (4): 475–501.

Young, I.M. 1995. "Polity and Group Difference: A Critique of the Idea of Universal Citizenship." In *Theorizing Citizenship*. ed. R. Beiner. Albany: State University of New York Press. 175–209.

Young, M.F.D. 1971. "An Approach to the Study of Curricula as Socially Organized Knowledge." In *Knowledge and Control*. ed. M.F.D. Young. London: Collier-Macmillan. 19–47.

Venezky, R.L. 1992. "Textbooks in School and Society." In *Handbook on Research on Curriculum*. ed. P.W. Jackson. New York: Macmillan. 436–465.

Verba, S., Nie, N. and Kim, J. 1978. *Participation and Political Equality: A Seven Nation Comparison*. New York: Cambridge University Press.

Whitty, G. 1985. "Social Studies and Political Education in England since 1945." In *Social Histories of the Secondary Curriculum: Subjects for Study*. ed. I. Goodson. London: Falmer. 269–289.

Zemach, M. and Zin, R. 1987. *Attitudes Concerning Democratic Values Among Israeli Youth*. Jerusalem: Van Leer. (In Hebrew).

7

Citizenship Education and Assessment: What Counts as Success?

Marie Clarke

INTRODUCTION

Learning requires individuals to progress from self-development to equip oneself for an occupation to self-development to allow autonomy, choice, and responsibility across all spheres of experience (Ranson 1994). Aristotle's conception of what it is to be and to develop as a person over a whole life is particularly relevant to citizenship education. It includes a quest for value, with each person seeking to reach beyond the self to create something of value. It also involves developing as a person toward what Aristotle described as "the excellences": perfecting a life, which is inescapably a struggle—an experience of failure as well as of success. As Held has pointed out, ultimately the most important virtue in this context is that of deliberation, a life of questioning and enquiry committed to revising both beliefs and action, so that learning moves from being a means to becoming the end in itself (Held 1989). To make this a reality for all, the unfolding of self depends on developing the necessary social conditions, which can provide a sense of purpose within society both for the self and others.

This is especially important in the twenty-first century, and the only way in which these conditions can be developed is by creating arenas for public discourse. Sen has made the point that the conditions for a learning society are, in the last resort, fundamentally political. They require the creation of a polity, which provides the foundation for personal and collective empowerment (Sen 1990). In the political tradition stemming from Greek city states and the Roman republic, citizenship has meant involvement in public affairs on the part of those who had the rights of citizens, namely, the right to take part in public debate and, directly or indirectly, shape the laws and decisions of a state. In modern times, however, democratic ideas shaped by both the American and French Revolutions led to constant demands to broaden the franchise from a narrow citizen class of the educated and property owners to a wider base. In the twentieth century this broadened again when female emancipation and a decrease in the voting age were achieved. Coupled with this was the expansion of the media and freedom of the press, which in turn opened up the processes of government.

Several trends have characterized the development of political education in Western democracies. Ichilov has made the point that the creation of mass education systems after World War II is considered a revolution that enabled modernization and democratization processes to occur (Ichilov 1998). Neo-Marxist and neo-Weberian theories of education and society, however, dispute the extent to which mass education reinforces democracy or the empowerment of citizens. They advance the argument that the progressive force of mass education in furthering democracy, tolerance, and welfare has been undermined by its use as part of the apparatus that perpetuates a class system based on economic and cultural dependence (Bowles and Gintis 1976; Carnoy and Levin 1985). The introduction of political education as part of the school curriculum was accompanied by public debates in many Western democracies when it was feared that political education might turn into manipulation, indoctrination, and the teaching of political partisanship (Ichilov 1998). As a result of these debates political education was narrowly defined, providing mainly factual knowledge about political institutions and avoiding the discussion of controversial issues. As Ichilov comments, it was normative rather than analytical (Ichilov 1998). In the world of the twenty-first century learning remains a source of hope as a human right, for which the ability to live together is an unavoidable condition. Learning to live together entails wishing to live together and learning how to do it. It entails knowledge, involves affectivity and the emotions, involves the construction of meaning, and is both a personal and a social challenge (UNESCO 2001).

THE ROLE OF SCHOOLS IN PROMOTING CITIZENSHIP EDUCATION

School has been the place where an attempt has been made to achieve the goals of a society in a structured way. As well as being used as a vehicle for social reform, an education system can also reproduce a society's status quo. Durkheim defined education as the influence by adult generations on those that are not yet ready for social life, and stated that its object is "to arouse and develop in the child a certain number of physical, intellectual and moral states, which are demanded of him [sic] by the political society as a whole and the special milieu for which he is specifically destined" (Durkheim 1956).

Education becomes an agent of social change, and while responding to social change, becomes tied up with both the economic and the cultural system. This is reflected in school curricula. During the last several decades, curriculum adaptations to social conditions have, in the words of McNeil, "swung between several orientations: academic (development of the mind through subject matter); social meliorist (the use of curriculum to improve society); social efficiency (school as preparation for a job); and student-centred (curriculum that offers students rich experiences)" (McNeill 1999). Within each of these orientations, choices have to be made between different learning and teaching objectives. As a result, criticisms may be levelled at the education system for failing to instill basic values; teach basic skills; develop higher order thinking and problem solving skills; develop creativity, flexibility, and cooperative working habits; and prepare young people for the unknown challenges of the future and the values that will inform future decisions (Le Métais 1997).

Le Métais has made the point that in an ideal world, national values that are clearly understood and shared by all would form a coherent thread that would permeate the education system from aims through to outcomes (Le Métais 1997). This would be reflected in educational structures, the institutional organization of pupils, and the time invested in this process. The curriculum would be consistent with aims and structure and would be supported by appropriate teaching styles. The methods and frequency of assessment would be chosen to enable all students to demonstrate the extent to which they had achieved the educational aims and internalized national values (Le Métais 1997). However, the reality is not so clearcut, and this is especially reflected in the area of citizenship education.

Heater has made the point that schools cannot possibly be expected to prepare young people for adult life as citizens without a complete and agreed understanding of what that status entails (Heater 1990). This view is also articulated by McLaughlin, who believes that "the absence of agreement about public virtues and the common good, actually gives rise to the various disputes about citizenship and 'education for citizenship'" (McLaughlin 1992). He goes on to argue that "if society is, through its schools, to educate for citizenship in a significant way, what is needed at the practical level is a wide ranging and informed national debate, to establish as far as possible a degree of agreement about the public virtues and the common good and about how citizenship and education for citizenship are to be understood" (McLaughlin 1992).

This is an important issue for all societies and, indeed, education systems and curriculum provision in this area. Each day in schools, teachers struggle to engage adolescent students' attention. Many students find their schooling irrelevant to their lives (Hargreaves, Earl and Ryan 1996).

As Holden and Clough have pointed out, "the process of assisting children to become active citizens requires the teacher to keep a delicate balance between providing security and offering challenge" (Holden and Clough 1998). They also argue that education for participation involves reflecting on values, assisting children to acquire the skills necessary for taking action, and ultimately providing opportunities for them to become involved as active citizens. Integral to the acquisition of skills is the acquisition of a values base from which to make one's decisions and responses. Such an approach has implications for teachers and others who work with children. Osler and Starkey have pointed out that if children are to be educated to participate, they will require a "range of skills, including social skills, and skills of communication and judgement" and the opportunity to practice and develop these skills (Osler and Starkey 1996).

This is further developed by McCollum, who states that there is a growing recognition from a number of educational theorists and practitioners that a conception of citizenship education is required that explicitly engages with issues of cultural diversity, addresses the problems of racism and social exclusion, and promotes open and inclusive forms of identity (McCollum 2000). She argues that educational and cultural traditions throughout Europe are highly resistant to such models of education and that there is currently a major and persistent gap between policy statements and educational practice in relation to citizenship education (McCollum 2000).

THE CHALLENGES FACED IN DEVELOPING CITIZENSHIP EDUCATION

It is evident that present-day societies are highly diverse and are becoming increasingly more ethnically, nationally, and racially heterogeneous, more regionally fragmented, more pluralistic culturally, and more strongly linked with global affairs (Ichilov 1998). The challenge for citizenship education at all levels is to enable the public as citizens to contribute to the development of their own society. Citizenship education is, perhaps, needed more than ever to provide a sense of purpose, solidarity, and guidance in a fragmented and rapidly changing world (Ichilov 1998). In many Western democracies there is a trend among citizens to claim their rights and retreat into their own privacy with a focus on the individual (Ichilov 1998). This inevitably results in what Ichilov describes as "a neglect of the community, of the national public place as well as of the international public space, which in turn results in the loss of the sense of trust, efficacy and neighbourliness" (Ichilov 1998). Linked to this is the way in which citizenship educators try to accommodate and reconcile individual and community values.

This refers to what Kerr describes as the tension between a "values-explicit" curriculum, which promotes distinct values that are part of a broader nationally accepted system of public values and beliefs, and a "values-neutral" or "values-free" curriculum that takes a neutral stance in relation to values and controversial issues, leaving the decision about values to the individual (Kerr 1999). Kerr points out that this tension is part of the broader debate about the balance between the "public" and the "private" dimensions of citizenship, leading to what McLaughlin termed "thick" and "thin" citizenship education (McLaughlin 1992). Those who view citizenship as a largely "public" concern see a major or "thick role" for education through the school and formal curriculum in the provision of citizenship education and, in particular, for teachers. Those who view citizenship as a largely "private" affair see a much more limited, or "thin," role for education and advocate a much stronger role for the family and community organizations (Kerr 1999). These tensions are reflected in the range and type of curriculum provision in the area of citizenship education.

CURRICULUM APPROACHES TO CITIZENSHIP EDUCATION

According to Kerr, three main curriculum approaches to citizenship education have developed over time: citizenship education as a specific subject, citizenship education as an integrated part of a broader course, and a cross-curricular approach whereby citizenship education permeates the entire curriculum and is included in all subjects (Kerr 1999).

McLaughlin has argued that citizenship is conceptualized and contested along a continuum that ranges from a minimal to a maximal interpretation (McLaughlin 1992). In his view minimal interpretations are characterized by a narrow definition of citizenship that seeks to promote particular exclusive and elitist interests, such as the granting of citizenship to certain groups in society but not all. Minimal interpretations lead to narrow, formal approaches to citizenship education—what has been termed "civics education." Kerr has argued that within the minimal continuum, the curriculum is largely content-led and knowledge-based. Its primary purpose is to inform through provision and transmission of information, lending itself to didactic teaching and learning approaches with little opportunity for student interaction and initiative (McLaughlin 1992; Kerr 1999). Kerr has pointed out that as the outcomes of minimal approaches are narrow, largely involving the acquisition of knowledge and understanding, it is much easier to measure how successfully the outcomes have been realized, and this can be achieved through traditional assessment methods (Kerr 1999).

On the other end of the continuum is the maximal interpretation. Maximal interpretations are characterized by a broad definition of citizenship that includes and involves all groups and interests in society. Kerr states that this type of citizenship education includes the content and knowledge components of minimal interpretations, but actively encourages investigation and interpretation of the many different ways in which these components (including the rights and responsibilities of citizens) are determined and carried out. Consequently the primary aim is not just to inform, but also to use that information to help students understand and enhance their capacity to participate. This lends itself to a broad mixture of teaching and learning approaches, from the didactic to the interactive, both inside and outside the classroom (Kerr 1999). It reflects the unity of both the process model of curriculum and the situational model of curriculum as developed by Stenhouse and Skilbeck, respectively. Kerr makes the point that viewed from this perspective, citizenship education comprises three strands, education about citizenship, education through citizenship and education for citizenship.

He believes that education about citizenship focuses on providing students with a sufficient knowledge and understanding of national history and the structures and processes of government and political life. Education through citizenship involves students learning by doing, through active, participative experiences in the school or local community and beyond (Kerr 1999). This learning reinforces the knowledge component. Education for citizenship encompasses the other two strands and involves equipping students with a set of tools (knowledge and understanding, skills and aptitudes, values and dispositions) that will enable them to participate actively and sensibly in the roles and responsibilities they will encounter in their adult lives. This strand links citizenship education with the whole educational experience of students (Kerr 1999). Beck has argued that the objective of educating for citizenship as distinct from educating about citizenship involves complex educational and practical difficulties that cannot be easily resolved (Beck 1996). As the outcomes of maximal approaches are broad, involving the acquisition of knowledge and understanding, the development of values, dispositions, skills, and attitudes, it is much more difficult to measure how successfully these outcomes have been achieved. This is particularly the case in relation to the formal assessment of citizenship education.

ASSESSMENT

Virtually all assessment, at least implicitly, examines the extent to which an individual student, school, or the system has achieved the aims set for a course or a system. The measurement of progress in relation to values presents many difficulties. While assessment of student performance in terms of knowledge and skills is widespread, there is little, if any, formal assessment of student growth in terms of attitudes, values, and moral judgements. Myers has made the point that the way students come to view citizenship in the future may be shaped by how they are assessed today (Myers 2000).

Measuring values is difficult and involves the complexity of the interaction of various elements, including the allocation of time to the assessment process, the methods employed, the criteria devised, and the consequences of the procedure. In relation to time, the question must be posed as to whether schools are able or willing to devote the amount of time necessary for meaningful assessment. There is also the issue of when assessment should take place. Students' moral judgements develop at different rates and in different ways, according to the experiences and opportunities that they have outside as well as inside of school. Traditional assessment approaches are generally based on hierarchies of knowledge and cognitive ability. If these hierarchies are applied to issues involving aims, attitudes, and values then the resultant interpretation of grades may be problematic. It has been argued that by failing to assess the more difficult area of personal qualities, attitudes, and social skills, we are implying to pupils, parents, and teachers that knowledge and skills are more important (Le Métais 1997). Short-answer and sentence-completion questions may tell you something about the breadth of knowledge students may have, but not about their deep and thoughtful understandings or their ability and willingness to apply what they know and can do towards making reasoned, informed judgements about citizenship issues (Le Métais 1997). There is a danger that when only behavioral responses are measured, the results of such procedures merely infer attitudes and beliefs that exist.

A number of important issues concerning citizenship education and assessment emerge from this discussion. The development of the concept of citizenship as expressed through political and democratic movements has been traced. The challenges facing modern society, particularly in relation to the tensions surrounding the private and public dimensions of citizenship, have been outlined. The role accorded to education in terms of the values articulated by societies in general, and the manner in which citizenship education has been considered within that overall context, have been explored. A central part of the education system is the role of assessment, and this is particularly challenging, as the measurement of progress in relation to student growth in terms of attitudes and values is complex.

The next section of this paper will focus on the Republic of Ireland context, in particular on the junior cycle program of citizenship education, which is offered to students in the final part of compulsory schooling. Educational values as expressed in official documentation will be examined and the aims of the junior certificate program will be outlined. This will serve as a background for understanding the development of the civic, social and political education program offered to students. The program itself will be considered in relation to its aims, methods, and assessment procedures.

EDUCATIONAL VALUES IN AN IRISH CONTEXT

The author contends that until the 1990s in the Republic of Ireland, a philosophy of education was rarely articulated, nor did the issues of values and aims feature frequently in official education documents. This changed with the publication of the White Paper on Education *Charting Our Education Future*, in 1995. It stated quite clearly that "the state's role in education arises as part of its overall concern to achieve economic prosperity, social well-being and a good quality of life within a democratic structured society" (DES 1995). In official documentation the role of the state in education is described thus: "The State's role in education is underpinned by the principles of pluralism and respect for diversity of values, beliefs, languages and traditions in Irish society. It is provided in a spirit of partnership among teachers and other staff, the community served by schools and other education institutions and the State." (DES 2001). The mission statement of the Department of Education and Science is outlined as follows: "The mission of the Department of Education and Science is to ensure the provision of a comprehensive, cost-effective and accessible education system of the highest quality, as measured by international standards, which will enable individuals to develop to their full potential as persons and to participate fully as citizens in society and contribute to Ireland's social and economic development" (DES 2001).

Similar language reflecting these aims and values can be found in curricula offered during primary and postprimary education. They are particularly pronounced in the aims and principles underlying the junior certificate program, a three-year program in the initial years of postprimary schooling that represents the final phase of compulsory schooling. This program was introduced into the Irish educational system in 1989 and was first examined in 1992. It is based on a number of principles that include breadth, balance, relevance, and quality. In the final phase of compulsory schooling, it is considered essential that every young person has a wide range of educational experiences. In the guidelines for the junior certificate program issued by the Department of Education and Science, teachers are advised that particular emphasis should be given to social and environmental education, science, technology, and modern languages. It is stated that the curriculum at this stage of education should be relevant to the immediate and prospective needs of the young person in the context of his or her cultural, economic, and social environment (DES 2000). Quality is a central component of this process. Coupled with this is the aspiration that every young person be challenged to achieve the highest possible standards of excellence, with due regard to different aptitudes and abilities and to international comparisons. The curriculum should provide a wide range of educational experiences within a supportive and formative environment by drawing on the aesthetic and creative, ethical, linguistic, mathematical, physical, scientific and technological, the social, environmental, political and spiritual domains (DES 1992). Each junior certificate subject syllabus including the current citizenship education program is presented for implementation within this general curriculum context.

CIVIC, SOCIAL AND POLITICAL EDUCATION

The current civic, social and political education program replaced the junior cycle civics syllabus. Citizenship education in the Republic of Ireland was nationally based, with a particular focus on the local community. In the primary, secondary and vocational sectors, civics education classes that focussed on nationalism and parochialism, with a strong emphasis on the Irish language and the maintenance of a Roman Catholic morality, were provided to students. The civics program offered at these levels of schooling concentrated on the accumulation of knowledge about specific topics, structures, and institutions, and very much represented the approach on the minimal continuum relating to education about citizenship. However, it was not assessed by formal examination. This remained the case until relatively recently.

In 1990 the National Council for Curriculum and Assessment (NCCA) prepared a junior certificate course in civic, social, and political education (CSPE)
with resource materials and guidelines for teachers (Hammond 1996). A pilot
project was initiated in the period 1993–1996, jointly developed by the Department of Education and Science and the National Council for Curriculum and
Assessment (NCCA). The pilot project tried to establish a balance between the
aspects of provision that catered for the personal and social development of
students and those that focussed more specifically on education for citizenship
in a democratic society (Hammond 1996).

In 1995 a draft strategy paper for the implementation of CSPE was published
by the NCCA. This document made the point that CSPE was a major curricular
innovation and consequently faced many challenges, which included limited
timetable provision for the area within schools and a nonexistent teaching cohort
for whom CSPE was their first teaching subject—the previous civics program
had failed in the past to establish itself within the curriculum in any meaningful
way. There was also a serious lack of teaching and learning resources specifically targeted for CSPE.

Since 1997 all postprimary schools have offered CSPE to their first-year students. The course is conducted around seven core concepts: democracy, rights
and responsibilities, human dignity, interdependence, development, law, and ste-
wardship (McCarthy 1998). Active learning is a key aspect of the program, and
student learning is to mirror the integrated occurrence of civic, social, and political phenomena in society and life. Participatory citizenship is the central aim
of CSPE. The affective and cognitive dimensions of active citizenship are emphasized throughout the syllabus (McCarthy 1998). It is recommended that
CSPE be timetabled for approximately seventy hours over a three-year period,
which works out to one forty-minute class period per week. The program consists of four units of study:

Unit 1   The Individual and Citizenship

Unit 2   The Community

Unit 3   The State—Ireland

Unit 4   Ireland and the World

The sequence of the four units of study are developmental, taking individual
pupils as their starting point and then exploring their citizenship in the context
of the communities in which they participate, their nation, and the wider world.
The sequence of the four units of study is neither discrete nor mutually exclusive
and, in practice, the implementation of the course should result in the over-
lapping of topics, ideas, and concepts that are common to all units. The CSPE
program aims to develop active citizens who have a sense of belonging to the
local, national, European, and global community; a capacity to gain access to

Table 7.1
Allocation of Time to CSPE by Schools Sampled

	First Year	Third Year
None	1.3%	9.1%
One period per week.	93.8%	88%
Two periods per week.	4.8%	2.9%

Source: *The Junior Cycle Review: Progress Report: Issues and Options for Development*, 1999.

information and structures; and an ability to fully participate in a democratic society.

The CSPE program is certainly innovative in the Republic of Ireland context, as it seeks to include the content and knowledge components of the minimal interpretation of citizenship education as outlined by McLaughlin. It also encourages active investigation and participation. In the view put forward by Kerr, the program seeks to educate about, through, and for citizenship. Postprimary schools in the Republic of Ireland context have traditionally focussed on the acquisition of knowledge as the primary function of education. This has resulted from the heavy emphasis on didactic teaching in many schools because of the pressure imposed by the examination system. The CSPE syllabus, while not denying a place for didactic education, places a greater emphasis on active and cooperatively structured learning situations in the classroom. The realization of the aims of the CSPE syllabus is dependent on the way the subject is treated within the school timetable, and the context in which the CSPE program is provided must be examined.

CSPE PROVISION IN THE JUNIOR CERTIFICATE PROGRAM

Polan has argued that students will value something if they perceive that the institution values it through a serious commitment of time and resources (Polan 1991). When one examines the actual provision in schools for CSPE as a subject area, an interesting picture emerges. In 1999 a report on the junior certificate entitled *The Junior Cycle Review: Progress Report: Issues and Options for Development* was published by the NCCA. This report documented subject provision at junior cycle (NCCA 1999). There are a total of 759 second level schools aided by the Department of Education and Science. Of the 345 schools selected in the sampling frame devised by researchers, 239 schools responded to a questionnaire in which principals of schools were asked about the number of subjects taken by first year and final year students (including nonexamination subjects) pursuing the junior certificate program. In relation to CSPE the data in Table 7.1 emerged.

These data indicate a decrease in the provision of CSPE as a subject between first and third year. This is very important in the context of citizenship education. Students who are maturing towards adulthood at 15 to 16 years of age are in reality receiving less citizenship education in their third year at a time when students are forming many ideas about themselves and the world in which they live. The main reason for this is that many schools have overloaded timetables with some students taking ten or eleven junior certificate subjects. Since the amount of time devoted to CSPE in reality decreases over the three-year period, there is a danger that students will not be exposed to a wide range of issues or active learning experiences as recommended in the syllabus guidelines. It is also worth noting that CSPE is the only subject at junior cycle examined at a single or common level. This has given rise to debate, particularly in relation to provision for less able students who are unable to cope with the requirements of the program. It should also be noted that there is currently no CSPE program on offer at senior cycle although work is ongoing in relation to senior cycle development of the program. However in the interim it means that ideas and themes surrounding citizenship cannot be further developed in a distinctive way as students move into the senior cycle level of their education.

One of the main difficulties in developing CSPE as a subject is the fact that there is a high turnover of teachers teaching this subject. During the academic year 1999–2000 (the last year of national in-service specifically designated for the program) 44 percent of teachers who attended for in-service were new to the subject.[1] This situation is directly linked to the fact that the subject is offered for only one period of 40 minutes per week. As a result, CSPE is used to cover shortages in teachers' timetables. A high turnover of teaching staff militates against good practice and disrupts continuity in the teaching of the subject. A large proportion of Higher Diploma in Education (preservice) teachers are asked to teach the subject while support at the preservice level for this subject is not strong in universities and teacher training colleges. These are exactly the issues referred to by Le Métais in terms of seeking to implement educational values and values associated with active citizenship within the contextual factors of school organization, timetabling, and culture. If one examines the way in which CSPE is assessed in the junior certificate program, the implications of this situation will become apparent.

ASSESSMENT ISSUES AT JUNIOR CYCLE

The National Council for Curriculum and Assessment has pointed out that the Republic of Ireland remains unique in its commitment to wholly externally assessed examinations at the interim stage of postprimary education. In 1990 the NCCA published a series of recommendations made to the minister for education on the junior certificate examination, stressing the need to use the widest possible range of assessment techniques, such as terminal written examinations, orals, aurals, practicals, project work, and assignments, that could be congruent with the aims and objectives of particular syllabi. However, the

1990 recommendations for the assessment of the junior certificate program were not fully implemented, and the terminal written examination paper remains the sole means of assessing the subjects taken by the majority of students (NCCA 1999). Hence the range of assessment techniques currently in use remains highly restricted. This restricted range of modes and techniques has a number of serious implications for the junior cycle program (NCCA 1999). As indicated by the NCCA, there is an ongoing mismatch between the aims and principles of the junior certificate program and the modes and techniques currently in use for the formal assessment of that program. This mismatch is particularly felt within individual subjects, which are built on a framework of broad and balanced aims and objectives of which only some can be assessed in this way.

CHIEF EXAMINER'S REPORTS ON CSPE IN THE JUNIOR CERTIFICATE EXAMINATIONS FOR YEARS 1999 AND 2000

Civic, social and personal education was examined for the first time at junior certificate level in 1999. Although CSPE is now a mandatory course for all junior certificate candidates, this particular examination had a limited entry of 16,663 candidates, who took the examination on a voluntary basis. This resulted from the fact that, following a three-year pilot project (1993–1996), schools were given the option of implementing this course with their first-year candidates in September 1996. All schools have had to offer this course to first year-candidates from September 1997 onward. The first full cohort of candidates took the examination in June 2000 (DES 2000). Assessment is carried out in two modes; a written terminal examination, which accounts for 40 percent (120 marks) of the final grade, and the presentation of either a report on an action project or course work assessment book, which accounts for 60 percent (180 marks) of the final grade. The Department of Education and Science issued guidelines to schools, which outlined the required format for the report on an action project (RAP) and also for the course work assessment book (CWAB). The RAP or CWAB is produced by the candidate before the terminal written examination. Table 7.2 illustrates the grades awarded in CSPE in the 1999 and 2000 examination. The grades E, F and NG denote failure in the examination. It is difficult from a statistical point of view to actually compare the results achieved by both cohorts of students. The 1999 cohort of students took this examination on a voluntary basis and represented only 28 percent of the available population that took the examination in 2000 when it was compulsory. This must be borne in mind when any analysis of this data is undertaken. What is particularly striking about the results is that five percent of those who participated in the assessment of CSPE did not achieve a pass in 2000. This begs the question as to what this assessment procedure is actually saying about these candidates in relation to citizenship education. It also highlights the need to explore the question as to whether the manner in which these pupils have been assessed will influence their views of citizenship and the values inherent in this

Table 7.2
Grades Awarded in CSPE in the Junior Certificate Examination 1999 and 2000

1999	A	B	C	D	E	F	NG	Total
No of candidates	2,052	5,215	5,033	3,185	784	344	50	16,663
% of candidates	12.3	31.3	30.2	19.1	4.7	2.1	0.3	100

2000	A	B	C	D	E	F	NG	Total
No of candidates	14861	19736	13980	7360	2048	732	79	58796
% of candidates	25.3	33.6	23.8	12.5	3.5	1.2	0.1	100

Source: Department of Education and Science, 2000. Republic of Ireland.

for the world in which they will have to live and work. When one analyzes the written examination component of the assessment, an interesting picture emerges.

THE WRITTEN EXAMINATION PAPER

The examination paper was divided into three sections. Section 1 examines the candidates' understanding of basic knowledge and information, which they should have encountered during the CSPE course in the form of multiple choice and sentence completion questions. The questions are short and require inserting missing words, checking off correct answers, and matching the names of organizations with their specific functions. Section 2 is composed of stimulus-based questions, which address one or more of the seven course concepts. A stimulus such as a photograph, cartoon, diagram, and so forth, is presented at the head of the question. In section 3 candidates complete open-ended or essay-type questions.

In the 1999 examination report the chief examiner was impressed with the levels of maturity and critical analysis candidates applied to these questions, commenting that "the general level of understanding and knowledge of national and international issues displayed by candidates in their answers belies the comment that is often made, that political issues are too complicated and beyond the general comprehension of thirteen to fifteen year old candidates" (DES 1999).

The 1999 and 2000 examination papers were topical because they asked about refugees, candidate councils, local government, by-elections and European elections, issues that were very prominent either at the time of the examination itself or during the school year. The vast majority of candidates completed this element of the examination satisfactorily in both years. In 1999 the paper was significant in ensuring that a number of candidates who scored less than 72 marks (40% or D) on the RAP or CWAB reached a grade D or higher in the overall examination. This was not in line with the general expectation that the vast majority of candidates would do better on their CWAB or RAP, and that the written paper would help candidates receive a higher grade in their overall result. This expectation was based on the fact that 60 percent of the final grade can be obtained from a CWAB or RAP, which is prepared in school outside formal examination conditions (DES 1999). In both years many students depended on the examination paper marks for vital grade marks rather than using the examination paper marks to enhance the grade achieved on the second component of the examination. In 2000 some candidates only presented an examination paper, and these failed the exam as they would have had to achieve a 100 percent score on the paper to reach a grade D overall (DES 2000). This indicates that students are very capable of performing in an examination setting but are not doing as well in assessments such as the RAP and CWAB, which are prepared prior to the examination. This is noteworthy in the context of what civic, social and political education as a subject is trying to achieve within the overall philosophical framework of the junior certificate program and in terms of its own aims and values related to issues of educating students for and through citizenship.

ACTION RESEARCH PROJECT/COURSE WORK ASSESSMENT BOOK

This element of the assessment is designed to assess candidates' active involvement in the course. The action project component is a compulsory part of each of these modules. In a report on an action project, a candidate presents a detailed description of an action project he or she has undertaken. This report must be presented in accordance with the format and procedures outlined in the CSPE guidelines on action projects and their assessment devised by the Department of Education and Science. These guidelines clearly outline what candidates should include and what they should avoid when completing these particular elements of the assessment.

The chief examiner reported in 1999 that in a number of cases, candidates seemed to be altogether unaware of the guidelines (DES 1999). In one particular case candidates from a school presented this particular element of their assessment on individual audiocassettes. What they presented was neither a course work assessment book nor a report on an action project but a peculiar hybrid, which proved difficult to mark. It is perhaps worth noting that if the culture of assessment was different at junior cycle then this approach taken by students would not have been a problem in the context of this particular subject. In one center, all candidates used the same photocopied material as part of their RAP, which they had apparently received from the same source (DES 1999).

Over 90 percent of candidates presented a RAP for assessment in 1999. The majority of reports were written on action projects appropriate to the CSPE course, but a significant number were not appropriate. The chief examiner pointed out that attention to guidelines was notably absent from a large number of RAPs. The report was divided into a number of sections. The first was the introduction, which most candidates completed well. However, they did badly when asked to provide a clear statement about the relevance of the action project to the CSPE course. The next section concerned activities undertaken. Part one of this section asked candidates to list and briefly describe the different activities undertaken during the course of the action project. Most candidates did this. Where a class action project was divided into different tasks and distributed among different groups in the class, a number of candidates failed to briefly describe what the other groups had done. Part two of this section asked candidates to describe in detail what they in particular had done. Most of the answers to this part of the report were poor. Part three asked them to identify and describe two particular skills and how they were applied. This was the weakest section of the whole report. Few candidates showed the capability to make the required explicit reference to skills (DES 1999).

In the 2000 report the chief examiner commented that there were some excellent examples of CWABs and RAPs presented by candidates, which ranged from painting a local Millennium Wall mural—including getting the planning permission to do so—to surveying knowledge about the Euro, to visiting a local dump, attending a Dail session, or meeting with various representatives from a wide range of local and national organizations. These activities indicated a significant improvement in understanding these processes (DES 2000). However, a small but significant number of candidates were quite unaware of the criteria for an action project and produced material relevant to other courses or limited research-based projects. In the public press during September 2001 it was reported that marks given to 1300 students in CSPE were based on the examination only because of concerns over the action project reports submitted in relation to the action project. The DES declined to say that students had cheated, but expressed grave concern about the work submitted. The minister for education commented that during the examination of the work, examiners noted significant similarities between the work of several candidates and suggested that the degree of similarity in the work of candidates in some instances presented a difficulty in relation to the validity of any assessment of the work (*Irish Times*, 12 September 2001).

The Department of Education and Science originally produced a pro-forma answer book for the course work assessment book in 1999, and following that examination a similar pro-forma answer book for the report on an action project was produced for the examination in 2000. The intention behind this booklet was that it would enable students to present their reports following the correct order or layout and procedure. From 2001 it was stipulated that all candidates presenting a RAP must do so on the pro-forma booklet. It was also stipulated that teachers of CSPE and their students should clearly understand that the action project(s) referred to in either the CWABs or RAPs should be based on one or more of the course concepts, should have a genuine action component, should be concerned with the human rights and/or social responsibilities perspective of civic, social, and political education and need not necessarily have a successful outcome (DES 2000). While this is a useful exercise in terms of providing guidance to both students and teachers, the format could nevertheless be regarded as too prescriptive and not really an assessment of what students believe and think in terms of values, attitudes, and outlook, encouraging students to follow prescribed guidelines with a focus on a process predefined as opposed to one that evolved.

COURSE WORK ASSESSMENT BOOK

Less than 10 percent of candidates opted for the CWAB in 1999, and less than 5 percent presented this format for assessment in 2000. In 1999 some candidates produced CWABs that were scrappy and repetitive. It was obvious that these candidates had been left to fill in the CWABs on their own with little or no direction and guidance (DES 1999). The section of the CWAB that candidates found the most difficult to complete was that relating to skills. Candidates were not aware of the particular skills relating to CSPE that they had developed and applied over the duration of the course. In 2000 students of all abilities scored very well if they had followed the CWAB format. It was generally felt that students scored easily when they understood the nature of the module and followed the official guidelines. The biggest problems encountered by examiners were those of repetition and the failure to complete the section dealing with the action project. Candidates were able to name the skills they had learned but often had difficulty describing how they had applied one of them. The chief examiner made a number of recommendations based on the analysis of performance in the subject. In summary, it was advocated that teachers need to be encouraged to focus more on skills, to use the language of skills, and to inform candidates of the skills that they are implementing and developing. Candidates should be aware of the skills related to civic, social, and personal education that they have acquired, developed, and employed over the duration of the course and be able to make explicit reference to them (DES 1999). Students who demonstrate the language associated with skills are just doing that; they are not expressing the attitudes and values they hold in relation to various issues.

As Holden and Clough have pointed out, a pupil who is action competent is one who can argue, reflect critically, and relate his or her opinions and actions to a values framework. Without action competence the pupil is in danger of engaging in participation at a superficial level (Holden and Clough 1998). These issues are vital to the successful development of citizenship education in the classroom. This highlights the real challenge that faces a program of this nature, which seeks to educate students through citizenship. Holden and Clough argue that "the introduction of such opportunities may require the management of a school to rethink its approach to pupil participation and may involve its teachers in a reassessment of their role." For teachers in the classroom, this will require reflection in terms of the values they hold, the freedom and autonomy they give their pupils, and the choices they make within the curriculum" (Holden and Clough 1998) and how this will be assessed or should be assessed. Little has been provided for teachers in the Republic of Ireland context at either preservice or in-service levels in terms of support for the development of a variety of assessment techniques. It is not clear that the current assessment modes in operation in relation to the CSPE actually enable students to reflect the values and attitudes that they have developed over the period of the course.

CONCLUSIONS

A number of themes emerge from this chapter in relation to citizenship education and assessment. These center on the values articulated in education systems and the gap that exists between policy documents and educational practice. This is particularly the case in relation to the aims and principles of the junior cycle program in the Republic of Ireland and the manner in which traditional assessment procedures remain in place. This paper has illustrated the inherent difficulties in a citizenship education program, which seeks to develop the active participatory dimension of citizenship education. These difficulties are reflected in the educational structures that exist, timetabling provision, the support offered to teachers, and the dominance of assessment methods that do not contribute to enabling students to voice their values and beliefs. It also reflects the need to consider the manner in which students perceive their citizenship education and—in the case of the five percent of those who were assessed in the Republic of Ireland—whether this will have any impact on their perceptions of citizenship education and what it is trying to achieve. Those who implement the program are operating in contexts that do not facilitate the translation into practice of the stated aims and objectives. The challenges faced in the Republic of Ireland are ones that citizenship educators face in many different contexts. If traditional forms of assessment continue to be used to offer legitimacy to programs of this nature and persist in testing traditional hierarchies of knowledge, then active participatory citizenship will never become a reality. If assessment procedures are not addressed as a key issue in this endeavor, then the aspirations, values and expectations of students who take such programs will never be acknowledged or developed in any real or meaningful way.

NOTE

1. Interview with one of the regional in-service co-ordinators.

REFERENCES

Beck, J. 1996. "Citizenship Education: Problems and Possibilities." *Curriculum Studies* 4 (3).

Bowles, S. and Gintis, H. 1976. *Schooling in Capitalist America*. New York: Basic.

Carnoy, M. and Levin, H.M. 1985. *School and Work in the Democratic State*. Stanford: Stanford University Press.

DES. 1992. *The Junior Certificate Aims and Principles*. Dublin: Department of Education and Science.

DES. 1995. *Charting Our Education Future*. Dublin: Government of Ireland Publications.

DES. 1999. *CSPE Chief Examiner's Report Junior Certificate Examinations*. Dublin: http://www.irlgov.ie/educ.

DES. 2000. *CSPE Chief Examiner's Report Junior Certificate Examinations*. Dublin: http://www.irlgov.ie/educ.

DES. 2001. *A Brief Description of the Irish Education System*. Dublin: Government of Ireland Publications.

Durkheim, E. 1956. *Education and Sociology*. New York: Free Press.

Hammond, J. 1996. *CSPE Pilot Project. Presented to NCCA and Department of Education and Science*. London: Department of Education and Science.

Hargreaves, A., Earl, L. and Ryan, J. 1996. *Schooling for Change: Reinventing Schooling for Early Adolescents*. London: Falmer.

Heater, D. 1990. *Citizenship: The Civic Ideal in World History, Politics and Education*. Harlow: Longman.

Held, D. 1989. *Political Theory and the Modern State*. Oxford: Polity.

Holden, C. and Clough, N. 1998. *Children as Citizens: Education for Participation*. London: Jessica Kingsley Publications.

Ichilov, O. 1998. "The Challenge of Citizenship Education in a Changing World." In *Citizenship and Citizenship Education in a Changing World*. ed. O. Ichilov. London: Woburn Press.

Irish Times. 2001. Editorial. Dublin: *The Irish Times*, 12 September.

Kerr, D. 1999. "Citizenship Education: An International Comparison." *International Review of Curriculum and Assessment Frameworks*. http://www.inca.org.uk

Le Métais, J. 1997. "Values and Aims in Curriculum and Assessment Frameworks." *International Review of Curriculum and Assessment Frameworks Project*. http://www.inca.org.uk

McCarthy, S. 1998. "Rewarding Activity: Assessment and Certification of the Junior Certificate Course in Civic, Social and Political Education." In *Innovations in Assessment in Irish Education*. ed. A. Hyland. Dublin: Education Department, UCC.

McCollum, A. 2000. "Whose Citizenship? Developing Practical Responses to Citizenship in the Curriculum." In *Developing Identities in Europe: Citizenship Education and Higher Education*. Proceedings of the Second Conference of the Childrens' Identity and Citizenship Education in Europe Thematic Network. ed. A. Ross.

McLaughlin, T.H. 1992. "Citizenship, Diversity and Education: A Philosophical Perspective." *Journal of Moral Education* 21 (3).

McNeil, J.D. 1999. *The Teachers' Initiative*. 2nd ed. Upper Saddle River, NJ: Prentice Hall.

Myers, J. 2000. *Contrived or Authentic Assessment in Citizenship Education? Taming the Beast*. Toronto: Ontario Institute for Studies in Education, University of Toronto.

National Council for Curriculum and Assessment. 1999. *The Junior Cycle Review: Progress Report: Issues and Options for Development*. Dublin: NCCA.

Osler, A. and Starkey, H. 1996. *Teacher Education and Human Rights*. London: David Fulton.

Polan, A.J. 1991. *Personal and Social Education: Citizenship and Biography*. London: David Fulton.

Ranson, S. 1994. "Education for Democracy." In *Education Reform and Its Consequences*. ed. S. Tomlinson. London: IPPR/Rivers Oram Press.

Sen, A. 1990. "Individual Freedom as Social Commitment." *New York Review of Books*. 14 June.

UNESCO. 2001. Forty-sixth International Conference on Education. http://www.ibe.unesco.org/international/ice/46english/46docintroe.htm

8

Citizenship Education and Teachers' Professional Awareness

Sigrún Adalbjarnardóttir

INTRODUCTION

In the struggle for human rights and justice, we must be seriously concerned about cultivating respect and care among humans, especially the young, within and among communities around the globe. This is the core of citizenship education. With increased globalization, we are constantly reminded of the need for such education.

In recent years, the conceptualization of citizenship has been changing from an emphasis on national citizenship, which refers to the rights and duties of each member within that society, toward a more universal model of global membership based on the notion of each person's universal rights (Soysal 1994). Urry (1999: 315) points out that along with this change a wide variety of citizenships has emerged:

Cultural citizenship, involving the rights of all social groups (ethnic, gender, sexual orientation, age) to full cultural participation within their society; *minority citizenship* involving the right to enter another society, remain within that society, and receive appropriate rights and duties; *ecological citizenship*, concerned with the rights and responsibilities of the citizen of the earth; *cosmopolitian citizenship*, concerned with how people may develop an orientation toward other citizens, societies, and cultures across the globe; *consumer citizenship*, concerned with the rights of people to be provided with appropriate goods, services and information from both the private and public sectors; *mobility citizenship*, concerned with the rights and responsibilities of visitors to other places and other cultures.

The common theme in these various types of citizenships is the universal rights and responsibilities each member has in our global community. They imply a notion of equality and a commitment to it. This notion of respect applies to all levels of human interaction: on the macro level both internationally and nationally, and on the micro level in daily interpersonal relationships in both private and public lives. In fact, young people construct their citizenship identities, values, and political views in social and interpersonal relations and activities within the family and among friends, at school, and in the community (Flanagan and Faison 2001; Yates and Youniss 1999). This is the pedagogical context for citizenship education.

The relatively recent emphasis on global or international citizenship is reflected in educational laws and national curriculum guidelines. Also, in this spirit, many people around the world have started programs in schools and published curricula with the general aim of promoting citizenship awareness. These programs focus on promoting children's social and moral thought and behavior, their active community involvement, and their political literacy by teaching the knowledge, skills, and values to make them effective in public life. National identity is emphasized in the broader perspective of global dimensions of citizenship (Holden 1999; Yates and Youniss 1999). These programs are interdisciplinary in their focus on important values and cross various traditional curricular boundaries, such as those of ethics, religious studies, history, social studies, and literature. Examples of these programs are *Education for Citizenship and the Teaching of Democracy* (QCA 1998), *Voices of Love and Freedom* (Walker 1996), *Education for Mutual Understanding* (Smith and Robinson 1996), and *Education for Public Inquiry and International Citizenship* (EPIIC 1999).

To understand the emphasis on citizenship education in various countries, it is important to explore the similarities and differences among educational laws, national curriculum guidelines, and curricula. However, given universal ethical values such as those involved in the conceptions of equality and human rights, and given educational laws, national curriculum guidelines, and text books that reflect important general aims of citizenship education, the crucial question remains, What happens in practice? Are these aims reflected in school and classroom work? That is, do the teachers' aims in their work with their students reflect the general aims of promoting citizenship awareness? Another question follows: How can we best support teachers to work effectively and responsibly in this area?

Surprisingly few studies have explored the effects of the various citizenship programs on students' progress in citizenship awareness (Flanagan and Faison 2001). Even fewer studies have focused on what this important work means to teachers as professionals and to their practice (Adalbjarnardóttir 1994; Adalbjarnardóttir and Selman 1997; Holden 1999). As teachers have a key role in organizing constructive and meaningful experiences for the students in citizenship education, it is important to explore how they make sense of this work both personally and professionally, as it affects their role as a teacher. Such understanding is important in the search for effective ways to support teachers in their work with students on citizenship issues.

For the last decade I have been exploring these concerns in schools in the Reykjavik area of Iceland. I have been running a joint intervention and research project called *Fostering Students' Sociomoral and Interpersonal Development*. This is a citizenship education program directed toward elementary-school teachers. Its major aim is to support teachers as they promote students' citizenship awareness and social and moral growth by fostering their autonomy and intimacy as a basis for community involvement and political literacy as they grow older.

In this chapter, I focus on how teachers can be effective and responsible in promoting students' citizenship awareness. I describe the intervention program in which the teachers participated and the findings of a study conducted during the program. One part of the study focused on students' progress in interpersonal understanding and skills as a result of their teachers' participation in the intervention program. The other part focused on the way teachers construct citizenship education, as reflected in their aims and teaching strategies. I will start by placing the intervention program in the educational context of Iceland.

EDUCATIONAL AIMS IN A CHANGING SOCIETY

During this century, particularly since World War II, Iceland has been undergoing rapid social, economic, and political changes, moving from a traditional agricultural community to a modern industrial society. Iceland is a parliamentary democracy with a president (republic). The state church is Lutheran and the educational system is centralized. Education and health care are almost free of charge to the recipient. The standard of living is high, with few extremes of poverty or wealth by international standards, and therefore a relatively modest discrepancy exists among the different social classes (Olafsson 1997). The country frequently ranks among the top five nations of the world according to such quality-of-life markers as levels of infant mortality, life expectancy, life satisfaction, and literacy rates (Euromonitor 1999; Olafsson 1997; United Nations 1997), as well as low unemployment rates (International Labor Office 1998). Following these radical economic changes have come sociological changes, for example, in family structure: fewer generations live together, the divorce rate has risen, in more families both parents are working outside the home, and fewer children are in each home. The population is around 280,000 and has been very homogeneous. In recent years, however, the number of immigrants has increased rapidly. In 1980 1.4 percent (3240) of the population were immigrants, in 1990 1.9 percent (4812), in 2000, 3.1 percent (8824) and in the first six months of 2001, 23 percent more people migrated than in the same period in 2000.

Within the education system the aims of education are outlined at three official levels: laws for each of the school levels (nursery, primary, secondary), general national curriculum guidelines (e.g., Adalnamskra grunnskola 1999), and national curriculum guidelines that are subject specific. Moreover, each school develops its own school-based curriculum guidelines.

The laws governing education (e.g., Log um grunnskola 1995) emphasize that "the role of the school is, in collaboration with the home, to prepare the students for participation in a democratic society that is constantly under development" (p. 2). This law also states that "school practice should be shaped by tolerance, Christian morality, and democratic collaboration" (p. 2). These basic values are further elaborated in the national curriculum guidelines for each school level (nursery schools, primary and secondary schools). They refer to the *equality* of all human beings, mutual *respect* and *responsibility*, *care* and *reconciliation*. The main obligation of the educational system, the law says, is to provide students with a good general education that emphasizes advanced-level educational opportunities for everyone and equal rights to study. General education is defined as being at the root of democracy. Its role and aims are to promote students' physical, social, moral, and emotional growth in a constantly changing world. This includes the development of autonomy, critical thinking, and solidarity with others through tolerance and respect toward other people and the environment. This includes developing personal relationships that are independent of gender, ethnicity, religion, or disability. Further, this includes promoting morality and equality, and constructing a social vision that respects society, enhances democratic methods, and fosters international awareness and sustainable development.

The national curriculum guidelines for specific subjects (e.g., social studies, ethics, health studies) further outline the values and aims of the laws and the national curriculum guideline. The above aims (and others) are to be reflected in each subject area. In addition, a new curriculum called "Life Skills" (Adalnamskra grunnskola: Lifsleikni 1999) has recently been formulated by the government to better ensure that schools are working to promote citizenship awareness, and to prepare students to participate in the information society.

PROMOTING CITIZENSHIP AWARENESS

There is a general agreement, at least in the so-called industrialized societies, on the importance of clearly stating the aims of education and outlining these aims in both laws and national curriculum guidelines (e.g., Pratt 1980). These are the umbrellas for the work in schools. Still, the question remains: Are these aims actually reflected in the school and classroom work, that is, do teachers' aims reflect the general aims of promoting citizenship awareness? Even more importantly: Can we help make teachers more effective as they work with their students on citizenship issues? In other words, are teachers who receive special training better able to promote their students' citizenship awareness than teachers who do not receive such training? And if so, the crucial question is: How can we best support teachers in the challenging profession of promoting their students' citizenship awareness?

In providing some preliminary answers to these questions, I will focus on what I have learned from designing and running the citizenship project I call "Fostering Students' Sociomoral and Interpersonal Development." In this project, I have guided teachers in working constructively with their students on sociomoral and interpersonal issues of friendship, the school community, and the family. I have also explored the students' developmental progress in interpersonal understanding and actions as a function of their participation in the intervention program. And finally, I have been tracing the teachers' own professional development during the intervention program while they work with their students on these issues.

THE THEORETICAL BASE OF THE INTERVENTION PROGRAM

Perspective-taking Ability

Basic to our ability to make sense of our interpersonal, social and moral worlds is the developing human capacity in social perspective-taking (Habermas 1979; Kohlberg 1969; Selman 1980). This competence refers to the developing ability among children, adolescents, and adults to differentiate between the perspectives of self and others, or of the individual and the society, and to coordinate these perspectives in constantly more flexible and mature ways (Selman 1980). In simpler terms, this competence refers to the different abilities to put oneself in the shoes of others. For example, children and adolescents may have different understandings of the universal ethical principle of the Golden Rule, found in various philosophies and religions (e.g., Confucianism, Buddhism, Christianity, Islam): "In everything do to others as you would have them do to you" (Matthew 7:12). A child might understand the Golden Rule in the following way: "This means that if a kid comes up and hits you, you hit back; do unto others like they do unto you." This response illustrates concrete thinking, which is quite natural for children. An adolescent, on the other hand, might respond differently: "Well, the Golden Rule is the best rule, because if you were rich you might dream that you were poor and how it felt, and then the dream would go back in your own head and you would remember and you would help make the laws that way." We can see that the adolescent goes beyond the concrete thinking of the child; she steps outside and makes connections between the perspectives of the individual and the society. She imagines a rich person who puts herself in the shoes of a poor person; not only does the rich person really feel how it feels for the poor person to be poor, but she starts to act politically by changing the law.

Those of us who work within this field claim that our perspective-taking ability underlies not only our understanding of ethical principles and values but also our skills in communicating with others (Adalbjarnardóttir and Selman 1989; Selman and Adalbjarnardóttir 2000; Selman and Schultz 1990). We claim that in general people who have more flexible skills and a deeper understanding of what it takes to communicate well have not only acquired the ability to function better in their closest interpersonal relationships but also to contribute to their communities and societies, both nationally and internationally, because they can operate with respect and care in their communications and negotiations (see also Noddings 1992). An important question is, How can we foster this core capacity of perspective-taking as a base for citizenship awareness?

Reflection

Recently, there has been an increased emphasis on the use of interpretive methods to understand teachers' reflections on their teaching (e.g., Richardson 1994; Schön 1987; Shulman 1987). In this spirit, reflective teaching becomes a form of inquiry in in-service approaches to teacher development (e.g., Brookfield 1995; Korthagen 1993). Even more importantly, reflection on one's own teaching appears essential for growth in professional awareness (e.g., Bartlett 1990). An important question is, How can we give teachers the support in reflecting on their work?

THE AIMS OF THE PROGRAM

This intervention program for practicing elementary school teachers aims to support teachers in their efforts to improve their students' citizenship awareness by fostering the students' autonomy and intimacy as a base for community involvement and political literacy as they grow older. Thus the program aims to provide students with opportunities to develop autonomy, as reflected in the freedom to raise different points of view as teachers encourage autonomous and critical thinking, and as reflected in the responsibility to share mutual rights and duties. It also aims to provide students with opportunities to develop their ability for intimacy as reflected in their care for each other, and their capacities for trust and truthfulness, goodness and generosity.

Conducting the Program

The intervention program has been ongoing since 1988. Each year a new group of teachers participates. Here, I describe the organization of the program during the year in which I systematically studied how the participating students progressed in their interpersonal understanding and actions in comparison with those not in the program.

The fourteen teachers, all female, taught children from 7 to 12 years of age. We held twenty group meetings every week or two throughout one school year, to give the teachers a context in which to gain knowledge, construct their understanding, challenge each others' ideas, share their concerns, work together to find ways to improve their teaching, analyze classroom experiences, and support each other. I decided to coordinate the program for the entire school year because it takes time for a teacher to create a comfortable atmosphere in the classroom, one in which students feel free to express their ideas, feel that they are heard, feel the need to listen to each other, and at the same time are motivated to argue, debate, and reach agreement (Adalbjarnardóttir and Edelstein, 1989). Also, this format was chosen so that the teachers' work could become more constructive, with the possibility that they would constantly *reflect* on it over an extended period. As teachers receive little support in considering what is important to teach and why (e.g., Johnston 1989; Rudduck 1988), an important part of the meetings was devoted to planning and deciding which tasks should be dealt with, why, and how.

The meetings had two related themes: (a) theories of children's sociomoral development, and (b) effective teaching strategies. To improve the teachers' understanding of how children gradually develop their sociomoral and interpersonal competence, I introduced them to several theories of children's social-cognitive development (e.g., Damon 1983; Edelstein, Keller and Wahlen 1984; Kohlberg 1969; Piaget 1965/1932; Selman 1980). I especially emphasized the theory of social development with a focus on interpersonal negotiation processes (Adalbjarnardóttir and Selman 1989; Selman and Schultz 1990).

Emphasis was also placed on teaching strategies that seem to have been effective in promoting children's social competence and skills (e.g., Adalbjarnardóttir and Edelstein 1989; Berkowitz and Gibbs 1985; Oser 1981; Power, Higgins and Kohlberg 1989). For example, these teaching strategies involve setting up a cognitive conflict in children's minds by using either real-life or hypothetical social dilemmas, followed by Socratic questioning. In this way students are encouraged to consider various points of view and to put themselves in each other's shoes.

The teachers used a curriculum constructed around three primary interpersonal themes: friendship, school community, and family (Adalbjarnardóttir and Elias-dottir 1992). The first of these was *friendship*. This included conflicts in friendship, what makes a good friend, how to make a friend, how to keep a friend, trust in friendship, and so forth. The second theme was the *school community*. This included on the one hand, social interactions during recess—conflicts between classmates such as teasing, fighting, and excluding, and prosocial behavior such as helping, supporting, and playing together. On the other hand classroom interactions were included, both between children—such as conflicts of opinion in cooperative work—and between students and teachers, such as differences in perspective regarding students' work or behavior. The third theme was the *family*. This included interactions between parents and children, including ideas such as "Every child owns . . . ," "Every child is allowed to . . . ," trust, and promises.

Teacher Reflections

Several techniques were used to encourage the teachers to reflect on their own teaching: interviews, meetings, reports, classroom tapes, and classroom observations. At the beginning of the program, I individually interviewed the teachers on the interpersonal aspects of their teaching, such as how they wanted teacher-student interactions to be and the attitudes they wanted their students to have toward them as a teacher, and vice versa. I also asked them about their classroom management and teaching strategies, such as the role of discussions, role-playing, group work, and how they solved social conflicts. Finally, I asked them about their aims; why they were going to participate in the program, and what professional expectations they had. The interviews were tape recorded and transcribed. Each teacher received her own interview as a base from which to develop.

At the evening group meetings I specifically encouraged the teachers to reflect on their pedagogical ideas, aims, attitudes, feelings, teaching choices, and actions. Activities such as discussion, writing, and role-playing (in groups, pairs, or individually) were used in this process of reflection (Korthagen 1993). This provided the teachers with a dialogue and context from which they could construct and reconstruct their new experiences by integrating their knowledge, understanding, and teaching practice through work with the students on interpersonal issues.

One part of individual teacher reflections was their own day-to-day teaching. After each lesson (or weekly theme) with the students on interpersonal issues, the teacher completed a report on her experience with regard to the aim of the lesson, how it went step by step, what had worked well and not so well, how the lesson could have been improved, and how the teacher felt about teaching the topic. Each teacher was also encouraged to tape record discussion sessions she led in the classroom and afterwards to listen to the tapes and reflect on her own teaching. The teachers also kept a diary in which they wrote down comments, discoveries, notions, and interesting events. At the end of each semester, each teacher wrote a report in which she summarized her experiences of her classroom practice as she reflected on how the project went step by step, the students' progress, her own changes and development as a teacher (ideas, attitudes, aims, skills), and changes in her interaction with her colleagues. In addition, I observed the teachers in their classrooms as they worked on sociomoral and interpersonal issues with the students and discussed each lesson with them afterwards. Finally, during the middle of the program and again at the end, I interviewed each teacher, encouraging her to reflect on four issues: (a) her perceptions of the students' progress in sociomoral growth, (b) her knowledge of students' social growth, (c) her own teaching skills; and (d) her own aims in working on interpersonal issues in the classroom as a part of citizenship education (Adalbjarnardóttir 1994).

Students' Progress in Social Growth

Overall, the participating teachers felt that their students made progress in the classroom. They reported that the students had become more friendly toward each other; expressed more empathy, tolerance, and understanding in their social relationships; and also tried more often to solve their conflicts in a constructive and responsible way. The results of the intervention study on the improvement of students' interpersonal understanding and actions testify to the teachers' feelings (Adalbjarnardóttir 1993).

The intervention study included four of the participating teachers, who taught children from ages eight to eleven. Four other classes outside the intervention program served as controls. Twelve students (six girls and six boys) were selected at random from each of eight classes to participate in the study. To assess the students' interpersonal understanding and skills, they were interviewed in the fall and again in the spring on interpersonal dilemmas that focused on negotiations about different perspectives with either a teacher or a classmate in relation to classroom activities. In one such dilemma, a student thinks she works hard on a group project, while her classmate feels she does not. The students were first asked to define the problem, also focusing on the feelings of those involved. They were then asked to find different ways to solve the problem, select the best solution, and finally evaluate the outcome. Students' responses in each of these four steps were classified at one of the four developmental levels of perspective coordination: impulsive, unilateral, reciprocal, and mutual (Adalbjarnardóttir and Selman 1989). In addition, the students' interactions with their classmates and teachers were observed in the classroom and coded, using the same assessment tool of levels of perspective-taking competence (see further, Adalbjarnardóttir 1993).

Overall, the findings were promising. They revealed that teachers in the intervention program were better able to improve their students' interpersonal understanding at both the level of thought and in real-life actions than were teachers with no such special training (Adalbjarnardóttir 1993). More precisely, with regard to *thought level*, students in the intervention program showed greater progress in reciprocity by more often considering both participants' perspectives when trying to resolve hypothetical classroom conflicts, compared to students in the normal program. Secondly, at the *action level*, when negotiating with classmates, students in the intervention program showed more improvement in negotiating conflicts in real-life situations compared to students in the normal program. This means that they used two-way strategies (reciprocity) more often. For example, the students in the intervention program tended to argue more frequently rather than fight with their classmates, ask questions instead of command, or engage in a discussion instead of a quarrel.

Teachers' Professional Awareness

The teachers felt strongly that as they participated in the intervention program aimed at fostering students' social competence and skills, they also grew more confident in dealing with interpersonal issues in the classroom (see Adalbjarnardóttir 1994). They felt more secure because they better understood the students' social capacity and because they had improved their own skills in dealing with various aspects of social interactions. Such understanding and such skills are important factors in promoting students' citizenship awareness (Oser 1992).

To identify developmental patterns within teachers as well as differences and similarities among them concerning the way they view their roles in working with their students on interpersonal and citizenship issues, we have postulated a developmental model that can provide us with a set of tools to conduct such an analysis (Adalbjarnardóttir and Selman 1997). The focus of the teachers' reflections is on three issues: their pedagogical ideas, aims, and classroom skills. We maintain that three dimensions of developmental awareness can be used to study the increased differentiation among teachers' reflections. These awareness dimensions range from focusing primarily on observable outcomes (e.g., students' classroom behavior) to emphasizing developmental processes (e.g., students' improved ability to differentiate and coordinate various perspectives and to resolve conflicts, which lead to active participation in society). The model is presented in Table 8.1. We propose that an important change in the professional development of teachers may occur when they can readily reflect on their thoughts and actions as teachers, that is, how their attitudes, competence, and teaching strategies relate and interact with the students' needs and growth. At that point, they have articulated insights that make it more meaningful for them to work constructively towards their aim of promoting students' citizenship awareness.

Below are examples of how two highly professional teachers, Anna and Disa, made sense of their work with their students on citizenship issues.

ANNA'S AIMS AND STRATEGIES

Anna taught 8- to 9-year-old children. Her themes were democracy, autonomy, and respect. Her focus on democracy was reflected in her aims of developing "more democracy" among the students in the classroom and that optimal communications between a teacher and students should be "very democratic." She also emphasized her aim of enhancing students' autonomy: "I view it as number one that the teacher respects the children and their opinions, because if we immediately start at school to strike their autonomy out of them, we cannot expect them to be independent individuals later in life." According to our model we would classify her perspective as integrated reflection, rather than integrated and context-based reflection, as her ideas about democracy and autonomy are rather general (see Table 8.1). In other words, even though her aims are future-

Table 8.1
An Analysis of Professional Development of Teachers' Perspectives: Awareness Dimensions and Issues

Awareness Dimensions	AIMS	Issues: ACT OF TEACHING		PEDAGOGICAL VISION
		Strategies	Progress	
Externally or internally based reflection	Focus on improving students' overt behavior and/or classroom atmosphere for both the students and self as a teacher. Short-term aims	Focus on additive teaching skills to improve students' overt behavior and/or the classroom atmosphere	Awareness of improvements in own teaching skills as noted by self and/or others	Pedagogical ideas, aims, and practice are differentiated but not integrated
Integrated reflection	Focus on the psychosocial needs of both the students and the teacher in relation to each other both within and beyond the classroom but not contextualized. Short- and long-term aims	Focus on various teaching strategies and activities to promote students' social growth and life skills but not contextualized	Awareness of the interplay between changes in own classroom strategies and the students' progress. Recognition of own strengths and weaknesses in teaching	Pedagogical ideas, aims, and practice are integrated with a psychosocial need-based orientation but not contextualized
Integrated and context-based reflection	Focus on preparing the students to participate actively in society. Reference to important individual life competencies and skills that are differentiated and contextualized. Both short- and long-term aims	Focus on various teaching strategies and activities to promote students' social growth and life skills that are contextualized with reference to different background, competencies ...	Awareness of the interplay between changes in own classroom strategies and the students' progress in relation to short- and long-term contextualized aims	Pedagogical ideas, aims and practice are both integrated and contextualized with an awareness of the relationship between students' social growth and the teachers' own professional growth

Adapted from Adalbjarnardóttir and Selman 1997.

oriented, particularly with regards to promoting autonomy, she does not at this point place them in a specific context.

Towards the end of the program, Anna seemed to put her aims more strongly into context: "It's important that they [the students] can stand up for themselves, dare to say no, and do not rely on the opinions of others. Dependence can lead to problems like drug abuse." Further, she expressed her perspective on the importance of fostering democracy by promoting the students' autonomy and respect for others' opinions.

It is natural in our society, characterized by democracy, that the children have the opportunity to take part, such as in what they want to study. In our society they have to learn to respect others, to listen to each other, and to make democratic decisions regarding various issues. In a democratic society like ours we take it for granted that everyone gets the opportunity to participate. But our society is controlled too much by a few people, so in general people don't express themselves on various issues. Thus, I find it important that the children get the opportunity to build up self-confidence by expressing themselves about their concerns and by experiencing the feeling that their idea is adopted or having to accept the fact that it hasn't been agreed to this time, [but] it might be next time. When I was in elementary school we were not allowed to decide anything by ourselves. That may be part of the reason why our society today isn't a very open one.

Here, we notice that Anna discusses her ideas about democracy from a broader perspective than at the beginning of the program. Now she places her aim of creating democracy among the students in educational, sociological, and political contexts. It is clear that she is preparing her students to participate actively in a democratic society, one she now feels is not democratic enough. She thinks that the school has not been responsible enough in this regard and refers to her own experience as a child. Thus, she is well aware of the students' psychosocial needs, which she associates with her own role as a teacher in preparing them to make democratic decisions. At the same time she emphasizes the interplay of being autonomous and respecting others: "You can be independent without putting other people down; we have to teach the children to respect others' opinions, to learn to listen." According to our model, we can now classify her reflections as integrated and context-based (see Table 8.1).

It was an adventure to visit Anna in her classroom. She had high expectations of her students; encouraged them to question, think critically, and to be creative; and was also conscious about student individual differences. She was independent in organizing her teaching around the sociomoral and interpersonal issues of the program. She both integrated our themes smoothly into other classroom work (e.g., Icelandic language), and also organized large projects (e.g., Friendship Island). She emphasized a variety of activities for the students, including discussions, role-play, painting, music, poetry, reading, and creative writing. In short, Anna was very active, integrative, creative, and sensitive to the students' opinions and feelings about the work. Her teaching style was characterized by encouragement and warmth. There was clearly a mutual respect between her and her students.

Anna felt she experienced some changes in her teaching strategies and skills by participating in the program. For example, she felt she was more systematic in her approach, in particular when working on interpersonal problems. Regarding her personal style she felt she had become more reflective about her work ("I have become more conscious and contemplative") and less emotional and more balanced ("I am a rather calm person, but I think I can say that I don't let my feelings take over as much as I did before. Previously, I often became angry or hurt and tended only to look at the issue from one perspective, most often [that of] the victim."). She also found it easier to deal with interpersonal issues ("I feel much better. Before I often felt a knot in my stomach when I had to deal with a conflict, but now I just do it."). Anna also felt that her students had made progress in their collaborative work, that they talked more together, listened to each other, and looked for the opinions of others in the group. She felt that they were more interested in discussing the issues and even solving conflicts themselves, being less judgmental than before.

One example of how Anna had gradually created a supportive community in the classroom arose when the class faced the responsibility of dealing with moral values. Three of the girls in the class were suspected of having taken some candy from a store together. Their classmates felt strongly that this had to be discussed in class. The reaction of the students reflected their awareness of their responsibility as members of a group, having to solve problems in order to keep a strong, trusting relationship alive in the classroom, and to follow moral rules. First, Anna decided to talk with the girls to understand their perspectives. They were very sincere about what they had done and expressed their own feelings as well as how they thought their classmates felt about the matter. Then Anna asked them to come to an agreement as to how to solve the problem with regard to their classmates. Next the girls presented their solution to their classmates for discussion. They agreed that all three of them were equally guilty, that they regretted having taken the candy, and that they would never do such a thing again. They also suggested that the problem did not need to be discussed any further in class. After some consideration and discussion the class agreed to this.

Further, Anna said that she felt convinced that the children would not have demonstrated such care and concern as a group and such competence in solving the problem, had they not taken part in our program on interpersonal issues. She said that the children had become such good friends, that they felt secure, so were ready to listen to each other, share their ideas, and reach an agreement. Anna was very proud of her students and reported that even she herself might not have been able to deal with the problem had she not taken part in the program. She saw her own progress as related to her students' progress.

This event is a good example of how, as a teacher, Anna aimed to promote her students' *understanding* of moral values, foster their *skills* in communicating about moral values, and deepen their understanding of moral values as this related to their real-life actions. In this work she was concerned about ensuring that her students were aware of different points of view and about coordinating these perspectives. We witnessed her deep respect and care for her students' voices (democratic decisions) by the way she fostered both their autonomy and intimacy.

DISA'S AIMS AND STRATEGIES

Disa taught 11- to 12-year-old students. Her themes were "tolerance," "mutual understanding," and "perspective-taking ability" as a basis for emotional and social growth. At the beginning of the program Disa expressed a broad and long-term educational aim: "I expect that [by participating in the program] I will succeed better than before in attaining my goals of making my students good people." At this point, however, her goal was relatively undifferentiated and not contextualized (see Table 8.1).

At the end of the program, she had changed her perspective on the importance of working on interpersonal issues in the classroom and on how the program had helped her in this respect: "I feel I have received a new vision." Her experiences had led her to develop a deeper *integration of the connection between general pedagogical aims*: "I now realize more clearly than before the importance of education with regard to emotional and social development . . . see how human beings need a much better understanding of each others' points of view. Look specifically at the problems that result from a lack of understanding. See, for example, from the low tolerance people in the world have for religions different from their own." *They also helped her develop more specific aims related to classroom practices*: "Positive social interactions among children are the basis for all other work with them." In other words, during the process of the work Disa has begun to differentiate and contextualize her aims to a greater extent (see Table 8.1).

Visits to Disa's classroom and observations on her classroom management abilities suggest she was very committed and active, both in her classroom and in her reflections on her teaching. She worked systematically and integratively on the interpersonal issues provided in the curriculum. She searched untiringly to find ideas in other curricula and integrate them into the interpersonal themes involved in the program. To motivate the students she used music, role-play, creative writing, drawings, and readings. She also was very active in using many everyday opportunities to discuss social conflicts in her classroom. Even though she expressed herself as insecure in dealing with these issues, she was courageous and independent in trying out ideas.

Disa reflected easily on the interpersonal aspects of her teaching, with respect to both her interpersonal style and her teaching skills. For example, she expressed a concern about her authoritarian style when she got upset about students' behavior; she said that she too often blamed the students, scolded them, and even shouted at them. She was rather "hard" on herself in these descriptions, as I observed her to be an affectionate teacher who was warm and friendly towards the students, even though she was also quite firm. Occasionally she showed her disapproval in unilateral ways. But she was motivated to improve her teaching skills and change her style.

In reflecting on her work, Disa claims that she deepened her understanding of working on interpersonal issues in the classroom by seeing theories work in practice. "I discovered in practice how important it was to get the students to consider different perspectives. I saw how it widened their understanding." She reflected on the important role she had in deepening students' understanding: "I saw that I had to help them to acquire this understanding by asking them to consider other peoples' opinions and feelings." Not only did she reflect on the importance of the work for students' interpersonal growth and her own role in that respect, she also realized how essential it was for her to experience directly the relationship between theory and practice as she became more secure in dealing with interpersonal issues. "It was important for me to experience how much my understanding had improved by seeing things work in practice. As a result I became more secure in dealing with interpersonal issues." In other words, Disa contextualized her pedagogy and experience by connecting improvements in students' interpersonal growth to her own development, and in becoming better able to deal with interpersonal issues. In short, as Disa acquired a deeper understanding of her pedagogical ideas, aims, and classroom management skills during the intervention program, the work helped her to bridge the gap between her pedagogical theory and practice.

Even though the themes of these two highly professional teachers may have differed in some ways, they shared a common meaning: the importance of promoting students' sociomoral growth and interpersonal understanding. In their aims, they looked both within and beyond the classroom with long-term concerns for students' active participation in society. In practice, they also had a clear overview of the work, which they related to their teaching strategies. They were clearly autonomous and committed, and appeared active and creative in dealing constructively with sociomoral and interpersonal issues.

Interestingly, neither these two teachers nor other participants in the intervention program referred directly to the aims outlined in the national curriculum guidelines when they reflected on their aims. And none of them referred directly to the aims of the intervention program, which had been introduced to them at the beginning. Instead, they clearly expressed their own special concerns. This is not to say that the aims of the national curriculum guidelines may not have influenced the aims of these teachers both directly and indirectly, but it seems not to have been the first thing they thought about when they reflected on their aims.

CLOSING CONSIDERATIONS

This chapter has focused on the key role that teachers play in promoting students' citizenship awareness. The citizenship intervention program described here, which aims to support teachers in their work with their students on citizenship issues, focuses directly on encouraging teachers to *reflect* on their pedagogical ideas, aims, and teaching strategies. The results of the intervention study are promising, indicating that students whose teachers participated in the program showed more progress in their interpersonal understanding and daily interactions compared to students whose teachers did not receive special training. They were better able to make allowance for the various relevant social perspectives.

The case study of the teachers Anna and Disa suggests that highly professional teachers can become even more insightful by constantly reflecting on their pedagogical ideas, aims, and teaching strategies as they work with their students on citizenship issues. They felt that they enhanced their understanding of their students' interpersonal competence and skills. They also felt that they improved their own teaching skills, style, and capacity to face and deal with interpersonal issues in the classroom. By seeing how their understanding of theories of students' sociomoral growth and of effective teaching strategies worked in their educational practice, they deepened the personal and professional sense that they made of the importance of the work, and hence of their pedagogical vision or philosophy. In this sense, this case study provides essential insights into the process of improving the integrative perspectives of highly professional teachers. As such, both Anna and Disa are among those teachers who may serve as models for other teachers (Gudmundsdottir 1990).

Given the essential role teachers can play in promoting students' citizenship awareness, we have to be aware of how we can best support them in working effectively and responsibly on citizenship education. Here, we argue that one important way to achieve this goal is to create a context for teachers that gives them an opportunity to reflect on their role in actively fostering their students' citizenship awareness (see e.g., Russell and Munby 1992; Richardson 1994; Schön 1987). In being capable of supporting them, we argue that it is crucial to explore how individual teachers make sense of the importance of their work on citizenship education, that is, how aware they are about their pedagogical vision and its effects on their work with their students.

Teachers' reflections on their work serve as an important factor in professional growth and effective teaching (e.g., Bartlett 1990). The teacher, as a professional, reflects on her own work, evaluating and criticizing what happens, aiming to improve herself as a teacher and never seeing herself as fully educated. Such a teacher actually works as a researcher. She collects data about her teaching, analyzes it, and evaluates and reevaluates it. She asks herself key questions such as: What am I going to teach? Why is that important? Why do I feel that is important? How am I going to teach this issue? Why are those teaching strategies important? Further, she asks herself challenging questions: How did I succeed? Did I succeed at my aims, for example, the aim of encouraging the students to think critically, raise independent opinions, put themselves in the shoes of others, and experience mutual trust, care, and solidarity? What can I do more successfully, and how? Reflection, whether individual or in collaboration with others, encourages the teacher to think about her work and rephrase her ideas. Simultaneously, she acquires more strength and security as a professional (see e.g., Zeichner 1994).

To guide practice and to inform policy, it is important that we continue to explore, on the one hand, the differences and similarities among teachers in the ways they make sense of citizenship education, and on the other, how teachers' professional competence relates to students' citizenship awareness.

REFERENCES

Adalbjarnardóttir, S. 1993. "Promoting Children's Social Growth in the Schools: An Intervention Study." *Journal of Applied Developmental Psychology* 14: 461–484.

Adalbjarnardóttir, S. 1994. "Understanding Children and Ourselves: Teachers' Reflections on Social Development in the Classroom." *Teaching and Teacher Education* 10: 409–421.

Adalbjarnardóttir, S. and Edelstein, W. 1989. "Listening to Children's Voices: Psychological Theory and Educational Implications." *Scandinavian Journal of Educational Research* 33: 79–97.

Adalbjarnardóttir, S. and Eliasdottir, A. 1992. *Samvera* [Being together]. Reykjavik: Namsgagnastofnun.

Adalbjarnardóttir, S. and Selman, R.L. 1989. "How Children Propose to Deal with the Criticism of Their Teachers and Classmates: Developmental and Stylistic Variations." *Child Development* 60: 539–550.

Adalbjarnardóttir, S. and Selman, R. L. 1997. " 'I Feel I Received a New Vision': An Analysis of Teachers Professonal Development as They Work with Students on Interpersonal Issues." *Teaching and Teacher Education* 13 (4): 409–428.

Adalnamskra grunnskola [National curriculum guideline]. 1999. Reykjavik: Menntamalaraduneytid.

Adalnamskra grunnskola: Lifsleikni [National curriculum guideline: Life Skills]. 1999. Reykjavik: Menntamalaraduneytid.

Bartlett, L. 1990. "Teacher Development through Reflective Teaching." In *Second Language Teacher Education.* eds. J.C. Richards and D. Nunan. Cambridge: Cambridge University Press. 202–214.

Berkowitz, M.W. and Gibbs, J.C. 1985. The Process of Moral Conflict Resolution and Moral Development. In *New Directions for Child Development: Peer Conflict and Psychological Growth.* ed. M.W. Berkowitz. San Francisco: Jossey-Bass. 71–84.

Brookfield, S.D. 1995. *Becoming a Critically Reflective Teacher.* San Francisco: Jossey-Bass.

Damon, W. 1983, *Social and Personality Development: Infancy through Adolescence.* New York: W.W. Norton.

Edelstein, W., Keller, M. and Wahlen, K. 1984. "Structure and Content in Social Cognition: Conceptual and Empirical Analyses." *Child Development* 55: 1514–1526.

EPIIC. *Education for Public Inquiry and International Citizenship.* 1999. Medford, MA: Tufts University Office of Publications.

Euromonitor. 1999. *International Marketing Data and Statistics 1999.* 23rd ed. London: Euromonitor.

Flanagan, C.A. and Faison, N. 2001. "Youth Civic Development: Implications of Research for Social Policy and Programs." *Social Policy Report* 15: 3–14.

Fridriksdottir, K. 2001. *Uppeldissyn og lifssaga kennara: Tilviksathugun* [Teachers' Pedagogical Vision and Life Stories: A Case Study.] Master's thesis, n.d. Reykjavik: University of Iceland.

Gudmundsdottir, S. 1990. "Values in Pedagogical Content Knowledge." *Journal of Teacher Education* 41 (3): 44–52.

Habermas, J. 1979. *Communication and the Evolution of Society.* Boston: Beacon Press.

Holden, C. 1999. *Education for Citizenship: The Contribution of Social, Moral, and Cultural Education.* In *Young Citizens in Europe.* ed. A. Ross. London: CiCe.

International Labour Office. 1998. *Yearbook of Labour Statistics.* Geneva, Switzerland: International Labour Office.

Johnston, M. 1989. "Moral Reasoning and Teachers' Understanding of Individualized Instruction." *Journal of Moral Education* 18: 45–59.

Kohlberg, L. 1969. "Stage and Sequence: The Cognitive-developmental Approach to Socialization." In *Handbook of Socialization on Theory and Research.* ed. D.A. Goslin. New York: Rand-McNally. 347–480.

Korthagen, F.A.J. 1993. "The Role of Reflection in Teachers' Professional Development." In *Teacher Professional Development: A Multiple Perspective Approach.* eds. L. Kremer-Hayon, H.C. Vonk and R. Fessler. Amsterdam/Lisse: Swets and Zeitlinger B.V. 133–145.

Log um grunnskola [Laws for elementary and secondary schooling]. 1995. *stj.tid.* A, nr. 66.

Noddings, N. 1992. *The Challenge to Care in Schools: An Alternative Approach to Education.* New York: Teachers College Press.

Olafsson, S. 1997. *Velferð Islendinga* [Welfare of Icelanders]. Rep. No. 26. Reykjavik, Haskoli Islands: Felagsvisindastofnun.

Oser, F.K. 1981. *Moralisches Urteil in Gruppen* [Moral judgment in groups]. Frankfurt am Main: Suhrkamp.

Oser, F.K. 1992. "Effective and Responsible Teaching." In *The New Synthesis.* eds. F.K. Oser, A. Dick and J. Patry. San Fransisco: Jossey-Bass.

Piaget, J. [1932] 1965. *The Moral Judgment of the Child.* New York: Free Press.

Power, F.C., Higgins, A. and Kohlberg, L. 1989. *Lawrence Kohlberg's Approach to Moral Education.* New York: Columbia University Press.

Pratt, D. 1980. *Curriculum: Design and Development.* London: Harcourt Brace Jovanovich.

QCA. 1998. *Education for Citizenship and the Teaching of Democracy in Schools.* London: QCA.

Richardson, V. 1994. "Conducting Research on Practice." *Educational Researcher* 23: 5–10.

Rudduck, J. 1988. "The Ownership of Change as a Basis for Teachers' Professional Learning." In *Teacher's Professional Learning.* ed. J. Calderhead. London: Falmer. 205–222.

Russell, T. and Munby, H., eds. 1992. *Teachers and Teaching: From Classroom to Reflection.* London: Falmer.

Schön, D.A. 1987. *Educating the Reflective Practitioner: Toward a New Design for Teaching and Learning in the Professions.* San Fransisco: Jossey-Bass.

Selman, R.L. 1980. *The Growth of Interpersonal Understanding*. New York: Academic Press.

Selman, R.L. and Adalbjarnardóttir, S. 2000. "A Developmental Method to Analyze the Personal Meaning Adolescents Make of Risk and Relationship: The Case of Drinking." *Applied Developmental Science* 4: 47–65.

Selman, R.L. and Schultz, L.H. 1990. *Making a Friend in Youth: Developmental Theory and Pair Theory*. Chicago: University of Chicago Press.

Shulman, L.S. 1987. "Knowledge and Teaching: Foundations of the New Reforms." *Harvard Educational Review* 57: 1–22.

Smith, A. and Robinson, A. 1996. *Education for Mutual Understanding*. Coleraine: Northern Ireland University of Ulster Centre for the Study of Conflict.

Soysal, Y. 1994. *Limits of Citizenship*. Chicago: University of Chicago Press.

United Nations. 1997. *Statistical Yearbook*. 42nd ed. New York: United Nations Department of Economic and Social Affairs.

Urry, J. 1999. "Globalization and Citizenship." *Journal of World Systems Research* 2: 311–324.

Walker, P. 1996. "An Introduction to Voices of Love and Freedom: A K–12 Multicultural Literature, Ethics, and Prevention Program." Family, Friends, and Community Project. London: Judge Baker Children's Center.

Yates, M. and Youniss, J. 1999. *Roots of Civic Identity: International Perspectives on Community Service and Activism in Youth*. Cambridge: Cambridge University Press.

Zeichner, K.M. 1994. "Research on Reflective Teaching and Different Views of Reflective Practice in Teaching and Teacher Education." In *Teachers' Minds and Actions—Research on Teachers' Thinking*. eds. I. Carlgren, G. Handal and S. Vaage. London: Falmer. 9–27.

9

Translating the National to the Global in Citizenship Education

Cameron White and Roger Openshaw

INTRODUCTION

Throughout the world, social studies educators and politicians alike have been quick to emphasize the role of the school in the promotion of global citizenship. To be sure, they often do this for different reasons. For social studies educators, the rationale is often claimed to be one of sensitizing young people to the issues and problems common to humanity. For some politicians, the goal seems more related to the concerns of employers that future citizens and workers become more cognizant of the benefits and responsibilities that will accrue to them as a direct consequence of the emerging global marketplace. The tensions between these goals, however, remain all too frequently unacknowledged. Furthermore, given the current promotion of global citizenship as a central component of social studies programs in many countries including the United States, the United Kingdom, Canada, Australia, and New Zealand, the question of multiple citizenship identities arises. As Scott and Lawson have recently observed, multiple citizenship identities of this type imply an intermingling of local, national, and global elements, with the strong implication that these diverse elements can and should be reconciled (Scott and Lawson, forthcoming).

A crucial issue relating to the whole global citizenship phenomenon concerns the place and role of the nation-state in the development of civic virtue. This chapter examines the role of the national state in the construction of citizenship identity. It concludes with the warning that unresolved tensions in citizenship education are being imported directly—and often uncritically—into current models of multinational and global citizenship. Two case studies are presented in support of this contention; one from the United States and the other from New Zealand. The contrast between these two national states is considerable, superficially. The United States is a global superpower, with a perceived mission as an international policeman committed to the active support of democratic structures. It is also, however, a trading nation dedicated to maintaining its position as the leading promoter and main beneficiary of a global free market economy. New Zealand on the other hand, is a small, geographically isolated and relatively recently colonized country. These factors have led to conflict between internationalist aspirations—which New Zealand left-liberals have historically shared with their Western counterparts abroad—and national priorities based on strategic realities, economic vulnerabilities, and growing social and cultural inequalities.

In this chapter, we will work from the smaller national context to the larger national context. First, we use the New Zealand case study to tease out some historic tensions and issues in citizenship education. We will then shift to the U.S. context to examine how some of these tensions and issues are continuing to influence contemporary global citizenship debates.

NEW ZEALAND

In New Zealand, unresolved historic tensions within schools that particularly relate to social studies have influenced citizenship education, be it national or global. A number of these tensions are examined in the New Zealand context under two broad headings, each containing a number of subheadings. The first focuses on national tensions that have subsequently been carried over into the global arena, while the second examines the way New Zealand looks at the world and projects itself on the international stage. It should be emphasized, however, that the problems and issues relevant to global citizenship are not as compartmentalized as this treatment would suggest, but are in fact strongly interlinked.

NATIONAL TENSIONS

Democracy and Authoritarianism

Like their U.S. counterparts, social studies educators in New Zealand have traditionally maintained a commitment to democracy and to democratic values, at least rhetorically speaking. Along with this commitment, successive curriculum documents have emphasized the importance of cooperation, mutual understanding, and social justice. An overarching contradiction, however, is that this rhetoric sharply conflicts with the structures within society and its schools. Writing in the early 1940s, Murdoch posed the provocative question of whether schools could realistically encourage students to work collaboratively for the benefit of the community, have respect for other peoples, uphold a high standard of international ethics, and appreciate spiritual values in their broadest sense, when that same community embraced individualism (narrowly defined as getting ahead), was fearful of external threats, and lauded a crass brand of materialism (Murdoch 1944: 440–453). Murdoch concluded that schools could make little headway when

a certain fear of thought is . . . painfully evident in our community. There is at once a professed desire for intellectual freedom and a dislike of the results of genuine thinking. We are a conventional people, and distrust originality—especially in our preachers and teachers. . . . All this, with our penchant for political control, reinforces our tendency towards democratic totalitarianism. The heavy handed father finds a little compulsion salutary; and the habit grows. So our educational institutions are consciously virtuous, and conscientiously paternal. (Murdoch 1944: 435–436)

Even within social studies classrooms, many teachers since Murdoch's time have chosen to take refuge in the safe and conventional in a manner that has confounded even the best intentions of social studies curriculum designers. Consequently, there has been a tendency for children to use social studies concepts in a conventional, moralistic way that does not always allow for their breadth and subtlety (Smythe 1992: 195). A large-scale social studies subject survey carried out in both primary and secondary schools during the early 1980s discovered that questioning and discussion were not always used effectively (McGee 1992: 170). A recent doctoral dissertation came to similar conclusions, arguing that "failure to teach higher order thinking might be due to teachers' imperfect understanding of the nature of higher order thinking in social studies and their imperfect understanding of the nature and purpose of social studies itself" (Barr 1998: 3).

Continuing problems in understanding the exact nature and purpose of social studies are common to both New Zealand and the United States (White 1999). Moreover, increasing resource constraints, together with the competitive environment that now dominates education in New Zealand, have acutely sharpened the dilemmas that so concerned Murdoch nearly sixty years ago. A crucial question for citizenship education, therefore, is whether the aim of building cooperation between people can coexist within an ethos that clearly demonstrates the efficacy of competition between individuals, companies, nations, and trading blocks (Codd, forthcoming).

Whose Social Criticism?

A related tension also exists between the historic mission of the school as a key institution in the maintenance of social order through the inculcation of citizenship values, and a wider commitment to more freely ranging social criticism that may lead to changes in the institutions and structures of society. Once again social studies is a crucial subject in respect to this tension. Barr has pointed out that while most New Zealanders accept that the ultimate aim of social studies is to produce democratic citizens, the best means of achieving this is debatable. A central issue here is whether a society should inculcate its current mores and beliefs, or whether it should teach students the skills necessary for critical thinking, even though this latter approach may lead to serious questioning of its underlying structures and values (Barr 1994).

Historical evidence suggests that the relationship between these two imperatives has long been an uneasy one for social studies educators. Although statements in social studies curriculum documents may appear broad and general, they reflect education policy at the national level. In turn this reflects what the state at any time has considered necessary and desirable for students to know (McGee 1998). In many ways the founding document for New Zealand social studies, the 1943 Thomas Report, asserted that social studies should aim to assist in the development of individuals able to become effective citizens of a democracy. The Report's definition of an "effective citizen," however, was "one who has a lively sense of responsibility towards civilized values, who can make firm social judgements, and who acts intelligently and in the common interest" (Thomas Report 1943: 27). Given the nature of New Zealand society during the war years, a certain vagueness of definition was perhaps understandable. One consequence, however, was that these phrases provoked considerable debate over subsequent decades. For instance, having "a lively sense of responsibility towards civilized values" appeared to encourage some support for a higher order value system than that affirmed by contemporary New Zealand politics. Conversely, references to social judgements and "common interest" tended to confirm support for existing national and community preoccupations.

F.G. Spurdle, the author of perhaps the earliest New Zealand social studies text, clearly reflects this tension between the relatively cautious brand of critical thinking apparently sanctioned by the writers of the Thomas Report, and the traditional responsibility of upholding the existing values of New Zealand society. Spurdle sought to interest children in community affairs, including many of the problems students might be expected to encounter as future citizens (Spurdle 1946: preface). He saw no fundamental conflict between the school's first duty, the creation of good citizens, and its second duty of "laying sound training foundations for housewives, shopkeepers, tradesmen and professional workers of tomorrow" (Spurdle 1946: 16). Nevertheless, Spurdle clearly intended the book as a reference to provoke critical thinking and to provide background for class discussion, rather than as a class reader. To this end he provided comprehensive and open-ended questions on several controversial issues such as compulsory trade unionism, defense, immigration, and race relations, at the end of each chapter.

The tensions within both the Thomas Report and within Spurdle's book are by no means merely academic and intellectual in nature. The very real risks social studies curriculum developers and teachers run in radically departing from avowedly mainstream thinking in New Zealand can be aptly illustrated by two subsequent controversies involving social studies. In 1964, *Washday at the Pa*, the first in an innovative series of school bulletins intended to deal with aspects of contemporary family life in New Zealand, was released. Within a matter of weeks strong objections from the Māori Women's Welfare League on the grounds that the depiction of Māori in the bulletin was culturally insulting obliged the government to hurriedly withdraw and subsequently destroy the entire production run. During the late 1970s, the introduction of *Man—a Course of Study (Macos)* in a limited number of New Zealand secondary schools sparked fierce controversy, necessitating a carefully planned series of responses from the New Zealand education department intended to defuse public concern (Openshaw 2001).

More recently, some social studies educators have advocated more overtly social meliorist approaches to citizenship education within social studies that draw on the theoretical work of Counts, Levi-Strauss, and others (Simon 1998; Harrison 1992). To a considerable extent, the 1994 draft social studies curriculum document drew on this tradition (New Zealand Ministry of Education 1994). However, the resulting controversy underlined the limits to this approach in the face of community and pressure group opposition. It also raised important questions about whose social criticism was to be judged acceptable for inclusion in a social studies curriculum, and who was to decide. It has been argued, for example, that the writers of the draft curriculum statement ignored some less attractive features of Māori society, such as cannibalism, while taking every opportunity to criticize British colonial society (Partington 1992). The result of this latter controversy was no less than three successive social studies curriculum documents, the last of which was finally declared to be definitive (New Zealand Ministry of Education 1998).

All this should lead us to ask serious questions concerning the process by which certain discourses are legitimated, while others remain submerged. In New Zealand, shortly following the release of the 1994 draft curriculum statement, the minister of education attempted to define just what were legitimate topics for social studies teachers to entertain a diversity of positions on, and which were permitting of one interpretation only. Smith maintained that there were some values such as honesty and respect for others with which no New Zealanders would disagree. There were some historical events, such as the holocaust, that permitted only one valid understanding. In other areas, however, such as the country's economic reforms over the past decade, it was right and proper for students to develop their own understandings based on the available facts. In the case of Māori land rights, where matters were more equivocal, teachers were to avoid promoting a particular view of a controversial issue that was still being debated (Openshaw 1998: 32).

The process of selecting which values are to be subjected to criticism and what issues are to be open or closed to student interpretation is always open to political influence. One might note the continuing utilization of avoidance strategies at the highest level. Once of the most powerful of these strategies has been the "one people" myth, which encourages an avoidance of race issues both historical and contemporary. This has led many social studies and history teachers to avoid controversial issues altogether and instead to cultivate a kind of social amnesia, especially where the history of racial and cultural conflict is concerned (Simon 1992). A more recent development has been the emergence of key nation-building concepts such as the Treaty of Waitangi and biculturalism. As a consequence of their symbolic power, these are sometimes held to be above and beyond questioning by students and teachers (Openshaw 1998).

Second, even when issues of national and cultural identity boil over, so to speak, there tends to be a sharp divergence concerning the nature of the issues. Both Smythe and Bloomfield believed that New Zealand social studies should challenge ethnocentrism, for instance, but Bloomfield favored a much more direct challenging of student beliefs (Smythe 1992; Bloomfield and Smythe 1992). More recently Harrison has argued that social studies be used to empower Māori children "to name the forces of history that acted brutally on their ancestors and visited misfortune on them." Additionally, teachers should aim to "liberate" European children from misconceptions and racial discrimination (Harrison 1992: 77). In opposition to this view, Partington has claimed that social studies will be neither rational nor coherent until it has a clear, defensible criterion of selection. In the absence of this, there is a danger that the subject will be driven by a narrow ideology that permits only one side's atrocities to be studied and only one side's cultural achievements to be praised (Partington 1992: 99).

Historical and contemporary experience with New Zealand social studies suggests that the question of which issues and values are open to debate and which are to be regarded as sacrosanct strongly depends on the ability of politically, morally, and culturally based groups to exercise influence over the curriculum writing process. Those groups able to sustain their message are likely to be those most capable of maintaining effective pressure on governments and bureaucracies, and in addition are able to function effectively as community watch dogs at the local school level.

Ironically, perhaps the only common ground between the various positions is a desire for social studies teachers to promote particular value positions on the presumably self-evident grounds that these are clearly the "right" ones for young New Zealanders to embrace. In this sense, citizenship transmission, broadly defined, remains the dominant tradition in New Zealand social studies, as indeed it does in the United States (Barr, Barth and Shermis 1978).

VIEWING THE WORLD FROM A NATIONAL PERSPECTIVE

The foregoing illustrates that a major difficulty with global citizenship programs in New Zealand is that they have been largely grafted onto existing social studies programs without much thought having gone into resolving the inherent tensions and difficulties. In addition, however, there are further contradictions, deeply rooted in New Zealand's own perception of the world.

Viewing the World Around Us

As a strategically and commercially isolated country, New Zealand's view of the surrounding world has been mindful of the opportunities presented while remaining apprehensive about their potential consequences. Strategic and internationalist considerations and latterly, commercial imperatives, have thus remained awkwardly juxtaposed in successive school history and social studies curriculum materials. In the early twentieth century, New Zealand was often viewed as being "the best of British" and this was reflected in the teachings of the school (McGeorge 1992). The 1929 school history syllabus, however, awkwardly juxtaposed traditional views of Empire and national security with newer internationalist hopes for the success of the League of Nations (Openshaw 1988). In introducing social studies, the Thomas Report likewise attempted to reconcile the specter of external threats with an emerging faith in a postwar world built on broadly humanist foundations. Spurdle's 1946 conviction that the world was "fast becoming one great community of peoples, regardless of colour, race or creed," was based on the increasing pace of travel and growing interdependence of economic relationships (Spurdle 1946: preface).

Again, however, it should be appreciated that the tension between national and international priorities has never been solely an academic or educational debate. In 1984, following controversy over the placing of advertisements in the *Education Gazette* sponsored by the Palestinian Human Rights Campaign and the New Zealand-Israel Information Center, the ministry of foreign affairs was consulted. The ministry subsequently advised the department concerning a number of countries and organizations to be currently considered "politically sensitive," and suggested various strategies for avoiding conflict when agencies sought leave to advertise teaching materials promoting particular points of view (*Sensitive Issues* 1984). More recently the current social studies curriculum document has been criticized for not placing a stronger emphasis on the economic dynamicism of the Asian economies. Evidently in the early twenty-first century, desirable and not so desirable countries for study are more likely to be ranked according to their value to New Zealand as trading partners than by their value or otherwise as cultural or strategic partners.

Self-image

The fate of the social studies bulletin, *Washday at the Pa*, was in part determined by the government's concern lest its international image as a country without racial conflict be tarnished. In the face of increasing globalization, the 1994 draft social studies curriculum document reflected a tendency to promote New Zealand's cultural diversity, particularly its bicultural heritage, as something valuable and "unique." In itself there may be nothing wrong with a positive self-image, but it becomes a matter of serious concern when New Zealand's problems are lamented and its solutions lauded as unique. To be sure, a number of submissions to the draft were critical of this aspect, but the definitive social studies curriculum document has done little to resolve the matter. Many of the issues the country faces, however, are by no means confined to New Zealand, but resonate globally. For instance, continuing global debate over the supposed evils of colonialism centers particularly on Western European colonialism but rarely on Muslim colonialism in regions such as the Balkans and the former Soviet Union. Nor, at least in United States and New Zealand schools, is there much discussion of Israeli colonialism in Palestine. However, it is precisely these legacies that feature nightly on our television screens, aptly illustrating that humanity as a whole faces common issues as well as unique ones.

Democracy as a Cultural Specific

Finally, notwithstanding the ongoing debate in New Zealand about values contradictions and which values social studies might support, very different culturally based claims are now asserting themselves at the global level. Although "democratic global citizenship" is a catch cry heard round the world at international educational conferences, there is a sharp division between Western and non-Western nations regarding what the term entails. It should be appreciated that many of the key concepts in nationally based democratic citizenship programs that have subsequently become translated into global ones, such as peace, human rights, gender equity, and environmentalism, are in actuality fairly culturally specific. As a number of leading historians have recently pointed out, they are eighteenth-century Western European enlightenment ideals. As a result, support elsewhere is often little more than pious lip service, reflecting a shrewd acknowledgement of current Western economic and financial power.

The same might also be said of the Western social studies emphasis on critical thinking. The International Forum on Educational Reform in the Asia Pacific Region held in Hong Kong during February 2001 acknowledged the importance of values and civic education. However, the conference also emphasized two common themes: decentralization, involving the enhanced involvement of parents in the education of children; and the need to reflect the values and traditional wisdom of the nation as a means of asserting national identity in a global world (Baker 2001). How these imperatives might reinforce or conflict with those values now associated with social studies is a complex issue to which we now turn, utilizing our second case study.

UNITED STATES

It is frequently asserted that there is little agreement on what it means to be a good citizen. What, for instance, do democracy and citizenship in the context of social education mean for the world today? What are the connections between critical democracy and citizenship education in social efficacy? How can we promote and enhance the voices of students and teachers?

A strong case can be made for a critical dialogue regarding education and schooling to develop an understanding of the issues and concerns with democracy and citizenship education. Citizenship education in the United States has historically perpetuated the status-quo. New forms of democracy being developed cast doubt on this limited aspiration. Citizenship education, it is suggested, should further the democratic principles in global society. It should also be encouraging teachers to facilitate, model, and practice these principles in their classrooms. Each generation deserves to experience democracy in all facets of society and each generation should be responsible for facilitating critical citizenship and democracy. The challenges faced by democracies have more to do with reinvigorating democracy and ensuring the transmission and transformation of its ideals, as well as a sense of its rights and responsibilities, to a new generation (Boyer and Pinhey 1997). What citizenship education might do is encourage students to become historical and political actors in order to further the goal of critical democracy and citizenship in the world.

Critical democracy and citizenship requires in-depth analysis. This necessitates that students gain access to the various competing discourses concerning the complex issues facing the world today. Uncertainty and conflict permeate many aspects of global society. Debates rage regarding direction or lack of direction from our leaders, the efficacy of solutions emanating from the political left or right, and the degree of cooperation and compromise required even to survive. Alternative approaches suggest a liberation from old, constraining and oppressive conditions and an affirmation of new developments, new terrains, and a forging of new discourses and ideas (Best and Kellner 1991).

Perhaps a key issue that has provided impetus for this thinking is the growing influence of corporations, technology, and capitalism in the world in the guise of globalization. The concepts of nation-state, democracy, and economic growth and development on a large scale and equality, human rights, and efficacy on a smaller individual scale are changing as a result of globalization. When citizenship education is assimilated into political socialization, many issues relating to facilitating democracy arise (Gutman 1990). Easy answers are not, and perhaps never were, available.

Social efficacy for policy makers continues to involve imparting the essential information and teaching students to be productive citizens in society. Most curriculum decisions emanate from the top and are subsequently devolved to "deskilled" teachers in the form of "teacher-proof" curricula. A more critical discourse is needed regarding the role of the education process to promote democracy and transform schooling. Despite current practice, society can understand schooling as an attempt to cope with multiple perspectives and lack of efficacy, rather than as a device to promote continued hegemony and disempowerment. The United States is increasingly employing ever more disempowering and demeaning techniques in its effort to deal with what is seen as societal, cultural, political, and economic turmoil. Using technology for drill and practice to train children for standardized tests and to achieve "effective and efficient" knowledge merely perpetuate this type of thinking. Insisting that children walk quietly, looking straight ahead, with their hands clasped behind them, all wearing the same uniform, while administrators are perched at obvious spots with walkie-talkies in hand might bring to mind other institutions, such as jails and large corporations, rather than schools. Classrooms that are quiet with children sitting in rows completing worksheets to prepare them for standardized tests and lunchrooms where children are required to be absolutely quiet have become the norm.

The goals and objectives of education require rethinking and reconceptualizing to meet the needs of students and society. Since a critical perspective is needed, schooling and education should be designed to facilitate a critical thinking and problem solving focus that allows for a variety of perspectives. A truly transformative education implies proactivity. The ultimate goal might very well be to change the social order toward a more just, equitable, and humane world for "everybody's children" (Holmes Group 1990).

DEMOCRACY AND SCHOOLING

In the United States the aim has been to inculcate traditional values. Teachers prepare citizens for the world of the industrial workplace by teaching them to be punctual, to sit silently and motionless for extended periods of time, to not question their role in the organization (classroom), and to interact appropriately while being "trained" with technology. Promoting allegiance and socialization to nationalistic ideals have become the primary goals of schools (Loewen 1995).

Prisons are now receiving more funding than higher education in many nations. The dissolution of social welfare and the increase of corporate and military welfare are contradictions that require questioning. The idea of civic competence as a goal in education suggests the development of a responsible citizenship for thinking, valuing, and acting, rather than for the promotion of particular thoughts, actions, or values (Stanley 1992).

What then is the role of schools and classrooms in this process? Schools and classrooms have served to socialize students into their roles as citizens in most societies. Schools and classrooms have been designed to perpetuate the status quo and remain very traditionally organized. Schools are designed to "educate the masses," using basically the same universal curriculum and instructional strategies to achieve a "liberal perspective." Schools remain isolated buildings with few connections to the outside world (except through technology). Classrooms are also isolated areas that remain for the most part teacher dominated and nondemocratic.

Schools and classrooms in this era need to be deconstructed and reconceptualized. Increasing efforts are underway within schools and classrooms to address the issues of social, cultural, political, and economic flux. Social injustice, social construction of knowledge, classroom culture, and the dissolution of identities are parts of this (McLaren and Gutierrez 1994). Only when these voices are recognized and heard and it is understood that schooling is a place where power is negotiated can we begin to address this angst as it relates to education. Evans and Saxe (1996) suggest that citizenship education is the application and manipulation of knowledge from traditional academic areas and other contemporary sources of social, political, and economic issues for the expressed purpose of furthering liberal-democratic ideals. Again, it is not the knowledge of these academic areas that is the only goal, but the student's ability to apply the knowledge to effect liberal-democratic goals.

Evans and Saxe (1996) suggest that a good citizen has a sense of fair play, dreams of justice and helps to transform society. The image that arises is a person who acts decently, who knows and cares about the affairs of his community, and who demonstrates this concern through overt actions. Merryfield and Remy (1995) extend citizenship to global attributes, including understanding of human values, seeing the connectedness of countries, tolerance of other cultures and ideas, a basic understanding of world history, realization of the impact of human choice, and the ability to analyze and evaluate information. They further argue that students should think globally while acting locally, clearly indicating that these ideas play not only into global education but into citizenship education in specific nations as well.

TRANSFORMING FOR EMPOWERMENT

A "powerful" social studies, as advocated by the U.S. National Council for the Social Studies (1994), which calls for teaching and learning that is meaningful, integrative, value-based, challenging, and active is an encouraging indication of what might be achieved. The issue remains, however, whether the United States really desires such an approach any more than did New Zealand society in the early post–World War II era. For both societies, it would appear antithetical to all that has gone before. Yet we must address these hard questions and move toward the empowerment of students and teachers at all levels of education. This is truly what is meant by social efficacy.

As is evidenced by the impositions throughout the world, schooling and education are subject to very close scrutiny, and in fact their very essence is being called into question. Schooling and education in society are currently faced with questions regarding efficacy. However, ideas such as democracy and empowerment, critical approaches to curriculum and instruction, and deconstructing the goals and objectives of education, schools, classrooms, and teachers are generally avoided in the education process. The idea has been to "train" individuals to meet the grand narrative regarding what it is to be a productive citizen in society. Unfortunately, with the societal, cultural, political, and economic transitions occurring, students, teachers and their schools have served as scapegoats when society at large is unable to find solutions to these perceived problems and issues. But schools have often accepted this and adapted to fit society's modernist and oppressive focus.

Students and teachers should be provided opportunities to be proactive rather than reactive. They must also be allowed to participate in decision-making throughout their entire schooling and education process. If we are to truly address these vital educational questions and to concentrate on these social, cultural, political, and economic transitions, schools must be willing to take the next step. Students and teachers need to be allowed to become transformative intellectuals who are able to affirm and practice the discourse of freedom and democracy (Giroux and McLaren 1996). They must be allowed to critically analyze curriculum, instruction, and technology's role in learning. For how can we possibly educate teachers and children by ignoring the ultimate goals of human progress?

On the other hand, does this perspective take too narrow a view of resistance and cultural production, and is the situation we describe actually a classic case of hegemony á la Gramsci (1971), in which oppressed groups come to align themselves with their oppressors' best interests rather than their own? If this is the case, then who might those oppressors be, and what is their agenda? Who are we, as teachers, to advance such an analysis? What is our responsibility to the state and to its people? How might we best take this case to them? In the end, there may be few, if any effective ways to respond to high-stakes accountability. We strongly suspect that the traditional schooling practices we have criticized will be with us as long as middle class students appear to be doing well within the system, the achievement measures themselves remain largely a mystery to the public, and the policy makers are able to hide behind the "high expectations" rhetoric while offering no concrete school improvement proposals.

Giroux and McLaren (1996) suggest some possible directions as the next steps toward encouraging a type of schooling and education that attempts to meet the needs of contemporary society. Their central contention is that critical citizenship education that concentrates on empowerment, emancipation, pluralism, and discourse should be the primary goal in schooling and education, both for students and teachers. Giroux and McLaren's four specific goals suggest that (1) democracy and empowerment require that citizens (students and teachers, too) be active agents in decision-making, questioning, and defining their relationship to their society, (2) an understanding and acceptance of the discourse of pluralism be part of any societal endeavor, (3) empowerment of all should not only focus on criticism, but also on problem solving to construct a variety of new societal possibilities; and (4) schools should be places that facilitate this transformation.

Social education requires a transformation that focuses on social efficacy, and in turn social efficacy can be enhanced so as to focus on social justice. An examination of social justice and critical theory for social education reveals the assumptions that underlie this perspective as it applies to teaching and learning.

The natures of progress, knowledge, education, and democracy are redrawn or redefined in such an investigation. Progress is defined in ethical, democratic, humanistic terms rather than the capitalistic, industrial, and technological terms so dominant in our schooling.

The transformational context suggests that social education can be empowering, but that it traditionally serves to demean and disempower. One of the benefits of social education in the United Kingdom according to proponents is knowledge of the past and appreciation of our culture. If nothing else, current approaches perpetuate enthocentric attitudes and a false sense of the world. And we still must recognize that access to this information is by no means equal; it is typically limited by wealth, race, and gender. Wealth, race, and gender often preclude access to an equity in ways of knowing and thinking about the information (Muffoletto 1994). Those in power do not encourage divergent ways of thinking among the marginalized.

A transformative approach to education and particularly social education provides a more humane and progressive alternative. The primary goal of social education should remain the development of civic competence through critical active participation, but the strategy should be critical thinking and problem solving rather than transmission of knowledge. We will only progress as individuals and as a society if we allow people to develop critical thinking and problem solving skills (Shor and Freire 1987). We need to move beyond the traditional mindset of social efficacy.

CONCLUSION

The two national exemplars we have provided in this chapter clearly illustrate that the place and role of the national state in the construction of global citizenship is pervasive, but problematic. Perhaps because of this reality, many issues have remained largely unexamined and unaddressed, if indeed they are capable of any fundamental resolution. The result has been that the unresolved tensions between fundamentally irreconcilable values that characterized twentieth-century citizenship education within social studies in the national context has carried over into twenty-first century global citizenship models. Emerging trends in non-Western countries likewise do not appear encouraging for the development of global citizenship models that promote genuinely free inquiry or criticism. For these reasons, it is unlikely that either the United States or New Zealand, or for that matter any other country on the planet, will adopt genuinely global perspectives in the near future.

We would argue, however, that there are some empowering approaches available that might serve to facilitate critical democracy and citizenship. Democracy is not a stagnant concept but an elastic one, a living political principle that needs to be exercised and stretched. Our students need to be able to analyze information about society, economic principles, political agendas, and have the desire to act on that analysis. If democracy is to continue and hopefully to expand, we need to foster in our students a sense of empowerment so that they can change the system. They need to be offered choices; one can be a victim of society or one can be an actor in changing society. Hopefully through citizenship education we can create more actors.

To accomplish this we must include a thorough discussion of the important questions so as to deconstruct the idea and goals of education, schools, classrooms, and teachers in society. Discourse regarding the issues of social, cultural, economic, and political transitions through a critical perspective must occur if there is any hope for the personal transformation of democracy and the idea of an empowered citizen. Democratic practice should be the goal (Parker 1996).

REFERENCES

Baker, R. 2001. "Educational Change and Reform." *Researched News* 32 (1). Wellington New Zealand Council for Educational Research. Pamphlet.

Barr, H. 1994. "Directions for New Zealand Social Studies." *New Zealand Journal of Social Studies* 3 (1): 10–14.

Barr, H. 1998. "Designing a Teacher Development Program to Enhance the Teaching of Higher Order Thinking and Conceptual Understanding in Primary School Social Studies." D.Phil dissertation, University of Waikato. Hamilton.

Barr, R., Barth, J.L. and Samuel, Shermis S. 1978. *The Nature of the Social Studies*. Irvine, California: ETC Publications.

Best, S. and Kellner, D. 1991. *Postmodern Theory: Critical Interrogations*. New York: Guilford Press.

Bloomfield, R. and Smythe, K. 1992. "Successful Social Studies: Forum." In *New Zealand Social Studies. Past, Present and Future*. ed. R. Openshaw. Palmerston North: Dunmore Press. 147–157.

Boyer, Candice L. and Pinhey, Laura A., eds. 1997. *Resources on Civic Education for Democracy: International Perspectives*. Sacramento, California: U.S. Department of Education.

Codd, J.A. "Neoliberalism, Democracy and Education for Citizenship in New Zealand." In *Democracy at the Crossroads: International Perspectives on Critical Citizenship Education*. eds. C. White, R. Openshaw and P. Benson. New York: Peter Lang Publishing. Forthcoming.

Evans, R. and Saxe, D.W. 1996. *Handbook on Teaching Social Issues*. Washington, D.C.: National Council for the Social Studies.

Giroux, H. and McLaren, P. 1996. "Teacher Education and the Politics of Engagement." In *Breaking Free: The Transformative Power of Critical Pedagogy*. eds. P. Leistyna, A. Woodrum and S. Sherblom. Cambridge, MA: Harvard Educational Review.

Gramsci, A. 1971. *Selections from the Prison Notebooks*. New York: International Publishers.

Gutman, A. 1990. "Democratic Education in Difficult Times." *Teachers College Record* 92: 7–20.

Hargreaves, A. and Jacka, N. 1995. "Induction or Seduction? Postmodern Patterns of Preparing to Teach." *Peabody Journal of Education* 70 (3): 41–63.

Harrison, K. 1992. "Social Studies in the New Zealand Curriculum: Dosing for Amnesia or Enemy of Ethnocentrism?" In *New Horizons for New Zealand Social Studies*. eds. P. Benson and R. Openshaw. Massey University, Palmerston North: ERDC Press. 63–82.

The Holmes Group. 1990. *Tomorrow's Schools* . . . East Lansing: Michigan State University.

Loewen, J. 1995. *Lies My Teacher Told Me*. New York: Touchstone.

McGee, C. 1992. "The Social Studies Subjects Survey." In *New Zealand Social Studies. Past, Present and Future*. ed. R. Openshaw. Palmerston North: Dunmore Press. 166–179.

McGee, J. 1998. "Curriculum in Conflict: Historical Development of Citizenship in Social Studies." In *New Horizons for New Zealand Social Studies*. eds. P. Benson and R. Openshaw. Massey University, Palmerston North: ERDC Press. 43–62.

McGeorge, C. 1992. "The Moral Curriculum: Forming the Kiwi Character." In *The School Curriculum in New Zealand. History, Theory, Policy and Practice*. ed. G. McCulloch. Palmerston North: Dunmore Press. 40–56.

McLaren, P. and Gutierrez, K. 1994. "Pedagogies of Dissent and Transformation." *International Journal of Educational Reform* 3 (3): 327–337.

Merryfield, M. and Remy, R. 1995. *Teaching about International Conflict and Peace*. New York: State University of New York Press.

Muffoletto, R. 1994. "Schools and Technology in a Democratic Society: Equity and Social Justice." *Equity and Social Justice* 34 (2): 52–54.

Murdoch, J.H. 1944. *The High Schools of New Zealand. A Critical Survey*. Educational Research Series No. 19. Christchurch: New Zealand Council for Educational Research.

National Council for the Social Studies. 1994. *Expectations for Excellence: Curriculum Standards for Social Studies*. Washington, D.C.: NCSS.

New Zealand Ministry of Education. 1994. *Social Studies in the New Zealand Curriculum*. Draft. Wellington: Learning Media.

New Zealand Ministry of Education. 1996. *Social Studies in the New Zealand Curriculum*. Revised draft. Wellington: Learning Media.

New Zealand Ministry of Education. 1998. *Social Studies in the New Zealand Curriculum*. Wellington: Learning Media.

Openshaw, R. 1988. "Imperialism, Patriotism and Kiwi Primary Schooling between the Wars." In *Benefits Bestowed? Education and British Imperialism*. ed. J.A. Mangan. Manchester: Manchester University Press. 113–131.

Openshaw, R. 1998. "Citizen Who? The Debate over Economic and Political Correctness in the Social Studies Curriculum." In *New Horizons for New Zealand Social Studies*. eds. P. Benson and R. Openshaw. Massey University, Palmerston North: ERDC Press. 19–42.

Openshaw, R. 2001. "Diverting the Flak: The response of the New Zealand Department of Education to Curriculum Controversy." *Change: Transformations in Education. A Journal of Theory, Research, Policy and Practice*.

Parker, W. ed.. 1996. *Educating the Democratic Mind*. Albany: State University of New York Press.

Partington, G. 1992. "Social Studies in the New Zealand Curriculum." In *New Horizons for New Zealand Social Studies*. eds. P. Benson and R. Openshaw. Massey University, Palmerston North: ERDC Press. 83–102.

Scott, D. and Lawson, H. "Democracy at the Crossroads: International Perspectives on Global Citizenship." In *Democracy at the Crossroads: International Perspectives on Critical Citizenship Education*. eds. C. White, R. Openshaw and P. Benson. New York: Peter Lang Publishing. Forthcoming.

Sensitive Issues. 1984. ABEP, W4262. Box 3676. NS 50/1/S1. National Archives: Wellington.

Shor, I. and Freire, P. 1987. *Freire for the Classroom: A Sourcebook for Liberatory Teaching*. Oxford: Boyton/Cook Publishers.

Simon, J. 1992. "Social Studies: the Cultivation of Social Amnesia?" In *The School Curriculum in New Zealand. History, Theory, Policy and Practice*. ed. G. McCulloch. Palmerston North: Dunmore Press. 252–272.

Smythe, K. 1992. "The Social Concepts of Children." In *New Zealand Social Studies. Past, Present and Future*. ed. R. Openshaw. Palmerston North: Dunmore Press. 180–196.

Spurdle, F.G. 1946. *New Zealand Community. An Integration of Geography, Civics and Elementary Economics*. Auckland, New Zealand and Melbourne, Australia: Whitcombe and Tombs.

Stanley, W. 1992. *Curriculum for Utopia . . .* Albany: State University of New York Press.

The Post-Primary School Curriculum. 1943. The Thomas Report of the committee appointed by the minister of education in November 1942. Wellington: Department of Education.

White, C. 1999. *Transforming Social Studies Education: A Critical Perspective*. Springfield, IL: Charles C. Thomas.

10

Endpiece: Citizenship Education and the Challenges of Cultural Diversity

Ann McCollum

INTRODUCTION

Three core principles underlie European Union directives and policies on citizenship education: the fostering of competencies and convictions capable of enhancing the quality of social relations, which rests on the natural alliance of education and training with equality and social justice; learning to live positively with difference and diversity as a core dimension of the practice of citizenship; and European citizenship as interdependent with other local, regional, and national identities within the social reality of a globalized world (European Commission 1997; 1998; 2000). Responding to these principles, a conception of citizenship education that aims to address contemporary challenges facing European societies will therefore have three dimensions:

- it will acknowledge the interdependent relationships between national, European, and global environments, engaging people in their local communities and cultures as a foundation for developing a sense of involvement and inclusion in wider regional, national, and European communities;
- it will take cultural identities and intercultural concerns into account. This will involve explicitly recognizing and challenging the racism that operates in schools and in societies at large, and developing pedagogic and research practices that engage with multiple identities, the complexity of identity construction, and the complex interactions between factors such as culture, gender, class, and race;
- it will adopt democratic and participatory pedagogies: the role of the teacher will be to facilitate and support the learner's creation of knowledge.

It is stated within "Learning for Active Citizenship" (European Commission 2000) that such learning builds on but moves significantly beyond the more familiar concepts and practices of civic and political/social education provided in formal schooling contexts. New conceptions of citizenship challenge us to rethink the ways in which educational systems engage with the needs of society, not simply in terms of educational content and pedagogies but in terms of how education relates to civil society (cf. Olssen and Arthur and Davison in this volume). For education to effectively engage with the challenges of citizenship, there is a need not simply to rethink educational interventions per se, but to rethink how we develop educational theory, policy, and practice.

CITIZENSHIP EDUCATION AND INTERCULTURAL UNDERSTANDING

The development of intercultural understanding is seen as a central component within the emerging conception of citizenship education, which therefore involves the inclusion of antiracist and multicultural education practices (cf. Osler in this volume). However, educational researchers and practitioners from different backgrounds are converging around the shared belief that there is a need to rethink educational approaches to issues of race, culture and ethnic diversity (Rattansi 1992; Torres 1998; Giroux 1980). Emergent attempts to define and frame the theoretical and pedagogical foundations of new educational approaches highlight the extent to which citizenship education is undertheorized, and identify the complex issues that citizenship education needs to address. Key challenges for contemporary forms of citizenship education include the need to develop a theory that undermines and challenges traditional citizenship concepts (Giroux 1980; Torres 1998); the need to rethink fundamental assumptions in relation to questions of representation, identity and difference, and cultural understanding (Lynch 1992; Rattansi 1992); and the need to rethink the development of educational theory.

A conception of citizenship education is required that explicitly engages with issues of cultural diversity, addresses the problems of racism and social exclusion, and promotes open and inclusive forms of identity. However, educational responses to these issues have hitherto failed to have a significant impact on mainstream educational practice, let alone on the wider society (Gillborn 1992; Troyna 1989). Furthermore, it has been argued that educational and cultural traditions throughout Europe are highly resistant to such models of education (Bell 1995). A recent analysis of the limitations of development, antiracist, and multicultural education identified a set of recurrent weaknesses that derived from the problematic relationships and gaps between theory, policy, and practice within the educational movements. These, in turn, reflected an inadequate understanding of the problems these movements faced (McCollum 2000a). The primary challenge facing citizenship education is to adequately grasp the nature of the problems faced and to develop corresponding programs of action based on an understanding of the complex and multifaceted interconnections between theory, policy, and practice.

CITIZENSHIP: A CONTESTED CONCEPT

A key reference point in the citizenship discourse has been Marshall's conceptualization of citizenship as comprising civil rights, political rights, and social rights (see also Olssen in this volume). Marshall's influential definition of citizenship involved a definite shift from a strict political definition of a citizen, which emphasizes the citizen's relation with the state, to a broader definition that emphasizes the citizen's relationship with society as a whole (van Steenbergen, 1994). Civil citizenship established the rights necessary for individual freedom, political citizenship encompassed the right to participate in public and political life, and social citizenship relates to the citizen's rights to economic and social security, as expressed in the welfare state (van Steenbergen 1994).

A number of political theorists and feminist writers (Arnot 1997; Pateman 1992; Habermas 1994) have offered critical analyses of Marshall's thesis. These view an extension of citizenship rights as a process of gradual incorporation of previously excluded groups (working classes, women, minority, and immigrant groups) for which citizenship expresses full membership in the national political community (Mason 1995). This conception of the citizenship narrative, with its emphasis on the progressive rise of democratic institutions, and a seemingly unproblematic extension of rights, has been identified in many studies of educational policy and curriculum (Gilbert 1992: 57). In England for example, the national curriculum documentation bases its citizenship education framework directly on Marshall's definition. However, it is argued elsewhere that the civil, social, and political elements in citizenship have created logical tensions and social conflicts in the concept's application, and that citizenship is in a contradictory relationship with its capitalist context (Gilbert 1992). From these perspectives, the citizenship narrative is therefore primarily a story of systematic exclusion, and a "disconnected series of struggles for people's rights contingent upon changing power relations at different times" (Gilbert 1992; Torres 1998). Furthermore it is argued that ethnic minorities and women are still denied full citizenship rights. Thus, while the concept of citizenship embodies the principle of equality, in practice it entails inclusion and exclusion. Its central motif is not that of universal equality but of social conflict and the struggles of marginalized groups for equal rights and recognition (cf. Olssen in this volume for a discussion of these issues in relation to New Zealand). Many writers therefore argue that contemporary changes such as immigration trends, the decline of the welfare state, and postmodern thinking, require a fundamental reappraisal of citizenship theory.

THE NATURE OF THE CHALLENGES FACING
CITIZENSHIP EDUCATION

Citizenship education is increasingly viewed as an educational agenda that has great potential for addressing the social and political challenges facing contemporary societies. As Torres argues, questions of citizenship, democracy, and multiculturalism are at the heart of discussions worldwide on educational reform, and affect most of the decisions we face in dealing with the challenges of contemporary education (Torres 1998). Renewed interest in citizenship education thus represents a response to profound social and political change. For example, an international comparison of citizenship education found that a range of educators from different countries identified a set of common challenges facing citizenship education:

- the rapid movement of people within and across national boundaries;
- a growing recognition of the rights of indigenous peoples and minorities;
- the collapse of political structures and the birth of new ones;
- the changing role of women in society;
- the impact of the global economy and changing patterns of work;
- the effect of a revolution in information and communication technologies;
- the increasing global population; and
- the creation of new forms of community (Kerr 1999).

The current social, political, and economic challenges facing societies today revolve around three central and interrelated issues: the phenomenon of globalization and new forms of governance at European and regional levels; the inadequate accommodation of social equity with cultural diversity; and the politics and theory of postmodernism, which challenge traditional, static notions of culture, identity, and the nation-state. As Hall argues, the place of culture has been revolutionized, and this has enabled people to enter society and influence its process in many new ways (Jacques and Hall 1997). However, while people are more willing to accept and recognize cultural and moral diversity, the legitimacy of cultural diversity and in particular its relationship to social equity represents one of the major contemporary problems facing societies today (cf. Ichilov in this volume for a discussion of the notion of citizenship equity in relation to Israeli education).

The tensions posed by the problematic and complex relationship between cultural diversity and social equity are reflected in the crisis of national identity in Western Europe. For example, while Rex argues that the rise of new nationalism in Europe is a response to increased immigration and European integration (Rex 1996), it has been argued elsewhere that the fundamental problem is the failure of the national model of the welfare state to provide for all groups, which results in deep social divisions and the fragmentation of social citizenship (Delanty 1996). Delanty's thesis has important implications for the ways in which education systems conceptualize their response to the challenges of nationalism, cultural diversity, and citizenship. He identifies the need to focus on the failure of social citizenship rather than the perceived threat of immigrants per se, in order to explain and understand the new nationalism.

THE IMPACT OF GLOBALIZATION ON EDUCATION POLICIES AND PRIORITIES

An understanding of the underlying tensions that have prompted the resurgence of citizenship as a significant educational issue and the contradictory responses from educational policy makers at national and European levels is the key to how we respond to the opportunities and challenges posed. The increasing privatization and instrumentalism of education, for example, circumscribes all other educational initiatives and often undermines the broader cultural and democratic goals of education. In a study of educational governance in response to the pressures of globalization, for example, Henry et al. (1999) identify the following trends:

- Educational governance has been radically implicated in the restructuring of the state.
- Institutions are bound to centrally determined policy and funding guidelines by a variety of accountability mechanisms.
- There has been a convergence of public and private spheres.
- Individually based notions of equity and disadvantage are resulting in greater inequality in educational outcomes.
- The dominance of instrumentalism and economic and vocational goals has undermined the social and cultural dimensions of education.
- Educational systems are becoming sites of contestation between backlash national chauvinisms, traditional representations of nationalism and emergent postnational forms, and the types of citizens and identities education ought to produce.

Within this context, education has become an issue of central concern to national governments and also to the European Union in terms of its potential role in supporting the development of competitive economies. However, parallel to the prioritization of the vocational and economic goals of education, the politics of identity and difference within education, and the role of education in the management of national and European diversity have also become central issues of concern (Marginson 1999). Research agendas in the European Union, and many other European nations, for example, have recently highlighted the importance of broader social concerns, such as social inclusion and exclusion. Key issues for consideration include how the principles of social rights and inclusion are expressed in civil societies that are characterized by diversity and rapid social change, and the need to understand changing sources of identity in relation to culture, lifestyle, religions and belief systems (ESRC Thematic Priorities 1997).

CITIZENSHIP EDUCATION IN EUROPE

Many European countries are now developing or rethinking their curricula in relation to issues of citizenship, identity, and the challenges of living in diverse societies. Most countries also specify, either explicitly or implicitly, the promotion of citizenship as a fundamental national aim, and often link this to the need to promote a sense of national identity and social cohesion (Kerr 1999). However, a recent survey of citizenship education in Europe shows that different countries interpret citizenship in very diverse ways, and that the concept can have a range of meanings, such as civics, political education, national identity, global education, interculturalism, and ethnic minority inclusion (Davies 1999).

A recent international comparison of citizenship education identified a range of contextual and structural factors underlying the diversity of approaches to citizenship education. The five main contextual factors are historical tradition, geographical tradition, sociopolitical structure, economic system, and global trends (for a further discussion of these in relation to Ireland, cf. Clarke in this volume). The three structural factors in national education systems that were identified as having a major impact on the varied definitions and approaches to citizenship education and the gaps between policy and practice included the organization of, and responsibilities for, education; educational values and aims; and the funding and regulatory arrangements relating to education (Kerr 1999).

These wide-ranging surveys are valuable for describing overall patterns of policies and practices in relation to citizenship education, but the inherent limitation of such surveys is that they are largely descriptive and quasi-analytical. While they provide an important basis or reference point for further research, they cannot provide insight into the complex interactions between the different levels of policy and practice, and they cannot effectively engage with the politics of policy making and educational change processes. Thus while they can identify some of the tensions that countries face in developing citizenship education programs, they cannot provide an adequate understanding of how policy makers and practitioners might seek to resolve these tensions.

One of the major tensions identified in the international comparison, for example, is the extent to which it is possible to identify and agree on the values and dispositions that underpin citizenship. Another is whether citizenship education can or should be "values explicit" and promote distinct values that are part of a broader, nationally accepted system of public values and beliefs. However, the Kerr Report fails to explicitly link these tensions with the issues of cultural and ethnic diversity, and the need to take cultural identities and intercultural concerns into account when developing citizenship education programs. The report refers in passing to the "complex issues concerning pluralism, multiculturalism, ethnic and cultural heritage and diversity" (Kerr 1999: 32). It simply states that educational systems are a vital part of the response to these challenges, which are prompting many countries to re-examine their underlying cultural traditions, values, and assumptions.

The European Union views the development of intercultural skills and understanding as a vital part of citizenship education, and views education as having a central role in promoting a broader idea of citizenship that can strengthen the meaning and experience of belonging to a shared social and cultural community. However, it is currently unclear how education can fulfill this role. While many European countries have traditionally had civic or civil education programs as part of the curriculum, current initiatives in relation to intercultural and citizenship education represent major innovations in that they involve (to varying degrees) a shift toward a new educational paradigm and a response to the challenges of democracy, human rights and civil society within the context of European diversity and global interdependence. However, while European nations recognize the need for education systems to respond to these challenges, there is very little understanding of what this means in practice and no coherent basis for new approaches to citizenship, as the following examples illustrate:

- The report of the Government Advisory Group in England acknowledged that there is no "coherent basis" for education for citizenship, and there is no consensus on its aims and purposes. Strong evidence for such a view was provided by national research, which found that the problems schools faced in trying to deal with citizenship included a lack of teacher understanding and commitment, and a lack of resources or advice and guidance (Kerr 1999; see also Ross and Arthur and Davison in this volume).
- In Ireland a national strategy paper for the implementation of citizenship education observed that the previous civics program had failed to establish itself in the curriculum. It stated that citizenship education was a major innovation that consequently faced many challenges, including limited timetable provision, a nonexistent teaching cohort for whom citizenship was their first subject, and a lack of teaching and learning resources (NCCA, in Clarke 2000 and in this volume).
- The Finnish National Board of Education recognizes that there is a need to increase the significance of international education and human rights education as part of ethical education in general. However, there is currently no specific provision for citizenship education, which remains without clear definitions or foundations, although promoting citizenship is an implicit aim of schooling in terms of the values that underpin the school system (Saine 2000).
- In the recent reform of the secondary education syllabus in Portugal (February 2000), education for citizenship appears as a main objective of schools. It is stated, for example, that education for citizenship must be an "integral part" of the schools' daily life and of learning and teaching. In 1993 the ministry of education established a department to promote and coordinate existing school projects that engage with cultural diversity and ethnic conflict (their views of identity and cultural diversity are closely linked to questions of citizenship) (Noronha 2000).

• In Germany the standing committee of the ministers of education and cultural affairs produced a policy paper on the need for cross-cultural education in all schools. Topics included in the curriculum that relate to citizenship include "Living in a Community," "Democracy and Human Rights," and "Living in One World." These are designed to promote project-oriented and interdisciplinary work (Behrens 2000).

PROBLEMS ASSOCIATED WITH THE IMPLEMENTATION OF CITIZENSHIP EDUCATION

The provision of citizenship education in schools is highly problematic for the following key reasons: the contested, controversial, and ambiguous nature and purposes of citizenship education; the need for participatory and democratic approaches to learning; the lack of understanding of what citizenship education means for and to teachers, the lack of guidance, resources, and support for teachers and schools; and the ambiguous nature of citizenship education. Studies of earlier attempts to introduce education for citizenship as a cross-curricular theme in England show that the theme was of "political as well as educational sensitivity"; that guidance was inconsistent and naive (in relation to the controversial nature of the subject); and that the response from schools and teachers was characterized by confusion and ambivalence (Beck 1996).

Participatory Learning

There is a need for increased encouragement of active and participatory learning in citizenship education, not only in the classroom but within the school's formal structures and policies. However, many schools' structures and policies are undemocratic, and there is a lack of coherence between the formal curriculum and the hidden curriculum. Ireland's citizenship education program places strong emphasis on active and cooperatively structured learning situations in the classroom; however, this is a major challenge to teachers because it seeks new and innovative ways of dealing with material in the classroom. As Clarke and Killeavy (2000) argue, the ability to achieve the aims of the syllabus is dependent on the way the subject is treated within the school's timetable and in the classroom. However, their research demonstrates that there were few opportunities for students to develop an action component or to develop the skills necessary to become involved as active citizens.

Teacher Training

In most countries, there is no specific initial training of teachers for citizenship education, and in-service for practicing teachers is very patchy. There are also limited opportunities for professional collaboration between teachers and schools (Kerr 1999; see also Adalbjarnardóttir in this volume in the Icelandic context). In Finland, for example, the National Board of Education requires that subjects such as internationalism, multiculturalism and tolerance are included in the curriculum, but multicultural education is a voluntary course within teacher training. Therefore only those teachers who are interested in international cooperation and multiculturalism participate in these courses (Saine 2000).

The international comparison of citizenship education claims that the main challenges for citizenship education are to achieve a clear definition and approach, secure its position and status in the curriculum, address teacher preparedness and teacher training, increase the range of appropriate teaching and learning approaches, improve the quality and range of resources, decide on appropriate assessment arrangements, and develop and disseminate more widely effective practice (Kerr 1999). While these are all valid aims in relation to citizenship education, they represent a partial response to the challenges faced, for the practical limitations identified above relate to a set of deeper tensions in relation to the perceived goals of education and contradictory policy initiatives. While many European countries have developed policies that apparently endorse the need for intercultural and citizenship education, these are rarely supported by adequate funding or resources or any attempts to introduce fundamental changes into school structures and/or cultures. The policy discourses may thus serve to disguise an unwillingness or incapacity to engage with the challenges of modern citizenship and cultural diversity. The educational system in England, for example, has over twenty years of experience in engaging with the issues of cultural diversity and equality. A review of their experiences and policies in this regard will thus serve to highlight the contradictory realities that underly the rhetoric regarding the role of education in pluralist democracies.

THE EDUCATIONAL RESPONSE TO CULTURAL DIVERSITY AND CITIZENSHIP IN ENGLAND

The 1984 Swann report, which was commissioned to review the educational needs of ethnic minority children in England is identified as the "one national stimulus for the study of equality in education" (Klein 1994: 168). As its title "Education for All" suggests, the report argued that multicultural education should be the basis of every child's education. However, while the report is recognized as providing a major contribution to the field, Troyna states that the failure of the report to stimulate real changes along multicultural and antiracist lines is profoundly disturbing (Troyna 1989).

Gorman (1994) argues that the 1988 Education Reform Act missed an opportunity to incorporate some of the recommendations of the Swann report into a coherent approach to cultural diversity in schools. The tendency of national curriculum reforms to sidestep the recommendations of government reports in relation to these issues has been exemplified again in response to the MacPherson Report (1999), which states that antiracist policies in education, even where they exist, are ineffective and that there must therefore be specific and coordinated action to counteract racism, particularly through the education system. The 1999 National Curriculum Review refers briefly to the MacPherson Report and claims that the issues raised in the report will be addressed through the review's proposals for citizenship education which can play a "vital role in promoting a greater understanding of the rights and responsibilities that underpin a democratic society" (QCA 1999a). The response thereby effectively dismisses the report's assertion that there is a need to amend the curriculum so that it explicitly engages with the problem of racism (Skinner and McCollum 2000).

One of the stated aims of the revised national curriculum is to support the development of citizens capable of contributing to a just society, to develop their knowledge and understanding of different beliefs and cultures, and to appreciate and understand the diverse nature of society (QCA 1999a). However, the curriculum documentation engagement with issues of social justice, national identity, and cultural diversity is superficial and fails to adequately explore the implications for educational policy and practice.

The Government Advisory Group on the Citizenship Education Report states that it recognizes "wider social questions" such as the increasingly complex nature of our society, greater cultural diversity, and the apparent loss of a value consensus (QCA 1998). However, the group's response to this issue emphasizes a unified British national culture that defines as un-British any but the most minimal manifestations of cultural difference (Mason 1995). These extracts from the advisory group's report represents the group's response to the need for a multicultural conception of citizenship:

3.12. Responding to these worries, a main aim for the whole community should be to find or restore a sense of common citizenship, including a national identity that is secure enough to find a place for the plurality of nations, cultures, ethnic identities and religions long found in the United Kingdom. Citizenship education creates common ground between different ethnic and religious identities. (QCA 1998: 17)

Majorities must respect, understand and tolerate minorities and minorities must learn and respect the laws, codes and conventions as much as the majority—not merely because it is useful to do so, but because this process helps foster common citizenship. (QCA 1998: 17–18)

Citizenship is conceptualized here in terms of a conformity to the core values of the "majority," a self-evident "us and them" is assumed, common ground is based on the rules of the "majority," and there is an implicit view that "minorities" potentially threaten the rules and security of the "majority." The minority groups are thus defined as outsiders; as "not really belonging, or as marginal to the mainstream of social life" (Mason 1995: 115). A multicultural conception of citizenship should be based on an understanding of the dynamic and constructed natures of both identity and culture; however, there is an implicit racism in the essentialist tones adopted in the report (see also Osler in this volume).

Lessons Arising

The response in England to issues of cultural diversity and citizenship demonstrate clearly that official government reports and policy recommendations are not necessarily indicative of clear and unequivocal support on these issues. Instead, they represent a "vague but unmistakable consensus" (Parekh 1992) that these issues need to be addressed. Thus, while the Advisory Group report claims to address the issue of cultural diversity, it has actually adopted a narrow and exclusive view of citizenship that fails to recognize the controversial nature of citizenship and the tensions posed, for example, in seeking a balance between individual and community rights, in defining the common values that underscore democratic and diverse societies, and in ensuring that all British citizens have a genuine sense of belonging to British society.

The report also overlooks the ways in which society is characterized by institutional racism and social and economic inequality, and the ways in which our educational system is characterized by distinctive exclusionary and discriminatory practices. Gillborn argues, in relation to schooling in the United Kingdom, for example, that schools teach a great deal about the realities of citizenship for black people through the operation of the hidden curriculum, and that these realities fundamentally challenge the ideology of the liberal, pluralist democracy presented in official national curriculum documents (Gillborn 1992).

Current E.U. rhetoric makes ambitious claims for the potential role of citizenship education in addressing issues of social equity and cultural diversity. However, previous reform efforts in relation to these issues have produced few tangible changes in education structures and highlight the dangers of superficial change whereby people absorb the language but not the substance of reform. Effective engagement with these issues requires fundamental shifts in the structure and culture of schools, but the core values at the heart of the current restructuring of education across Europe are in tension with the values of citizenship education.

MOVING FORWARD

A consensus is emerging that traditional forms of citizenship education fail to engage with the realities of living in culturally diverse societies and that there is a need for debates on education for citizenship to explicitly articulate and engage with the realities of existing inequalities that operate through race, gender, class, and disability codes, and to attend to the ways in which education currently addresses and formulates citizenship and cultural diversity in its practice. The questions at the heart of these discussions have far-reaching implications for the way we conceptualize educational responses to the needs of culturally diverse democratic societies:

• How should schools participate in the struggle for social justice and civil rights?

• How can education support in children the development of an open sense of identity, in which they embrace rather than suppress difference? (Parekh 1999)

• Whose cultural practices, values, and beliefs should constitute the school curriculum?

The Need to Rethink Core Concepts

While many writers are arguing that we need to develop new forms of citizenship education, it is currently very difficult to say what this means in practice. It has been argued, for example, that there is a need to rethink fundamental assumptions in relation to the nature of identity and cultural pluralism. However, there are few practical programs that engage with these issues.

Lynch (1992) argues that educational practice is limited by a false perception of what cultural pluralism actually means in the daily construction and negotiation of reality in the lives of ordinary pupils. Neither the multiculturalist nor the antiracist movements in education have engaged with "new ethnicities" or developed creative ways to explore the shifting contours of black and white cultural and political identities. Rattansi (1992) states that there has been very little serious thinking about how cultural understanding actually occurs and highlights the need to reexamine the underlying assumptions that inform current educational practices. Intolerance, for example, is conceptualized basically as a matter of attitudes and is said to be constituted by prejudice: the basic educational prescription is the sympathetic teaching about other cultures. Prejudice is defined as hostile or negative attitudes based on ignorance and faulty or incomplete knowledge. There is a common assumption that individuals hold prejudiced views consistently and express them systematically, and a concomitant tendency to essentialize the prejudiced individual.

Educational approaches are needed that transform the underlying cultural-valuational structures so that, for example, the dominant cultural ideology is made transparent and learning processes are aimed toward changing everyone's sense of self so that all pupils understand the nature of their own identity (Fraser 1997).

The Need to Link Theory, Policy, and Practice

To translate the vague but unmistakable consensus about the need for citizenship education into a real commitment to tackle these issues, it is necessary to engage directly with the contradictions at the heart of educational change processes; develop a clearer conceptualization of the relationships between theory, policy, and practice; and facilitate new forms of collaboration in response to the integrated realities of educational change processes (McCollum 2000b).

In terms of theoretical development, critical analyses of conceptual weaknesses inherent in educational practice tend to be divorced from the historical context and constraints on practice. New thinking in relation to citizenship education is complex and controversial. There is therefore a need to explore how to make complex theoretical concepts accessible to practitioners and policy makers and to identify the practical conditions that facilitate engagement with complexity. Rather than producing prescriptive models or blueprints for citizenship education, there is a need to identify core principles and concepts that are widely debated and negotiated and tested collaboratively in the development of new practices.

While citizenship education is apparently high on education policy agendas, other policy agendas may serve to undermine the citizenship agenda: the problem of the gap between policy and practice is often formulated in terms of practice "lagging behind" policy. However, the limitations of practice in citizenship education partly relate to deeper tensions in relation to contradictory policy initiatives at different levels.

While policies may be contradictory, they nevertheless provide important opportunities and spaces for the development of effective citizenship education programs. There is a need therefore not to simply "develop and disseminate good practice," but to identify the possibilities for change within a set of shifting and contradictory conditions and to identify problem solving approaches that engage people in developing solutions to the problems they face in their particular contexts.

These problem solving approaches need to combine the capacity to be experimental and innovative with an appreciation of the opportunities for and constraints on educational change that operate at micro and macro levels, making them dependent on new forms of collaborative research and practice (Halpin 1999).

To effectively address the challenges for theory, policy, and practice in citizenship education, there is a need to develop strategies that engage with the dynamic connections between areas such as research, policy and the professional development of teachers, as well as ways of working that bring educational practitioners, students, trainers, researchers, and policy makers together to collaborate in the development of new policies and practices.

REFERENCES

Arnot, M. 1997. "Gendered Citizenry. New Feminist Perspectives on Education and Citizenship." *British Educational Research Journal* 23 (3): 275–295.

Beck, J. 1996. "Citizenship Education: Problems and Possibilities." *Curriculum Studies* 4 (3).

Behrens, U. 2000. "An Overview of Education Policies and Practice in Relation to Citizenship Education in Germany." University of Koblenz, Germany.

Bell, G.H. 1995. "Towards the Europe School: Partnership in European Dimension of Teacher Development." *British Journal of In-service Education* 21 (3).

Clarke, M. and Killeavy, M. 2000. "Citizenship Education in the Irish Curriculum: Processes of Teacher-child Interaction in Social Learning." In *Second European Conference, Curricula for Citizenship in Europe: The Role of Higher Education.* ed. A. Ross. London: CiCe.

Clay, J. and Cole, M. 1992. "Euroracism, Citizenship and Democracy: The Role of Teacher Education." *International Studies in Sociology of Education* 2 (1).

Dale, R. 1999. "Specifying Globalisation Effects on National Policy: A Focus on the Mechanisms." *Journal of Education Policy* 14 (1): 1–18.

Davies, L. 1999. *A Summary of Developments in Citizenship and Human Rights Education in Key Countries.* London: British Council.

Delanty, G. 1996. "Beyond the Nation-state: National Identity and Citizenship in a Multicultural Society." A response to Rex, *Sociological Research Online.* http://www.socresonline.org.uk/socresonline/1/3/1.html

Departmento de Ensino Secundario do Ministerio da Educao. Fevereiro 2000, *Revisao curricular no ensino secundario.* Lisbon, Portugal: Departmento de Ensino Secundario do Ministerio da Educao.

European Commission. 1997. *Accomplishing Europe through Education and Training.* Report of the Study Group on Education and Training. Luxembourg: Office of Official Publications.

European Commission. 1997. *Towards a Knowledge of Europe.* Luxembourg: Office of Official Publications.

European Commission. 1998. *Education and Active Citizenship in the European Union.* Luxembourg: Office of Official Publications.

European Commission. 2000. *Learning for Active Citizenship.* http://europa.eu.int/comm/education/citizen/citiz-en.ht

Fraser, N. 1997. *Justice Interruptus.* New York: Routledge.

Gilbert, R. 1992. "Citizenship, Education and Postmodernity." *British Journal of Sociology of Education* 13: 51–68.

Gillborn, D. 1992. "Citizenship, Race, and the Hidden Curriculum." *International Studies in Sociology of Education* 2 (1): 57–73.

Gillborn, D. 1997. "Racism and Reform: New Ethnicities/Old Inequalities?" *British Educational Research Journal* 23 (3): 345–360.

Giroux, H. 1980. "Critical Theory and Rationality in Citizenship Education." *Curriculum Inquiry* 10: 329–336.

Gorman, M. 1994. "Education for Citizenship." In *Cross Curricular Contexts, Themes and Dimensions in Primary Schools.* eds. G. Verma and P.D. Pumfrey. London: Falmer.

Habermas, J. 1994. "Citizenship and National Identity." In *The Condition of Citizenship.* ed. B. van Steenbergen. London: Sage.

Halpin, D. 1999. "Utopian Realism and a New Politics of Education: Developing a Critical Theory without Guarantees." *Journal of Education Policy* 14 (4): 345–361.

Henry, M., Lingard, B., Rizvi, F. and Taylor, S. 1999. "Working with/against Globalisation in Education." *Journal of Education Policy* 14 (1): 85–97.

Jacques, M. and Hall, S. 1997. "Cultural Revolutions." *New Statesman,* 5 December 1997.

Kerr, D. 1999. *Citizenship Education: An International Comparison.* QCA/NFER. http://www.qca.org.uk

Klein, G. 1994. "Equal Rights in the Classroom? The Role of Teacher Education in Ensuring Equality of Educational Opportunities." *Educational Review* 46 (2): 167–177.

Lynch, J. 1992. *Education for Citizenship in a Multicultural World.* London: Cassell.

Lynch, J. 1989. *Multicultural Education in a Global Society*. London: Falmer.

Marshall, T.H. 1950. "Citizenship and Social Class." In *Citizenship and Social Class and Other Essays*. ed. T.H Marshall. Cambridge: Cambridge University Press.

Mason, D. 1995. *Ethnicity and Race in Modern Britain*. Oxford: Oxford University Press.

Mattinheikki-Kokko, K. 1999. "Towards the New Paradigm of Multicultural Education." In *Multicultural Education—Theory and Experiences*. ed. K. Matinheikki-Kokko. Helsinki, Finland: Opetushallitus.

Marginson, S. 1999. "After Globalisation: Emerging Politics of Education." *Journal of Education Policy* 14 (1): 19–31.

May, S., ed. 1999. *Critical Multiculturalism Rethinking Multicultural and Anti Racist Education*. London: Falmer.

Menezes, I. et al. 1997. *Educacao Civica em Portugal nos programas e manuais do ensino basico*. Lisboa: Instituto de Inovacao Educacional.

McCollum, A. 2000a. "Education for Global Citizenship: Towards a Core Agenda for Addressing Contemporary Challenges Facing Education." Seminar paper. University of Manchester.

McCollum, A. 2000b. "Whose Citizenship? Developing Practical Responses to Citizenship in the Curriculum." In *Second European Conference. Curricula for Citizenship in Europe: The Role of Higher Education*. ed. A. Ross. London: CiCe.

National Council for Curriculum and Assessment 1999. *The Junior Cycle Review: Progress Report: Issues and Options for Development*. Dublin: National Council for Curriculum and Assessment.

Noronha, R. 2000. "An Overview of Education Policies and Practice in Relation to Citizenship Education in Portugal." Paper. Universidade de Lisboa, Portugal.

Pateman, C. 1992. "Equality, Difference, Subordination: The Politics of Motherhood and Women's Citizenship." In *Beyond Equality and Difference: Citizenship, Feminist Politics and Female Subjectivity*. eds. G. Bock and B. James. London: Routledge.

Parekh, B. 1999. Keynote speech, Teachers in Development Education (Tide) conference, June 1999, School of Education, University of Birmingham.

Parekh, B. 1992. "The Hermeneutics of the Swann Report." In *Racism and Education: Structures and Strategies*. eds. Gill et al. London: Sage.

QCA. 1998. Final report of the advisory Group on Citizenship: *Education for Citizenship and the Teaching of Democracy in Schools*. London: QCA.

QCA. The review of the national curriculum in England, the secretary of state's proposals. May–July 1999, London: QCA.

QCA. 1999a. The review of the national curriculum in England, the consultation materials. May–June 1999, London. QCA.

Rattansi, A. 1992. "Changing the Subject?" In *Race, Culture and Difference*. eds. Donald, J. and Rattansi, A. London: Sage.

Rex, J. 1996. "National Identity in the Democratic Multicultural State." *Sociological Research Online*. http://www.socresonline.org.uk/socresonline/1/3/1.html

Rosenau, J.N. and Durfee, M. 1995. *Thinking Theory Thoroughly*. Oxford: Westview Press.

Saine, N. 2000. "An Overview of Education Policies and Practice in Relation to Citizenship Education in Finland." Paper. University of Jyvaskyla, Finland.

Short, G. and Carrington, B. 1996. "Anti-racist Education, Multiculturalism and the New Racism." *Educational Review* 48 (1): 65–77.

Skinner, G. and McCollum, A. 2000. "Intercultural Education." In *Teaching Values and*

Citizenship in Schools: New Directions for the Modern World. ed. R. Bailey. London: Kogan Page.

Standing Committee of the Ministers of Education and Cultural Affairs in the Federal Republic of Germany. 1996. *Cross-Cultural Education in Schools*. Bonn: Department of Education and Cultural Affairs.

Stationery Office. 1999. *The Stephen Lawrence Inquiry*. Report of an inquiry by Sir William Macpherson of Cluny. London: Stationery Office.

Torres, C.A. 1998. "Democracy, Education, and Multiculturalism: Dilemmas of Citizenship in a Global World." *Comparative Education Review* 24 (4): 421–447.

Troyna, B. 1989. " 'A New Planet'? Tackling Racial Inequality in All-white Schools and Colleges." In *Cultural Diversity and the National Curriculum. vol 4: Cross Curricular Themes in Primary Schools*. eds. G.V. Verma and P. Pumfrey. London: Falmer.

Troyna, B. 1989. "Beyond Multiculturalism: Towards the Enactment of Antiracist Education in Policy, Provision and Pedagogy." In *Policies for the Curriculum*. eds. B. Moon et al. London: Hodder and Stoughton.

Verma, G.V., ed. 1989. *Education for All: A Landmark in Pluralism*. London: Falmer.

Verma, G.V. and Pumfrey, P. eds. 1994. *Cultural Diversity and the National Curriculum. vol. 4: Cross-Curricular Themes in Primary Schools*. London: Falmer.

van Steenbergen, B. ed. 1994. *The Condition of Citizenship*. London: Sage Publications.

Index

About the Editors and Contributors

SIGRÚN ADALBJARNARDÓTTIR is professor of education in the faculty of Social Sciences at the University of Iceland. She received her doctoral degree (1988) and master's degree (1984) from the Harvard University Graduate School of Education in Human Development and Psychology, her B.A. degree in education (1983) from the University of Iceland, and her teacher's diploma (1969) from the Teacher Training College in Iceland. She was previously an elementary school teacher and teacher trainer and a curricula developer and curriculum writer in social studies in the Department of Research and Development within the Ministry of Education.

JAMES ARTHUR is professor and head of educational research at Canterbury Christ Church University College. He has written and published books on citizenship, communitarianism, virtues, and character education and has been a member of a number of Department for Education and Skills' committees on citizenship education. He is currently completing a book on *Character Education*.

MARIE CLARKE is a college lecturer in the Education Department, UCD/NUI, Dublin, Republic of Ireland. She lectures in the areas of curriculum development and adult education at preservice teacher training and in-service levels, and supervises postgraduate research in these areas. She has published in the areas of citizenship education, adult education, educational disadvantage, and vocational education. She is a member of the European Thematic Network, Children's Identity and Citizenship Education (CiCe) and serves as the Irish representative in its Data Collection Group.

JON DAVISON is professor of education and head of the School of Education at the University of North London. Formerly, he was professor of teacher education at University College, Northampton. His research interests include sociolinguistics, citizenship education, and personal and social education. He has published widely on social literacy and citizenship education, the teaching and learning of English, and teacher education. His recent publications include *Subject Mentoring in the Secondary School*, *Issues in Teaching English*, and *Social Literacy, Citizenship and the National Curriculum*.

ORIT ICHILOV is professor of education at Tel-Aviv University. She chaired the Department of Educational Sciences and was vice-president of the International Society of Political Psychology. She is the author of *The Political World of Children and Adolescents* (1984, in Hebrew) and *Citizenship Education in an Emerging Society* (1993, in Hebrew); coauthor of *Between State and Church: Life History of a French-Catholic School in Jaffa* (1996); and editor of *Political Socialization, Citizenship Education, and Democracy* (1990), *Education for Democratic Citizenship* (1994, in Hebrew), and *Citizenship and Citizenship Education in a Changing World* (1998). Her publications also include articles in professional journals, chapters in books, and encyclopedia entries. She is the Israeli National Representative to the International Education Association (IEA) Civic Education Study, and she was a member of the City Council of Tel-Aviv-Jaffa (1993–1998), working to advance equality of educational opportunities and education for democracy. She is now chairing a subcommittee on education in a committee advising the Israeli Ministry of Justice on the implementation of legislation on the United Nations Children's Rights Covenant.

HELEN LAWSON is a research fellow at the Open University and a visiting research fellow at the University of York, where she is researching techniques for evaluating education for sustainable development. She has acted as an education evaluation consultant to a number of nongovernmental organizations such as the Commonwealth Institute, the International Broadcasting Trust, and the Development Education Association. She is a consultant to the University of Nottingham, where she is assisting with the integration of citizenship education into the university's teacher training courses. She is working on the Citizenship Education Project at the Open University and has published on sustainable development and international perspectives on citizenship identity.

ANN McCOLLUM works as a consultant specializing in strategic planning and evaluation advice for development education organizations. Current projects include work for DEC Birmingham, Somerset Goes Global, and the Children and Youth Partnership Foundation. Ms. McCollum was the Sarah Fielden Research Fellow in the Faculty of Education at the University of Manchester from 1998 to 2001. Her research interests include the development of critical theory and practice in citizenship education and the relationship between different forms of socially critical education. She is the author of many articles and reports on citizenship education and development education. She has also written distance learning materials on development education and developed a postgraduate certificate in citizenship education.

MARK OLSSEN is reader in Education and director of Doctoral Programs at the University of Surrey, England. He is the editor of *Mental Testing in New Zealand: Critical and Oppositional Perspectives* (1988), author (with Elaine Papps) of *The Doctoring of Childbirth* (1997), editor (with Kay Morris Mathews) of *Education Policy in New Zealand: The 1990s and Beyond* (1997), and sole author of the book, *Michel Foucault: Materialism and Education*, published in 1999 by Bergin and Garvey, a division of the Greenwood Publishing Group of Connecticut. He has recently published articles in the *Journal of Education Policy*, the *British Journal of Educational Studies, Educational Psychology*, and *Educational Philosophy and Theory*. Formerly from New Zealand, he is presently on the editorial boards of *Access, Educational Philosophy and Theory*, and *New Zealand Sociology*.

ROGER OPENSHAW is an associate professor in the Department of Social and Policy Studies, Massey University College of Education, Palmerston North, New Zealand. Since completing his Ph.D. on the history of patriotism in New Zealand schools, he has written, cowritten, edited, and coedited nine books and some sixty articles and book chapters. He has extensively researched the histories of education and curricula. His most recent publications have dealt with the sociopolitical and historical contexts of reading, social studies, and citizenship education.

AUDREY OSLER is professor of education and director of the Center for Citizenship Studies in Education at the University of Leicester. Her recent books include *The Education and Careers of Black Teachers: Changing Identities Changing Lives* (1997); *Citizenship and Democracy in Schools: Diversity, Identity, Equality* (2000); and *Inspecting Schools for Race Equality: OFSTED, Strengths and Weaknesses* (2000, with Marlene Morrison). Her research focuses on issues of human rights and social justice in education, with a number of projects addressing the issue of exclusion from school. The most recent of these is a study of girls and school exclusion funded by the Joseph Rowntree Foundation and conducted in collaboration with colleagues from the New Policy Institute.

ALISTAIR ROSS is professor of education, director of the Institute of Policy Studies at the University of North London, and international coordinator of the Erasmus Thematic Project Network "Children's Citizenship and Identity in Europe." Formerly a primary teacher in inner London, he has had a longstanding interest in children's political and economic education, and has written on the social studies curriculum, economic and industrial understanding, and citizenship education. He also has research interest in teachers' careers and in social inclusion and recruitment to higher education. His most recent book is *Curriculum: Construction and Critique* (2000). He has also recently edited a series of books on citizenship education in Europe: *Young Citizens in Europe* (1999), *Developing Identities in Europe* (2000), *Learning for a Democratic Europe* (2001), *Preparing Professionals in Education for Issues of Citizenship and Identity in Europe*, and *Children's Understanding in the New Europe* (2002).

DAVID SCOTT is a professor of educational leadership at Lincoln University in the United Kingdom. He has previously worked at the Universities of Warwick, Southampton, and London. He has published widely in the fields of curriculum, assessment, and research methodology. His most recent books include *Reading Educational Research and Literacy, Realism and Educational Research: New Perspectives and Possibilities* and (with Robin Usher) *Researching Education: Data, Methods and Theory in Educational Enquiry*. He is the current editor of the *Curriculum Journal*.

CAMERON WHITE is associate professor of social education and curriculum and instruction at the University of Houston. His professional interests include international and comparative education, critical pedagogy, popular culture, social education for social reconstruction, and progressive praxis. He has published four books and numerous articles focusing on various aspects of social education.